Disciplines in Art Education: Contexts of Understanding
General Series Editor, Ralph A. Smith

FE

Aesthetics and Education

AESTHETICS
AND
EDUCATION

*Michael J. Parsons and
H. Gene Blocker*

UNIVERSITY OF ILLINOIS PRESS
Urbana and Chicago

©1993 by the Board of Trustees of the University of Illinois
Manufactured in the United States of America
1 2 3 4 5 C P 5 4 3 2 1

This book is printed on acid-free paper.

This volume and the others in the series Disciplines in Art Education: Contexts of Understanding are made possible by a grant from the Getty Center for Education in the Arts. The J. Paul Getty Trust retains all publishing rights to the individual essays in the series. The views expressed in the volumes are those of the authors and not necessarily those of the J. Paul Getty Trust.

Library of Congress Cataloging-in-Publication Data

Parsons, Michael J.
    Aesthetics and education / Michael J. Parsons and H. Gene Blocker.
       p.   cm. — (Disciplines in art education)
    Includes bibliographical references and index.
    ISBN 0-252-01988-1 (cl.) — ISBN 0-252-06293-0 (pbk.)
    1. Art—Study and teaching—United States. 2. Art appreciation—
Study and teaching—United States. I. Blocker, H. Gene.
II. Title. III. Series.
N353.P27   1993
701'.17'07073—dc20
                                            92-21377
                                            CIP

Contents

General Series Preface

Since the early 1980s, the Getty Center for Education in the Arts, an operating entity of the J. Paul Getty Trust, has been committed to improving the quality of aesthetic learning in our nation's schools and museums. According to the organizing idea of the center's educational policy, teaching about the visual arts can be rendered more effective through the incorporation of concepts and activities from a number of interrelated disciplines, namely, artistic creation, art history, art criticism, and aesthetics.

The resultant discipline-based approach to art education does not, however, mandate that these four disciplines be taught separately; rather, the disciplines are to provide justifications, subject matter, and methods as well as exemplify attitudes that are relevant to the cultivation of percipience in matters of art. They offer different analytical contexts to aid our understanding and aesthetic enjoyment, contexts such as the making of unique objects of visual interest (artistic creation), the apprehension of art under the aspects of time, tradition, and style (art history), the reasoned judgment of artistic merit (art criticism), and the critical analysis of basic aesthetic concepts and puzzling issues (aesthetics). Discipline-based art education thus assumes that our ability to engage works of art intelligently requires not only our having attempted to produce artworks and gained some awareness of the mysteries and difficulties of artistic creation in the process, but also our having acquired familiarity with art's history, its principles of judgment, and its conundrums. All are prerequisite to building a sense of art in the young, which is the overarching objective of aesthetic learning.

Although no consensus exists on precisely how the various components of aesthetic learning should be orchestrated in order to accomplish the goals of discipline-based art education, progress toward these objectives will require that those charged with designing art education programs bring an adequate understanding of the four disciplines to bear on their work. It is toward generating such needed understanding that a five-volume series was conceived as part of the Getty Center's publication program. To narrow the distance separating the disciplines from classroom teaching, each book following the introductory volume is coauthored by a scholar or practitioner in one of the disciplines (an artist, an art historian, an art critic, and a philosopher of art) and an educational specialist with an interest or competence in a given art discipline. The introductory volume provides a philosophical rationale for the idea of discipline-based art education. It is hoped that the series, which is intended primarily for art teachers in elementary and secondary education, for those who prepare these teachers, and for museum educators, will make a significant contribution to the literature of art education.

Ralph A. Smith
General Series Editor

General Editor's Introduction

A philosopher of art and an educational theorist with a strong interest in philosophical aesthetics and art education have cooperated to produce this volume. H. Gene Blocker is currently a professor in the department of philosophy at Ohio University, where he teaches courses in general philosophy and served as chairman of the department from 1984 to 1987. A prolific writer, his *Philosophy of Art* is still considered one of the better introductions to aesthetics, and he has since authored and edited a number of books, among them *Fundamentals of Philosophy* (coauthor), *The Aesthetics of Primitive Art*, and *Aesthetics Reader* (editor). A frequent visiting professor and lecturer, Professor Blocker has taught at Bendel State University in Nigeria, where he was Fulbright Professor and head of the department of philosophy from 1982 to 1984, and at Fudan University, Shanghai, where in 1988 he was visiting foreign expert in philosophy. Michael J. Parsons is currently head of the art education department at The Ohio State University, where he teaches courses in philosophy of art education and administers a department recognized for the excellence of its faculty and programs. Professor Parsons's principal interests lie in the study of aesthetic growth, in connection with which his *How We Understand Art: A Cognitive Developmental Account of Aesthetic Experience*, the result of ten years of research, has become a standard reference in the field. He is also interested in curriculum design and evaluation and the social and institutional factors that influence the understanding and appreciation of art. The philosophical, psychological, and educational expertise and wisdom the authors bring to their subject have resulted in an uncommonly successful example of the kind of collaboration across disciplines and areas of interest that this series was intended to achieve.

Among the fields included in a discipline-based approach to art education — artistic creation, art history, art criticism, and aesthetics — the latter is perhaps the most daunting to art teachers who may consider teaching philosophy of art a remote, arcane, and difficult endeavor. Professors Blocker and Parsons quickly dispel such misgivings.

Philosophy as they define it is based on experience; it arises when a situation becomes puzzling and our ideas and understandings are inadequate to resolve it. Such puzzles have proved frustrating to most persons without special training in art when they attempt to come to terms with an artwork, and this is especially true of young people in our schools. Hence, the authors propose that "to teach aesthetics is to promote and exploit the questions which in any case arise in the classroom," particularly when the appreciation and understanding of art rather than its production is the primary objective. However, this does not imply that aesthetics must be taught rigorously and systematically as a separate subject that characterizes its teaching in higher education. Nor need teachers themselves become scholars in aesthetics. An understanding of aesthetics simply helps them to guide students, even very young ones, in their thinking about art and how to experience it more effectively.

This conception of the teaching of aesthetics underlies a great number of extremely helpful suggestions regarding what art teachers ought to know and how they should conduct themselves in the classroom, suggestions that are dispersed throughout the book but concentrated mainly in its last chapter. Teachers are counseled to be deliberately open-minded, facilitative, and provocative rather than authoritative; they should aid students in identifying, articulating, and discussing philosophical issues related to art rather than provide definitive answers. But to do all this successfully, teachers need to be familiar with the developmental stages of children's thinking about art, and they should also deploy strategies for finding out what students already know, take for granted, are interested in, and create a classroom atmosphere that is supportive of discussion. This means that each teacher has to design a "homegrown" curriculum adapted to the composition and characteristics of a particular art class. Many activities can be structured around what students have said and written, but, the authors warn, not every topic is worth pursuing, nor is every student interpretation fully adequate. To be able to decide which student responses are aesthetically relevant, the art teacher must understand aesthetic theory.

The assistance the authors offer to art educators who must try to orient themselves toward aesthetics is of two kinds: (1) introducing art teachers to some of the problems and questions that have occupied philosophers of art throughout the ages; and (2) encouraging art teachers to form a personal outlook on these and related issues that will allow them to go about their work fully attentive to the demands of the times.

Under the first heading, the authors discuss several of the more traditional aesthetic theories, for example, art conceived as the imitation of nature, art and the representation of external or internal (subjective) reality, the difficulties of accounting for art's apparent capacity to express emotions, the role of artists and their intentions, and the problem of beauty seen as an objective property of artworks. A good organizing device suggested by the authors is the arrangement of theories along a continuum from those that insist on isolating the artwork from its many relations to those that would require consideration of the largest possible context — including social, political, and economic conditions — for determining a work's meaning.

It is through the second sort of help Parsons and Blocker lend to art teachers — that is, aid in framing their own aesthetic viewpoints — that their book would appear to make its most distinctive and valuable contribution. Although in their writing the authors maintain the stance of open-mindedness and sensitivity to divergent opinions that they urge on teachers, they do insist that no position can be defensible today that does not recognize and accommodate itself to some extent to postmodernism and multiculturalism.

Multiculturalism both shares the postmodern temper and reflects the realities of contemporary society — and hence of art classrooms — in the United States, namely, the increasing ethnic and cultural diversity of the population. The authors state: "We expect schools to help students understand and be proud of their cultural background. We also expect schools to teach understanding across cultural differences, so that students will respect and be willing to learn from each other." Having asserted cross-cultural understanding as a desideratum for art education, Blocker and Parsons might be said to have positioned themselves between two extremes. They distance themselves from strident voices that proclaim ethnic pride as the overarching concern and demand that students be instructed exclusively in their own cultural heritage, a course that according to some educational observers would lead to pernicious cultural particularism. On the other hand, neither do the authors recommend that cross-cultural studies be undertaken as a means for discovering possible commonalities among groups that could form elements in a shared national culture. Tolerance of diversity and respect for difference are the main considerations.

If multiculturalism is in accord with present-day social and political realities, postmodernism mirrors current conditions in the art world, where many often contradictory movements coexist and no dominant trend or direction is discernible. "Postmodernism" itself is merely a collective name for a multiplicity of philosophical stances that are united only by their rejection of modernism. To their credit, Parsons and

Blocker espouse postmodernist philosophy only up to the point where it would conflict with the art-educational aim of teaching for cross-cultural understanding (or, in fact, with teaching art in any meaningful way at all), and they caution art teachers against adopting radical positions that are educational dead ends. It is therefore important as well as profitable for readers to pay careful attention to the authors' lucid and well-reasoned exposition.

At a minimum, claim Blocker and Parsons, postmodernism should make us more aware of and modest about our assumptions. Assumptions are the concepts we use to understand the world, and these concepts are involved even in what we take to be the unmediated perception of sense qualities. We are thus unable to differentiate the way things seem to us from the way they are, to compare claims about reality with reality itself. Students often find it difficult to accept that properties they see "in" an artwork, there for all to observe and agree about, do not appear the same way to others — to those, that is, who operate with a different set of assumptions. This leads to another important postulate of postmodernism: humans learn assumptions from the social circumstances in which they grow up, and what they take to be reality is thus culturally conditioned.

It follows that artworks from a different civilization, or those from a past period of one's own, were shaped under the influence of assumptions different from the ones currently in use. Some postmodernist theorists have pursued this realization to its logical extreme and claim that a work of art can be correctly interpreted only by persons who are conversant with the full range of the assumptions operant in the work's indigenous or historical environment. Acceptance of this imperative would make the teaching of cross-cultural understanding inordinately difficult, especially since teachers of art would also have to make allowance for the fact that students can appropriate knowledge of other cultures only through the conceptual and cultural framework they now have. The authors write: "Unless connections are made with the art and interests of our times and the culturally different placed somehow within the orbit of our perspective and concerns, we cannot understand it." But if we make an honest effort to learn as much as we can about another group's expectations and cultural conventions — and just how much of this background needs to be filled in depends on the artwork in question and on what students already know — we can achieve at least the sort of partial understanding that, though relevant, is always subject to revision and improvement. The authors, in other words, do hold out prospects for cross-cultural art appreciation.

An even better understanding of artworks can of course be attained within communities that share assumptions and expectations. Not only can members of a linguistic and cultural group give reasons for their judgments and come to an agreement about truth but they can also reach a sufficient degree of objectivity and differentiate between appearance and substance, fact and interpretation — always with the awareness that validity is not universal but exists only for and within that particular culture. Keeping this important proviso in mind, Parsons and Blocker have secured for art teachers the ground on which that species of reasoned classroom discourse can take place. Without such reasoning it would not be feasible to teach art along the lines the authors suggest.

Another strain of postmodernist thinking has traced the alleged impossibility of arriving at a correct interpretation of art to the irreducibility of individual differences. It is not only the cultural context that is brought to bear on an art object, but also the way contextual relations are refracted by each person's life experiences. Consequently there are as many discrete, incompatible, but equally valuable interpretations of an artwork as there are percipients. What art teaching under such a prescription would amount to is hard to say. But it is clear that extremes of individualism would complicate communication even within the same cultural group. It is also obvious that it would no longer make sense to speak of artistic traditions, institutions, genres, and styles — ideas that Blocker and Parsons think it important to retain. Students, they say, should know about well-established artistic conventions in order to make sense of artworks. Older art and works from other cultures where meaning is largely determined by rules governing art production in that particular society at that particular time should be interpreted in terms of such conventions. It would seem then that although art teachers enjoy great latitude in selecting approaches to art teaching and are in fact called upon to expose students to a wide variety of views, their freedom is restricted to a degree by the nature and provenance of each work of art.

A third variant of postmodernism goes beyond insisting that the properties of an artwork are conditioned almost wholly by its cultural background, while the work itself determines little. This position holds that it is primarily a society's political realities, namely, its prevailing power relationships, that are the most crucial determinants of any artwork's meaning. According to this view, the art and art history prominent in a given period and place are those that reflect, and help perpetuate, the ideology of the dominant class, usually at the expense of subordinate groups. Choices among artworks and art histories are thus at base always political and indicate only which group the chooser favors. "In this way," say the authors, "most questions of value in art are interpreted as matters not of aesthetics but of power." Parsons and Blocker do acknowledge and condemn the blindness to the substantial influence of the dominant social strata on the shape and form of art and the insensitivity to the aspirations of other groups that have marred so much of traditional thinking about art, and they enjoin teachers to correct this bias. But they also reject the radical position just sketched and persist in identifying the aesthetic dimension as separable from the political. And one could say that here again they select a position not arbitrarily but for reasons having to do with maintaining the very possibility of art education. These reasons may be discussed under three rubrics.

First, if art served exclusively or even primarily to reveal the political symptoms and power relations of its culture, it would be indistinguishable from other cultural products that equally bear the imprint of their age. There would be no reason for cherishing art (and some theorists today are indeed saying there is none). By contrast, the authors could be understood as positing something like a universal aesthetic impulse, that is, the delight humans everywhere seem to take in visual appearance for its own sake. Which qualities are enjoyed and which combinations of them called "beautiful" varies greatly from culture to culture; still, aesthetic objects generally, and works of art in particular, appear to satisfy a genuine human interest and are therefore valuable in their own right, apart from whatever other social, practical, economic, or political functions they may serve. In short, the desire to preserve opportunities for aesthetic experiences and aesthetic enjoyment — and for the induction of students into these value aspects of life — can be one reason for retaining the aesthetic as a separate category.

Second, we also need to separate the aesthetic from political and other considerations if we believe that a significant connection exists between art and the affective life of its percipients. Blocker and Parsons maintain that emotions become available when they are articulated in a public medium and that such emotions are most accessible in the medium of art. Art is therefore the main source for understanding our own emotional life and provides an excellent means for helping students toward the maturation of theirs. Which emotions are embodied in art varies among groups, but in all cultures emotional expression tends gradually to become stereotyped and inadequate to altered collective and individual conditions. It is especially in periods of profound changes that we rely on artists to experiment with hitherto unknown feelings, devise artistic expressions for them, and lead their contemporaries to new insights.

Third, unless we uphold the possibility of separating aesthetic values from other values, we cannot see the difference between, for instance, art and mere propaganda. And unless we allow for the existence of gradations of aesthetic value, that is, its presence in objects to different degrees, we cannot distinguish great art from mediocre art. It is important to Parsons and Blocker that we continue to be able to do so, that, in other words, aesthetic judgments can be made and defended. This position has curricular consequences. The authors agree that the traditional canon of works discussed in art classes should be amended. Some works from the Western tradition should be replaced with artworks that originated in other cultures or within groups that have thus far been underrepresented. But aesthetic judgment should be exercised in selecting the newcomers. "Most cultural pluralists," the authors state, "want to see works form other cultures in the curriculum because they are valuable as artworks and are therefore worth study. They do not want trivial or worthless pieces to be chosen just because they are from a particular culture."

Blocker and Parsons have pointed out two basic motivations for doing philosophy: solving puzzles and gaining consistency among our ideas. When we have achieved consistency of ideas we have in effect achieved a theory. One is impressed with the many consistencies found throughout this book, not only in the seamless writing but also across chapters and topics. Indeed, readers may conclude that Parsons and Blocker have exceeded their modestly stated goal and provided a fully articulated theory for teaching aesthetics within the framework of discipline-based art education.

Ralph A. Smith

Preface

Writing this book has been a challenging and rewarding experience for both of us. One reason is that we have tried to integrate in one book two normally distinct approaches to thinking about art — those of philosophical aesthetics and of art education. The simplest strategy would have been to divide the chapters between us, some being written from an art education standpoint and others from a philosophical one. But we decided against this approach because we felt that this book, aimed at integrating aesthetics into the study of art in the school curriculum, would be better if it integrated aesthetics and art education to begin with. As a result, each of us has written and rewritten every part of the book and there is scarcely a paragraph for which either of us can claim exclusive credit (or blame).

Another kind of challenge has been the effort to focus on the main issues and keep our discussion of them up-to-date in terms of the new challenges in both art education and aesthetics: to stay relevant to new developments in schools and in aesthetics. There are rapid and often radical changes occurring in art, in philosophy, and in education today, including especially the many-headed postmodernist movement. Many of the principles and goals that we learned in graduate school are now challenged as inadequate or irrelevant. There is a temptation to ignore or resist these challenges or to jump on the bandwagon. We have tried to use the occasion of writing this book to assess our response to many of these contemporary issues, working them through until we have at least reached agreement ourselves. Sometimes we support new movements as pointing to long-ignored factors in our understanding of art; sometimes we are critical of them as exaggerations or misunderstandings; and sometimes we are not quite sure what to think. We try to make these differences clear to the reader. The result does not fit neatly into any current camp or stereotype but we feel that the book in that way represents some of the current difficulties and controversies.

There has also been the challenge of finding a suitable style and tone to address the audience for which this book, and this series, is intended: practicing schoolteachers, especially art teachers, who have a good but not necessarily scholarly background in art and in education. We have tried to avoid being too academic or abstract, on the one hand, or too simplistic or slow-moving, on the other.

We would like to thank Ralph A. Smith for his constant support throughout this process. We also thank those at the Getty Center who have reviewed drafts of this book and facilitated its writing: Stephen Dobbs and Mary Ann Stankiewicz.

Aesthetics and Education

Introduction

A movement is underway today to have aesthetics taught in our schools. The intention is not so much to teach philosophy to children as to amplify the existing curriculum in the art classroom. Aesthetics is to be taught for its ability to help students understand art, as one of the kinds of studies thought appropriate for that purpose.[1] Such a movement raises many questions. What is the appropriate content of aesthetics for students at different age levels? How can it best be taught? How should it be combined with studio work and other art disciplines? These questions are far from settled, and the movement is still relatively untested in the classroom. There is, too, the question whether teachers in our schools are equipped to teach aesthetics, since their training rarely includes much work in the subject and since philosophy seems to call for very different interests and skills than does art.

This book is addressed primarily to teachers. It tries to answer the questions mentioned above in at least a preliminary way. In what follows we try especially to help teachers understand the nature of aesthetics and some of its content. Our discussion of topics in aesthetics is intended to help the understanding of the teacher, though many of these topics might, with appropriate materials, be introduced into the art classroom. For we take it as obvious that one cannot teach aesthetics without knowing something of the subject, especially without a feel for the kind of enterprise it is, the kind of thinking it calls for, and the educational goals and means it represents.

We speak of a feel for the subject rather than of the scholarly mastery of it, though of course the two together are better than either one alone. This is because of our conception of aesthetics and of why we should teach it in the art classroom. If one thinks of teaching aesthetics as a distinct discipline with its own content, then one imagines a standard set of topics that should be covered, with a set of standard questions and perhaps of answers. One thinks of textbooks, lectures, exercises, examinations, all having to do with the views of philosophers such as Plato and Collingwood on the standard topics. In that case, teachers may well wonder whether they personally have the time required to achieve the mastery of the subject to teach it. They may also wonder whether their students would benefit from such study and whether they might not better spend the time studying more artworks.

We prefer to think of aesthetics as thinking hard about some of the questions that occur to us in our interactions with art. The topics of aesthetics arise naturally in the course of making, enjoying, and discussing art. If we think of it in this way, there is no completely new discipline to master, no foreign subject matter to introduce, and no sudden break in the curriculum when we move from the study of art to the study of aesthetics. Students do not lose time away from the study of art when they think about topics in aesthetics. Rather, aesthetics can be used to promote and exploit the questions about art that already arise inside and outside the classroom. Occasions that allow one to raise philosophical questions about art in this way abound; a teacher who does so will find that students are already interested in many of them and often have strong opinions about them.

We say "raise philosophical questions" because raising questions is as much a part of aesthetics as is answering them. To raise a question is first of all to focus attention on an issue, to bring it into consciousness. We do this by "thematizing" the issue, that is, by articulating it and showing where it is present in what has been already done or said. Attention is drawn to some part of the issue that seems troubling or to some idea that is taken for granted as the issue is first formulated. One begins to ask questions about the ideas presupposed by this formulation, to uncover for a fuller view the assumptions on which it is based. "Raising a question" in this way is already an achievement of philosophy because it makes us more aware of some assumption that we were making and of the way in which this may be problematic.

An example has to do with the topic of beauty. Suppose we are talking with students about the painting by Ivan Albright, *Into the World Came a Soul Called Ida* (fig. 1). This often strikes children as an ugly and unpleasant work, and reactions to it can be quite pronounced (see chapter 3 for an actual example of such a reaction). In that case, the teacher may decide to thematize the issue of ugliness and beauty in art — to get the students to think about the assumptions that they are making. For example, is it the woman or the painting that they find ugly? Do they assume that paintings of ugly subjects are also ugly? Is there a difference between ugliness in nature, in people, and in paintings? Can ugliness be an appropriate aim in art? Why is ugliness sometimes so interesting? And what really is the difference between beauty and ugliness? Such questions can be highly motivating for children who have a strong negative reaction to the painting, because

Figure 1. Ivan Albright. *Into the World Came a Soul Called Ida*, 1930. The Art Institute of Chicago.

they bring into view assumptions that are presupposed by their reaction. Raising such questions gets students to examine ideas and feelings they already have as well as the work itself and to learn something about themselves as well as about art. Doing this is in effect a way of taking advantage of the emotional power of the painting. A good discussion would require repeated references to the work and to other works that the children find beautiful or ugly and references also to the reactions of the children, all considered as examples of the general points being made.

With a different group of students it might be more appropriate to use a work like the Albright to raise questions about the social character of our views of beauty and ugliness. Especially one might thematize the issue of our expectations about beauty in women. What does the work suggest about our stereotypes of people? Why does the image have the power it has? Would it have that power if Ida were a man or a younger woman? Is it better to react with sympathy for Ida rather than with horror? Why would that reaction be better? Is it a virtue in art to make its viewers more sympathetic? Questions such as these are most appropriately raised if the students react sympathetically to Ida or can be brought to do so.

Skillfully managed, the discussion of such questions can develop its own intrinsic motivation and can enrich the way students interpret particular artworks. It can also help them understand art better in general and to become more aware of associated issues such as, in this example, our gender and age related stereotypes.

We intend this brief example to suggest several things. One we have already mentioned: philosophy lies as much in the raising of questions as in answering them. It is a truism that getting the question right is the hardest part of philosophy. Another point the example makes is that, handled well, the study of aesthetics does not compete with the study of art but is a natural part of it. One reason for this has to do with developments in contemporary art itself. We live in a time when art has become puzzling to most people, when an artist may make an artwork by erasing a drawing or wrapping a gallery with paper. Such works often provoke questions and confusion about the nature of art. We also live in a time when we can no longer take for granted the dominance of "mainstream" art, when different movements and styles coexist and various art traditions demand attention, including folk art and art from various non-European cultures. This development leads to questions about the social functions of art, the connections of art with culture, and the possibility of cross-cultural understanding. So it appears that the study of art increasingly invites the discussion of philosophical topics, and to be knowledgeable about contemporary art is to be aware of the broad outlines of those topics.

We can arrive at the same conclusion by considering the diverse cultural makeup of our schools. Students increasingly come from different cultural backgrounds and are familiar with different traditions of art. This fact calls for a change in the curriculum, one that helps students understand both their own art traditions and those of other students. A multicultural curriculum easily gives rise to philosophical questions for the students. Why is something beautiful in one culture and not in another? What assumptions about art does a particular culture have? Can one really understand art that comes from a different culture? These are questions that students need to discuss openly if they are to deal with art from more than one tradition and to achieve the kinds of understandings our complex society demands. Such inquiries are therefore stressed in the chapters that follow.

Obviously, the authors believe that students can do aesthetics in a meaningful way and that teachers can teach it if they are willing to try. More than that: we think children are naturally inclined to philosophical questioning and that the chief thing teachers need, if they are to incorporate aesthetics into their classroom, is a sense of the philosophical questions that are profitable to raise with their particular students. This book is intended primarily to help develop that sense. The bulk of the book is a discussion of the nature of aesthetics as an activity and as a group of topics and an account of some of the standard arguments on these topics, along with some suggestions about where they might arise in a classroom. From time to time we include some advice on goals, procedures, and topics in aesthetics, though this is in no sense a how-to book on teaching aesthetics, nor an outline of a curriculum. We hope that the whole will provide teachers with the knowledge and encouragement they need to enrich their teaching of art with the pleasures and insights of aesthetics.

NOTES

1. Much has been written about this movement, which is often known as DBAE (Discipline-based Art Education). Some of the basic references are Gilbert Clark, Michael Day, and Dwaine Greer, "Discipline-based Art Education: Becoming Students of Art," and Ralph Smith, "The Changing Image of Art Education: Theoretical Antecedents of Discipline-based Art Education." Both articles are in a special issue of *The Journal of Aesthetic Education* 21:2 (Summer 1987), reprinted as Ralph A. Smith, ed., *Discipline-based Art Education: Origins, Meanings, and Development* (Urbana: University of Illinois Press, 1988). See also *Beyond Creating: The Place for Art in America's Schools* (Los Angeles: The Getty Center for Education in the Arts, 1985); Elliot W. Eisner, *The Role of Discipline-based Art Education in America's Schools* (Los Angeles: The Getty Center for Education in the Arts, reprinted in *Art Education* (Sept. 1987); Stephem Dobbs, ed., *Research Readings for Discipline-based Art Education* (Reston, Va.: National Association of Art Educators, 1988); Albert Levi and Ralph A. Smith, *Art Education: A Critical Necessity* (Urbana: University of Illinois Press, 1991.)

1

Aesthetics, Art, and the Aesthetic Object

Aesthetics

We will begin with a discussion of what "aesthetics" is. Sometimes people are unfamiliar with aesthetics, even though they are otherwise sophisticated about art. They may feel comfortable talking about art criticism or history but lack confidence with aesthetics. If they are teachers, that leads to the avoidance of teaching aesthetics. But it is not a mysterious discipline, and in many ways it is a natural activity.

Aesthetics is the branch of philosophy that has art for its subject matter. Unfortunately, philosophers themselves don't always agree on what philosophy is. Traditionally, it has been considered the supreme science, concerned with ultimate topics such as God, morality, the nature of the world, beauty, and the human soul. Philosophy has been thought of as a kind of super science that provides answers to life's most perplexing problems. But this idea, which still lingers in popular conceptions of philosophy, has come under enormous opposition in recent years. In light of the increasing successes of the various sciences, few philosophers today believe that philosophy is a science of any kind.

A more recent view is that philosophy is an analytical discipline for clarifying the way we think. On this view, it analyzes not the world but the ideas with which we think about the world. The notion is that human beings see the world through a filter of ideas, or "concepts"; and, whereas the sciences examine the empirical facts of the world, philosophy examines the way we think about those facts.

If we take this view, we can distinguish the different branches of philosophy in terms of the kinds of ideas they examine. For instance, we typically use ideas like the sacred, faith, and miracles when thinking about religion, and so if we examine these ideas we will be doing philosophy of religion. In the same way, ethics analyzes the ideas we use in moral discussions, such as rights, obligations, law, and conscience. Aesthetics, on this account, is the analysis of the ideas with which we think about the arts. Some of these ideas are rather specific to the arts — for example, design, form, rhythm — but others are not — for example, emotion, beauty, reality, communication, and judgment. These latter are drawn from everyday life more than from a specialized discourse, and we use them to discuss much else besides the arts. For this reason aestheticians often find themselves discussing quite general topics, like the nature of emotion or how we can understand one another. In this regard, aesthetics reflects the connections of art with life and, we think, this makes it all the more interesting.

Aesthetics, then, looks at the ways we think about art — "we" meaning anyone who does think about art, including critics, art educators, art historians, ordinary lovers of art, and even those who do not care much about art. It examines the conceptual problems arising out of the way people behave and talk — problems surrounding the meaning of ideas like those mentioned above. Because it is concerned primarily with questions of meaning, philosophy is sometimes thought of as a second-order discipline. The artist creates an artwork and the critic talks about it (first-order); the aesthetician talks about the artist's and the critic's talk (second-order). The philosopher therefore operates at a distance from the actual world, talking not about individual artworks (except as examples) but about other people's talk about, and behavior regarding, artworks. The aesthetician is primarily concerned not with artworks, but with the way we think about them.

It is a mistake, though, to imagine that aestheticians are interested only in words or that the analysis of meanings makes no practical difference. This is because the actual world, including the artworks we love, comes to us in perception already organized by our ideas and our language. When we look at something, we do not first see unrelated fragments of sensations and then relate them together; we immediately recognize objects in a comprehensible relation — a cup of coffee on the table, trees in a park. Perception comes to us not as a bunch of raw, unprocessed sensations, but a number of objects already organized by ideas, such as "a cup," "a table," "trees," and arranged into some order, such as "after-dinner coffee," or "lunch in the park." We cannot accept the world innocent of language, much as we might wish to do so. So an analysis of our concepts of the world is also an analysis of our world.

It follows that there is no distinction between describing how things are and describing how we think they are. Suppose you divide a sheet of paper into two columns. On the right you jot down what a given object is really like; on the left you put down what you think it is like. How would the two lists differ? Since you will not put anything on the right side (the "is" side) which you do not think is so, they will be exactly alike. What you say things are is precisely what you *think* they are, and what you think they are is precisely what you will say they are. You cannot distinguish in your own case how things actually are from how you think they are.

The same sort of thought experiment works for whole societies. What a particular society says is real or true is just what it thinks is real or true. A group of people may perceive the world in terms of witchcraft or atomic structures, but they will not think of witchcraft or atomic structures as only cultural phenomena. Instead, they think of them as part of the actual world. In short, we perceive the world in terms of ideas, most of which are shaped by our culture, but they are not for us *only* ideas. They are real properties of the actual world, descriptions of what exists.

Thus philosophy is useful. Since we see the world in terms of our ideas, to analyze our ideas is to analyze the world — as we understand it. Moreover, we are not always aware of the ideas with which we understand the world, especially when we learned them young. We are often unaware of them and in that case they are called assumptions. In doing philosophy we may become aware of our assumptions for the first time, and this awareness is a valuable outcome of doing philosophy. It amounts to a knowledge of the way one thinks, a reflection on one's own understanding of the world, something that philosophers have valued ever since Socrates said that the unexamined life is not worth living.

There is a somewhat different view of the nature of philosophy that has become popular recently. This popularity is due in part to the influence of Continental traditions in philosophy, which are often different from Anglo-American traditions. In this view philosophy is the attempt to reach rather general, though nonscientific, conclusions about the nature of things. It differs from science in that the kinds of questions it addresses are not answered by discovering more facts but rather by thinking through the consequences of what we already know. There are a number of basic questions that are difficult to answer, but their difficulty is not due to information that we don't have. It is due rather to the difficulty of making consistent sense of what we do know. Take, for example, the nest of questions that emerge when we think of art as communicating emotions. We might ask: How is it possible for us to communicate about our emotions? If you say you are angry, how do I know what you mean? Do you mean that you have the same feeling that I have when I am angry? But how do you know our two feelings are the same, since it seems that they can never be compared? You cannot examine my feelings directly since you cannot experience them, nor can I examine yours. How, then, do you know that I don't use the word "anger" to mean what you would call outrage or perhaps jealousy? For example, if you say that Picasso's *Guernica*, to which *Woman Crying with a Handkerchief*, also know as *Weeping Woman with Hands*, (see fig. 2) is related, is an expression of Picasso's outrage at war, how do I know what feeling you have in mind or what Picasso may have felt? How do I even know that Picasso expressed any feelings at all in the *Guernica?* In short, since emotions appear to be privately experienced and are not the sorts of things that we can point to or share, how can we talk about them reliably – in art or in life? Yet it seems that we do talk about emotions and often understand each other. Is this mutual understanding an illusion? And if the understanding is genuine, what does that imply about the nature of emotions and communication in general?

We will take these particular questions up again in chapter 3; the point here is that they are not the sort of questions that can be answered by the discovery of new facts about emotions. Neither do they seem to be questions only about the *meanings* of words like anger, outrage, and jealousy, though certainly those meanings are relevant. They seem to call for a more general theory about what kinds of things emotions are and how we can communicate them. This kind of theory is reached by trying to think through the implications of what we already know about emotions and the situations in which we seem to be able to communicate about them. When we have thought about these implications, we may reach a point where we can answer the above questions consistently, and we will have a theory that explains what happens in our experience. This alternative view of philosophy, then, holds that the purpose of aesthetics is to give an account of our experience of art that is consistent with everything we know about it. On this view, much of aesthetics will be expressed in terms of theories about such things as the nature of emotions, or of communication in general.

Philosophers who take this second view of what philosophy is – that it is the search for a general explanatory account of experience – usually believe that the first view – that it is the analysis of ideas – is too limited. But they do believe that the analysis of ideas is a very useful tool for doing philosophy, and increasingly the difference between two approaches has become blurred. Philosophical analyses of meanings can be, and often are, expressed as theories about the world, and vice versa. Philosophers may either discuss the meaning of the word "emotion," or they may advance a theory of what emotions are. Today they are increasingly likely to switch back and forth between the two approaches, without stopping to mark the difference. More and more, philosophers from both traditions, the Anglo-American and the Continental, talk

Figure 2. Picasso, *Woman Crying with a Handkerchief*, 1936, the Prado, Madrid. 1992 ARS, N.Y./SPADEM, Paris; Bridgemean/Art Resource, New York.

to each other about topics such as the nature of emotions or of communication. What makes both traditions philosophical is not so much their method as that they try to answer such important questions without trying to discover new facts or empirical proofs. They discuss ideas, using what is already known, usually what everyone knows.

Therefore, to reflect the field as it now exists, we speak in both idioms in this book. We have organized the book into chapters, each of which is about a traditional theory or topic in aesthetics, but much of the discussion of the theories and topics proceeds through the analysis of particular concepts.

Art

An example may help. Take the question "what is art?" Traditionally, this was taken to mean "what is the true nature of art?" that is, as a question calling for a theory about art, especially about what it is that makes art valuable. Continental philosophers often understood the question to mean: "What must be true of human life if what we call art is to occur as it does?" Forty years or so ago, philosophers in the Anglo-American world took the question to mean: "What is the meaning of the word 'art?'" And now, more recently, we have seen interest in theories emerge again, and the question is taken to be "What is it about an artwork that enables us to identify it as art, as distinct from an ordinary object or event?" Yet, through all these changes, many of the same topics keep arising, often provoked by developments in art itself.

Consider, for example, the moment when Marcel Duchamp first began exhibiting "ready-mades" in galleries — a snow shovel, a bicycle wheel, a urinal from a men's room — and treating them as artworks. This project is considered by many philosophers to be one of the more critical moments in a progressive history of challenges by nineteenth- and twentieth-century artists to the reigning idea of what art is, and for that reason it is one of their favorite examples. The category system of Duchamp's time did not regard ready-made objects like these as artworks but as industrial products. By claiming that they are artworks, Duchamps forced the reconsideration of the idea of art in general. This effect has continually been repeated by artists since Duchamps, in an easily discernible cycle. At any given time, there are limits to what can be considered art; an artist creates something that exceeds these limits in a particular way and claims that it is art, usually by exhibiting it as if it were art and often with an argument about why it is art; the work is considerably discussed and eventually either accepted or rejected as an artwork. In this way the boundaries of art have continually been widened. One could easily list a sample of things that have been advanced as artworks in this same way. For example: a simple rock; a building filled with cement; ruts bulldozed across the Nevada landscape; some stones gathered together in a city park; a plastic curtain stretched across miles of California landscape; a program on a computer disk; a blank canvas with some words written on it; an idea; an unrehearsed "performance"; an artist mutilating himself. Each of these kinds of things have in their time raised questions about what art really is.

It should be clear that the questions involved are not about empirical facts. The facts about such objects are usually agreed upon, both by those who maintain that they are works of art and by those who disagree. The facts are, for example, that a canvas had the words painted across it: NOTE: MAKE A PAINTING OF A NOTE AS A PAINTING and that it was exhibited in an art gallery by a man known as an artist. Similarly, a rather ordinary rock was exhibited in a museum by an artist.[1] The question remained (for a while) whether the canvas or the rock was an artwork. And this question can be construed to mean, is this the sort of thing that should be *called* an artwork, that is, does it conform to our idea of a work of art? Or it can be construed to mean: does this sort of thing fit with our theory of what art is? or: Does it have the kinds of values we attribute to artworks? Which ever way we intend the question, philosophy begins at this point, after all the facts are in. The question requires us to think about what we already know about works of art.

How do we set about answering the question? We begin by "raising" such a question but we cannot leave it at that. Formulating a question is the beginning of philosophy, but it is not the end of it. Note that one thing we usually do *not* do is to answer right away with a definition. A definition is more like the product than the process of philosophy. We must begin where we already are, with our intuitive but unarticulated knowledge and understandings. We don't need a definition to recognize many artworks because we already have an intuitive idea of what they are, that is, we generally "know one when we see one." Making that intuitive idea explicit is a large part of the task of philosophy, and when we have done that we may have a definition we can use.

We usually begin by reminding ourselves of what we already know. It helps to collect some obvious and varied cases of our idea of an artwork. For example, we may think of a Rembrandt portrait, a medieval cathedral, a Japanese print, Duchamp's *Fountain*. These are cases, let us say, where we feel rather sure that these things are works of art. They are clear, exemplary cases of what we *mean* by "a work of art." It helps also to collect some cases that are obviously not works of art: grass, cigarettes, a pipe-wrench. Then there is the most interesting category, cases where we're not quite sure or about which there is dispute. We may not be sure, for example, what to call the blank canvas with the words painted on it: NOTE: MAKE A PAINTING OF A NOTE AS A PAINTING or the rather ordinary rock. With these three kinds of cases — those that clearly are works of art, those that clearly are not, and those where we are unsure — we can begin to discern the shape of our own inarticulate but pre-existent idea. We can then think of some tentative definitions and try them out by seeing if they apply to the clear cases appropriately and what kinds of trouble they have with the unclear ones. Much of the point of this, though, will lie in making some progress with the unclear cases, rather than in the establishment of an all-encompassing definition.

We can think of an idea as a space in which are placed all those things that the idea covers. Some things will lie well within the area of the idea — the exemplary or "paradigm" cases; some will lie well outside the area — the cases that are obviously not instances; and others will lie close to the boundaries. It will be unclear about these latter whether or not they lie within the boundaries of the idea, that is, whether they are examples of it. This is especially true when, as with most ideas about art, they are embodied in our ordinary language, which is almost always vague and imprecise about boundaries. By focusing on these borderline cases, we can try to draw the idea's outlines more precisely. If we do this well, the result will be a clearer account of the disputed boundary; if we did it exceedingly well, it could be a clearly articulated account of all of the boundaries of our original intuitive idea, something like an accurate map of a space that was previously unmapped.

There is a sense, also, in which we will change the original idea. For one thing, if we draw the boundaries more precisely, the idea will be different just because it will now be clear where it once was fuzzy and it will clearly include either more or less than it clearly did before. There is also the possibility that when we have seen the outlines of our original idea we will consciously decide to change them for some reason. The reason may be that we did not previously take account of all the facts we have now recognized or because of something that strikes us as inconsistent when we make it explicit. In other words, we may decide that we had a wrong (incomplete, misleading) idea of art. Before we made our idea explicit we did not have the choice whether or not to change it in this way; now we do.

It follows from this account that those who display objects like those mentioned above as if they are works of art are really trying to reshape the boundaries of our idea of art. Those who resist giving these objects the status of artworks are defending the boundaries we already have. The dispute about these works, in other words, is a dispute about ideas. And it is obviously an important dispute. At stake are the kinds of things that will be produced and accepted as art in the future in our society.

One reason that an idea such as "art" is not fixed with precision is that it changes as the practices of artists change. As new meanings emerge, however, they do not replace the older ones so much as coexist with them. And since the old and the new meanings are somewhat different, the idea of "art" becomes simultaneously richer in content and more ambiguous in meaning. At first "art" meant the skill required to make any kind of man-made object, whether a brick wall or a statue. And when we speak of the art of cooking or growing roses we still use the word in this way. Similarly, in Aristotle's time the word translated as "poetics" meant making anything skillfully, not only poems.

Only later, in the eighteenth century, did we begin systematically to distinguish between skillfully made objects that serve utilitarian purposes, like furniture and ships, and others whose purpose was not utilitarian but *only* "aesthetic." The former were called the useful arts and the latter the fine arts. The list of fine arts included painting, sculpture, music, and dancing and has been constantly expanded over the centuries. Nowadays the fine arts are usually just called "art," whereas the useful arts are usually called "crafts." So part of what we inherit from the eighteenth century is a categorical distinction between the artist who paints paintings and the craftsman who makes chairs and other useful objects; but we also retain the inheritance from the older tradition in which they were both thought of in the same way, as skillful makers of objects. More recently, many crafts have been allowed back onto the "art" list so long as they have aesthetic purposes as well as utilitarian ones. We now generally think that there is no reason not to call a pot an artwork so long as it rewards our looking at it as well as our using it.

In addition to these two notions of art as skillful making and as the creation of beautiful objects, the nineteenth century added the idea that the artist is a person of special vision, someone who has important ideas or deep feelings that must be expressed. Art therefore is also thought of as a means of expressing significant ideas and feelings. And more recently we have added the modern idea that art must be original and innovative.

These four basic ideas all live alongside each other in contemporary consciousness, none having succeeded in wholly replacing its predecessors. They are different from each other, but not incompatibly so. In the Renaissance, it seems that artists tried to produce works that met all of these conditions: works that were skillfully made, beautiful, expressive of profound ideas, and original. In the modern period many artists have emphasized one of these criteria at the expense of the others. This enriches art but confuses us about what art is. When Duchamp created his *Fountain*, for example, it seems that he did not make it skillfully nor did he intend it to be beautiful. Its chief significance lies in the ironic comment it makes about art itself. On the other hand, we may consider many baskets as artworks not because they are innovative or express significant ideas but because they are well made and aesthetically pleasing. It appears that we cannot limit the idea of art to only those objects that fulfill all the criteria that have evolved over the centuries. We must also allow objects to be artworks that fulfill some of the criteria and not others — though just which combinations of criteria are not clear.

One conclusion is that it is often useful to look at the history of an idea, which is a part of the history of philosophy. The history may help one understand some of the elements of our intuitive ideas and why some kinds of things are borderline cases. It may help us to see why, for instance, some people still think of quilting as only a craft and others regard it an art form. The first group is influenced by the historical distinction between the useful and the fine arts; the second is more influenced by the equally historical distinction between the aesthetic and the nonaesthetic. In other words, the dispute has a historical basis that allows us to understand it, and when we draw the map of our own idea of quilting we may find that these historical issues still affect us.

How does philosophy help us to settle such disputes? What do we do once we realize that we are unclear about an idea? It has already helped us to see where the fogginess lies, which boundary we are unclear about. Let us pursue for a moment the question whether quilting is a form of art. It is an old-fashioned example where little controversy remains today, but that may make the structure of the discussion all the clearer. On the one side of the issue we have the fact that a quilt is a useful object and that part of our heritage distinguishes useful objects from fine art. Later, we will look at the reasons why this distinction arose. On the other side of the issue we have three kinds of facts to consider. One is that making quilts by hand requires skill. Another is that they are usually intended and treated as aesthetic objects as well as useful objects; that is, they are designed to be looked at for the reward that looking brings. Indeed, many quilts are hung on the wall and not spread on a bed at all. A third fact is that some quilts are understood by some people as expressions of significant ideas or emotions. The question is, which of these facts about quilting shall we judge most important in deciding whether it is an art form?

We may begin, perhaps, by deciding that the matter of skillful making is not terribly important to us: there have been too many cases of artworks where the artist did not need to be skillful. As an example, we cite one from our original list of clear cases: Duchamp's *Fountain*. We may also decide that the question of usefulness seems unimportant, because there are plenty of cases where artworks have been useful. For example, there is a medieval cathedral in our list of exemplary cases. What seems more important is whether quilts are looked at for their aesthetic qualities, for the way they look. If people are commonly interested in quilts for the way they look, then they should count as art. It is irrelevant to this judgment whether their aesthetic qualities are understood as qualities of beauty or of significant expression. This judgment conforms, let us suppose, with our intuitive sense of what is important about art.

This account is actually a rough map of a collective decision about many crafts that has been made during this century. A number of points stand out. One is that the final outcome is determined by a decision — in the end a collective decision — rather than simply by the discovery of facts. When a part of the boundary is too vague, we have to decide where to draw it more precisely. Of course the decision is made in light of the facts we considered but in most cases these were facts that we already knew. The decision is also influenced by the categories we used in the analysis, whether or not they are new to us: in this case, the categories of skillful making, useful versus nonuseful, aesthetic qualities, significant expression. But the decision is determined, in the end, by a judgment about what we think is most important in the case. We cannot avoid the fact that such judgments are matters for which we must take responsibility. They often have quite practical consequences. They can determine, as in this case, whether a whole range of activities will count as art and thus what happens in the careers of individual people, what kind of curriculum takes place in schools, and so on. In this sense, such judgments are inevitably evaluative and even "political." In short, contrary to what many believe, philosophers often take sides in disputes. Even when we think of philosophy as the analysis of concepts, it is usually more than just the description of a received idea. It usually is more like a reordering of the elements of a complex and unclear set of tendencies. In fact, most of the major theories in aesthetics have been advanced and defended to explain and justify new movements in art. In that sense they have always involved decisions that had consequences.

Another point to notice is that at virtually any point in the decision about quilting it would have been possible to raise further questions about the meaning of the different criteria being used. For example, we talked about the aesthetic qualities of objects. It is not always clear just what these qualities are. Are they simply the qualities that can be seen in an object, as distinct from what can be known about it? But there is considerable disagreement about what can be seen in an object, depending largely on how much contextual information we think is relevant. Is irony, for example, something that can be seen, or is it something that must be inferred? And whether we consider it a perceptual quality or not, is it an aesthetic one?

Similarly, we talked about the distinction between useful objects and objects that have no uses. Is it clear what "useful" means in this connection? In what way is a cathedral useful? Is its use simply to lend a sense of dignity to a particular place and to the activities taking place in it? In that case, perhaps we can say that a painting is useful because it lends a certain feeling to a house or office. And quilts, it may seem, are used to give pleasure to the beholder as much as to keep people warm at night. Is the difference between these two latter — keeping people warm and giving pleasure to the beholder — really a difference between two uses or between a use and something else? And, either way, why was this difference once thought to be so important? This latter is perhaps the most important question here, and we will return to it later.

Perhaps the most difficult idea in the quilt discussion is that of significant expression. Just what is "significant expression?" Does it mean expressing ideas? Expressing ideas in the way language expresses ideas? Or is there another way to do it? Or do we mean expressing not ideas but emotions, or feelings, or something else? And in that case, how are these expressed? Can we identify a few specific cases? Does the *Fountain* express an idea? What idea? How do we tell if it is a significant idea? Significant to whom? This nest of questions is so large and also so traditional that we will spend the whole of chapter 4 discussing it.

In short, further questions can arise in the course of deciding whether quilts are to count as artworks, and for a teacher in class it is a matter of judgment whether to deal with them right away or to leave them for another day. On the one hand, these questions may be importantly related to the original question and settling them may help resolve that.

Furthermore, the connections between such ideas is one of the things that aesthetics should teach. On the other hand, one cannot discuss everything at the same time. If one stops to discuss every question as it arises, one may never get back to the original problem. Often, the best solution is to explore the new question briefly, enough to see whether it is important, and then to put it aside, keeping it on a list of questions that one could return to later.

One can see from the anatomy of the quilt discussion why philosophy is more than just the analysis of ideas. Certainly, the analysis of ideas is part of it. But the more one finds questions related to each other in complicated ways, the more it appears that general views about substantive matters are involved. For example, we came across the topic of expression in art. To give an account of what expression is, of how it works and of the kinds of things that can be expressed, seems to require more than an explanation of what our concepts already are. The reason is that our ordinary concepts are vague and contain conflicting elements, whereas to give a satisfactory account of the topic requires more clarity and more consistency. We may have to explain, for example, how language works to express ideas and how the visual arts are similar to or different from language in this regard.[2] Or we may have to develop some systematic ideas about what kinds of things emotions are and how they relate to ideas, and whether and how they can be communicated from one person to another.[3] Topics of this kind seem to call for speculation and theory of a general kind, in addition to the analysis of concepts.

Aesthetics As the Solving of Problems

In most cases, the motivation for doing aesthetics comes from something that puzzles us in our interactions with artworks. When we encounter a work that does not fit our assumptions, it raises questions about how to understand it. For example, we may assume that art should be pleasant and that it should be realistic. Normally, we hold these two assumptions side by side. But then we may see a work that is very disturbing but also very realistic. Perhaps it is Goya's *Lo Mismo* (see fig. 3). Then what are we to think about it? Why should we want to look at such a disturbing work? We are motivated to answer the question because we feel a tension between our assumptions and the power of the work. If we pursue the question in a deliberate and general way, we will be doing aesthetics. For most people, therefore, aesthetics is a problem-solving activity, where the problem is how to think about some artistic situation. We can say that aesthetics arises

Figure 3. Goya, *Lo Mismo*, from *The Disasters of War*, 1810–20. Pomona College, Claremont, California.

naturally from encounters with art, and that means that everyone can be an aesthetician, at least in a beginning way. This includes children and teachers. The discipline of aesthetics is just the attempt to pursue such problems persistently and with as much intellectual rigor as we can manage.

We are also sometimes impelled to think philosophically by recognizing an inconsistency in our views about different topics. For example, suppose we have thought about both the way we know our emotions and, separately, the role of the artist's intentions in interpreting artworks. We may conclude, on the first topic, that it is in general possible to be mistaken about what one's own emotions are. After thinking about it, it seems to us that we don't always know accurately what we are feeling or intending and that actually it is quite possible to deceive oneself about such things. On the second topic, we may also conclude that disputes about the meaning of an artwork should be settled by consulting the artist's intentions. The artist seems to be in a unique position to speak about the work and that means she should decide between alternative interpretations. But then we are brought to notice that these two views about apparently unrelated topics are inconsistent with each other. For if it is possible to be mistaken about one's own feelings and intentions, then the artist may be mistaken about her intentions for the work. In that case, the artist's unique relation to the work will not guarantee that there is no self-deception in the work or in the artist; and the viewer after all may be in a better position to interpret the work as it actually appears.

Of course, much of the time we do not notice such inconsistencies in our own thinking. Indeed, we may *avoid* noticing them and even resent someone who points them out to us. For when we do notice them, we are likely to feel uncomfortable until we have reached a resolution of the tension induced by the inconsistency. The motivation to be consistent in one's thinking is characteristic of philosophy. Part of the art of teaching aesthetics is to structure situations that will present the learner with problems of these sorts.

Philosophical problems can also arise from the activities of art critics and art historians. In fact, when people talk about art, their assumptions may become more noticeable and their inconsistencies more obvious. For that reason, much of aesthetics is reflection on what people say about art, rather than on artworks themselves. Sometimes people say things about artworks that are more puzzling than the works themselves. For example, many people have thought it puzzling when critics say something like the following: This is an angry, or an anxious, work. The puzzle is how we can ascribe emotions to works when emotions seem to be the sorts of things that are the property of people only. Sometimes critics will offer puzzling reasons for judgments. For example, they may suggest that we have to know certain things about the circumstances in which the work was produced if we are to understand it. Consider the photograph by Cindy Sherman reproduced in figure 4. A critic may claim that we need to know a number of facts about this photograph if we are to appreciate it as an artwork: for instance, that it is one of a series of photographs titled *Movie Stills*, each of which pictures Cindy Sherman dressed and posed in a different way, and that Sherman intends this series to be about, not herself, but about women in general in contemporary America.[4] We are forced to wonder whether this demand that we know more is legitimate and how it can be justified. What if we look at this photograph without knowing what the critic claims we should know? Why can't we look at it with an "innocent eye?" Does it have the same *visual* properties regardless of what we know? Is it an artwork only in the context of the series and of our knowledge of what the series is intended to signify? And in that case is the artwork the individual photograph

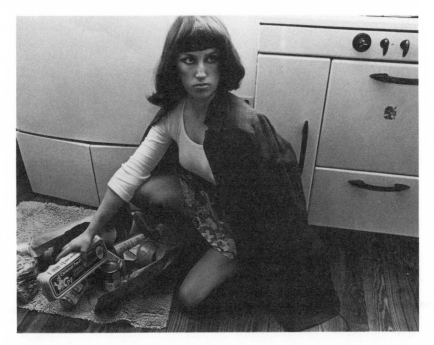

Figure 4. Cindy Sherman, *Untitled Film Still, #10*, 1978. Metro Pictures, New York.

or the series as a whole? These questions touch on philosophical discussions of the nature of perception, of meaning, and of the relation of both to art. In fact, contemporary critics often have theories of art in general, whether or not they are overtly stated, and these theories may be crucially important to their practice as critics.[5] At such points, art criticism and the philosophy of art are mutually dependent and not easily distinguished from each other.

It is much the same with the talk of art historians: they sometimes say baffling things and they often imply or announce theories that touch on philosophical topics. For example, Linda Nochlin, an art historian, says that Seurat, in his *La Grande Jatte*, deliberately "removes himself" from the painting. Nochlin says:

> [The] historical presence of the painting is above all embodied in the notorious dotted brushstroke — the petit pointe — which is and was the first thing everyone noticed about the work — and which in fact constitutes the irreducible atomic particle of the new vision. For Seurat, with the dot, resolutely and consciously removed himself as a unique being projected by a personal handwriting. He himself is absent from his

stroke. . . . The Western tradition of representation has been under-
mined, if not nullified, here by a dominant language that is resolutely
anti-expressive, rejecting the notion of a hidden inner meaning to be
externalized by the artist. Rather, in these machine-turned profiles,
defined by regularized dots, we may discover coded references to modern
science, to modern industry with its mass production, to the department
store with its cheap and multiple copies, to the mass press with its endless
pictorial reproductions.[6]

This claim may puzzle us first because it is not clear just what Nochlin
means when she speaks of the artist removing himself from the painting.
He was never *pictured* in it, as Sherman is pictured in her photographs,
so it cannot mean removing his picture from the painting. In what other
sense can an artist be "in" a painting such that Seurat can remove himself
from this one? The answer, no doubt, has something to do with the
way the Impressionists, Seurat's contemporaries, are generally thought
to have put themselves in their paintings: by trying to capture their
awareness of the fleeting appearances of things and by using a brush-
work and palette that reflected their mood as they worked. Seurat,
according to Nochlin, refused to do this. He did not just fail to do
it but he knowingly and deliberately avoided doing it. The refusal,
according to Nochlin, is significant because it affects the meaning of
the work and the qualities it possesses. There is, then, a claim presupposed by this art historical remark about Seurat that a philosopher
might thematize. It is the claim that it is important to consider what
Seurat did *not* do. This is a specifically art historical piece of reasoning
because many artists, living at other times, have also not done what
Seurat did not do and in their case this fact has no special significance
for the meaning of their works. How can something, or the absence
of something, be aesthetically significant at one time and not at another?
Again, that is the sort of question that philosophers typically debate.

In short, the philosophy of art is related to the several disciplines
of art — to the production of art, to art criticism, to art history — as
well as to our general understanding of artworks. Some have argued
that aesthetics can integrate the study of these other disciplines in the
art classroom and avert the danger that they will each appear to the
students to be quite independent studies.[7] We agree with this. The
various disciplines for the study of art are complexly interrelated and
their interdependence is most clearly shown by aesthetics — and is in
fact a topic within aesthetics.

Oversimplifying, we could say that there are three levels of experience in dealing with art, each associated with particular disciplines:
the direct perceptual or creative experience with the art object; the level

at which we interpret artworks historically or critically; and the level at which we reflect on the general implications of our interpretations. But these three levels of experience interpenetrate and affect each other constantly. We can distinguish them theoretically but they are very much connected together in experience. The creation of a work may express some prior feelings and ideas; its critical interpretation may illuminate our actual experience and response to it; a philosophical analysis may clarify the ideas used in the interpretation; and this in turn may enrich our subsequent attempts at creation. There are multiple connections between the levels and disciplines, and we move back and forth among them, often without noticing, whether in the studio, the gallery, or the study.

Sometimes we are told that the experience of art is quite different from the understanding of art, that the one is an emotional and intuitive response and the other is an unemotional and intellectual analysis. But this is a simplistic picture. If we reflect on our actual experience, we find that direct response and critical analysis, creation and reflection, are not sharply differentiated but rather flow into one another, affecting each other, merging into one experience. That complexity is why art is so challenging and so rewarding.

Educationally, there is a tension here. On the one hand, it is a desirable goal that students should know the differences between the various disciplines of art, that they should know the kinds of inquiry they represent, the kinds of means they employ and the kinds of criteria appropriate for success. Students should be able to tell when they are doing aesthetics, when criticism, and so on. Such an awareness enables one to monitor one's activity and gives one much greater control. On the other hand, in the art classroom the various disciplines are not so much an end in themselves as a means to an end. The end is an understanding of art and artworks. The disciplines should be experienced in that connection and not as separate academic school subjects, ends in themselves. There has been discussion of the problem of integrating the art disciplines in school, how to bring them together in the students' experience. Our view is that the problem should not become acute if we keep the students' attention on a particular topic and not on the discipline used to solve it. The disciplines do not need integrating if they are not first separated in the students' experience. They will not be separated if they are constantly experienced in the context of thinking about problems, because in that context they naturally interrelate and feed each other. The teacher, as is so often the case, is required to maintain a balance.

On the one hand, it is desirable, from time to time, to draw students' attention to the character of the question being discussed and the kind of claims and arguments being made. This will help them become reflectively aware of what they are doing. On the other hand, it is important for them to experience the relatedness of the disciplines to each other and their relevance to problems. It is a matter of judgment in each case whether to halt a discussion in order to draw attention to the nature of the discourse at issue or to continue with the substance of the discussion. The long-term goal is that students can distinguish the disciplines in a reflective way but experience their interrelations in connection with problems.

Aesthetic Objects

We have discussed aesthetics as the philosophy of art. That is what this book is about. But there are other meanings to the word "aesthetic," and we will review the important ones here. For instance, we sometimes talk about somebody's "aesthetic," meaning, roughly, their artistic tastes, their characteristic stylistic choices and preferences. For example, some people prefer bold patterns, vivid colors, direct statements; others like simpler forms, subtler colors, indirect reference. We speak of these kinds of stylistic preferences as their "aesthetic." In this sense we can debate, for example, whether there is a distinctive Latin American or African American "aesthetic." The evidence in the debate would be the kinds of art and other works characteristically produced and preferred by Latin Americans or African Americans.

Sometimes "aesthetic" is used as an adjective, rather than a noun. We speak of aesthetic objects and of the aesthetic qualities of objects. We also speak of aesthetic experiences, aesthetic attitudes, and the aesthetic point of view. These are important usages and there is a considerable history of discussion of them in the philosophy of art.

We will speak first of aesthetic objects and aesthetic qualities of objects. The meaning of "aesthetic" is much the same in these cases. What is aesthetic about an object is its appearance, that which can be perceived, and its aesthetic qualities are those qualities that appear to the senses that can be grasped in perception. Such qualities exhibit an enormous range. They begin with the simple qualities of the medium like being smooth of texture, blue in color, irregular in form. They can also be qualities that carry a sense of human significance or meaning, such as seeming angry or suggesting a kind of religious grandeur. These latter kind of qualities can become immensely complex, subtle, and particular, as with Paul Klee's *Head of a Man* (fig. 5), which offers first a sense of naive fun, then a sophisticated combination of

Figure 5. Paul Klee, *Head of a Man* (sometimes called *Senecio*), 1922, the Kunstmuseum, Basel. Giraudon, Paris/ARS, N.Y.

reticence and allusiveness, and finally an ambiguous and mute response to a threatening world. Of course, in such a case we might want to debate exactly how to describe these qualities and not be able to reach agreement. It is also possible that to see these qualities at all one might need an acquaintance with a certain background or contextual information. But the important point is that, in principle and given an observer with the right background and information, such qualities can be seen; they are part of the visual qualities of the object. And that makes them aesthetic qualities. In the same usage, an object that has aesthetic qualities is an aesthetic object.

Obviously, artworks are aesthetic objects. They are the paradigm cases of aesthetic objects. They can be thought of as objects that have been made deliberately to have such qualities, qualities that we will find particularly interesting or meaningful. But other kinds of things can also have aesthetic qualities and therefore can be aesthetic objects. For example, we often look at trees, mountains, pebbles, for their aesthetic qualities, that is, for how they look. Not only natural things but artifacts as well: city streets, automobiles, buildings. It is true also of living things: horses, birds, even people. They all can be perceived, hence have appearances, hence have aesthetic qualities. Often such qualities are relatively simple or lacking in meaning, not worth looking long at, when compared with artworks. But, interesting or not, they have aesthetic qualities.

There is an implicit contrast of aesthetic qualities with what we might, with some hesitation, call real qualities. Aesthetic qualities belong to appearances; real qualities belong to reality. Imagine a structure that looks fragile, though in fact it is very strong. Then its aesthetic qualities — weakness, fragility — are the opposite of its real qualities — strength, toughness. Or an automobile may look fast and sporty and yet be actually slow and sedate. Ideally, of course — at least from the designer's point of view — the aesthetic and the actual qualities will be very similar.

"Aesthetic" can also be used as an adjective to describe states of mind of the observer, as in the aesthetic attitude, experience, point of view, perception. This is the other side of the usage we have just discussed. If aesthetic qualities are what can be perceived, then there must be someone that perceives them. And the state of mind of that someone as she looks at aesthetic qualities — at the appearances of things — is an aesthetic state of mind. If our interest is in the aesthetic qualities of things as we look at them, then our point of view is the aesthetic point of view, our experience is aesthetic experience, and so on. Our state of mind is aesthetic whenever we look at things for the qualities and significance of their appearances.

Notice that there are two slightly different ways of speaking of aesthetic qualities and our experience of them. One is as if their character is wholly perceptual and our grasp of them is unmediated by thinking, somewhat as we perceive colors. In this case, we are likely to speak of the quality of aesthetic experience and the pleasure it brings. The other way of speaking is as if aesthetic qualities are more like meanings and we have to interpret their significance in order to understand them. In this case we are likely to speak of the depth of art and the insight it brings. These two ways of speaking are not necessarily at odds with each other and we will treat them as alternative ways of speaking of the same things. Nevertheless the second way, that of speaking of significance and interpretation, is currently gaining on the older way, of speaking of quality and direct perception.

We will consider a case, speaking of it first in the older way that is becoming less popular and then in the newer way. In doing so we will retrace some of the key distinctions we inherit from the eighteenth century that have affected our idea of the aesthetic. Suppose I am looking at a pond nestled between wooded hills. This experience might be aesthetic and it might not. According to what we have said, it would be aesthetic if I am paying attention to its perceptual qualities for their own sake; that is, if my motivation for looking is the pleasure or interest of apprehending the qualities of its appearance. We could put this latter condition in a negative form. My experience would not be aesthetic if my motive were to see whether it will supply enough water for my cattle, or whether it appears to be stocked with game fish, or some other practical concern. In that case, the thought is, I am concerned with some part of the reality of the pond and not with its appearance; and though in my looking I might be paying attention to perceptual qualities, my state of mind is oriented to the actuality that they may reveal. Is the pond really as big as it looks? Do the changes of tone in the water's surface reveal changes of depth beneath? If these are my questions, then we would say that my experience is not aesthetic.

At this point we have re-created the distinction made by eighteenth-century aestheticians, who tended to see their primary task as identifying the distinctiveness of aesthetic experience. They identified the aesthetic with the perceptual, as we did above; and additionally they focused on the absence of practical motives, which they called "disinterestedness." It is important to realize that disinterested does not mean uninterested and is really a kind of technical term of philosophers. The idea gained its importance as part of an attack in the eighteenth century on Hobbes's theory that all human activity is really self-interested, that is, "interested." Hobbes argued that, despite some appearances and many protestations, all human actions are selfishly motivated. If I help a friend, he said, it is only because she may someday help me in return, or because it makes me feel good, or to avoid feeling guilty, or from some other similarly "interested" motive. Opponents of this view looked for kinds of experience that were not self-interested, namely, those that were "disinterested." One much discussed example was that of a judge trying to decide a case on the merits of the evidence, where nothing personal for the judge depends on the outcome. Another case was our response to beauty, whether in art or nature. Why do we enjoy looking at beautiful things? We needn't have any other motive, was the answer, than simply the pleasure of looking at them. That is, we look at them "for their own sake." This is what "disinterested" means, that we are disengaged personally, unmotivated by any personal interest in the outcome. Our attention is only on the qualities of the object and is not on practical consequences of any kind.

This negative way of describing aesthetic response has had a bad reception in the twentieth century. The reason is that it suggests that art is removed from the problems of life and that our response to it is unemotional and of no consequence to us personally. Of course this suggestion is misleading. Artists are often deeply engaged in social, political, or religious problems and movements. Many artworks deal with social or psychological problems and often they make political points; for example, Goya's *Lo Mismo* (fig.3) is surely a passionate protest against war. And our response to artworks may be tense and moving and may relate to important emotional and moral themes. In short, art is by no means cut off from life and individual passion, and for that reason words such as "disinterested" no longer seem to do justice to aesthetic experience.

But it helps to see that there is some truth in the old way of putting things. Sometimes, or for some people, a personal involvement with an issue can be too great to be able to deal well with it in art. Artists may be too personally engaged with an issue like rape to be able to translate their feelings effectively into artistic terms. Viewers may be too preoccupied with their personal situations to be able to attend well to a work that strikes psychologically close. Many people feel that issues like gang rape, lynching, Nazi atrocities, are too horrible to even talk about, much less to explore artistically. Many viewers have recently found Robert Mapplethorpe's explicit photographic pictures of homoerotic acts too repulsive to enjoy or to contemplate aesthetically.

Even a nonemotional but practical motive *may* diminish the aesthetic experience for us. Suppose you are a keen fisherman looking at the pond. You may focus only on the question of just which spot to cast a line from and ignore all the other aspects of the pond's appearance. Imagine a race of creatures just like us except that everything they did was motivated in a utilitarian way. They are Martians, perhaps, or computer-driven robots. Such a race would never look at things or listen to them *just* for pleasure, would never be interested in appearances for their own sake. They might be as intelligent as humans are in other ways, but they would not be human because they would be incapable of aesthetic experience. In this sense, it is true that aesthetic experience is quite unlike much of our other experience: it is enjoyed for its own sake, it has no motive other than itself. It is a taste of heaven.

It might be said, in response to this, that the reverse is also true. Sometimes an artist creates her best work out of personal crises and the strength of her emotional engagement adds strength to her work. The same thing is sometimes true of the response to art: we may find a work more powerful when it touches on our own emotional problems. And the fisherman may have a heightened aesthetic response to the pond just because he attends so much more closely to its nuances, to its ripples and variations of shadow, its quietness and varying depths. We agree with this. We would even say that one of the important by-products of interacting seriously with art is the ability to reflect on and to talk about deeply disturbing emotions and issues. The summary is that sometimes it helps and sometimes it hinders our aesthetic response to be personally engaged with the theme of a work. What makes the difference is a function of the person and the circumstances as well as of the artwork, though we are tempted to say that the less experience one has with art in general the more personal motive hinders one's aesthetic response.

We therefore prefer to put the point positively rather than negatively. We prefer to talk about what one does attend to in aesthetic experience rather than what one does not. In aesthetic experience we are interested in the qualities of appearances, the way things look to us. The pond, for instance, appears calm and peaceful in the evening, or perhaps a little eerie and mysterious. These qualities — peacefulness, eeriness — are visual qualities of the pond that we can apprehend and savor for their own sake. We may also be aware that it is a three-acre body of water, stocked with bass and blue gill, and that the evening is a good one for fishing. In that case it is a question whether we can combine our interest in catching fish with a continued attention to the general qualities of the lake. Peacefulness, eeriness, can also be thought of as a kind of meaningfulness seen in the pond, symbolic overtones of the pond's appearance. The symbolic overtones might be elaborated and made more particular by further attention to the pond: perhaps the quietness suggests peace, the peacefulness of sleep, of death; the dark ripples suggest the smallness of individuals and their impermanence; the mass of water unmoving beneath the ripples suggests permanence, eternity, and so on. These may all be aesthetic qualities of the pond and our experience of them will be aesthetic experience so long as we are actively interested in them. No doubt there is an element of cliche in this example, but so long as the qualities are seen in the pond itself, experienced as part of its appearance, they are aesthetic qualities. This will be so whether or not we want to catch fish for supper.

This is the positive way to say it. Notice that we must not take the expression "for its own sake," too exclusively. When Susan is asked why she is majoring in history ("I mean, what can you do with it?") and she replies that she likes it "for its own sake," she does not mean that she sees no relationship between history and the real world. She means that she is not taking it simply to get a job, fulfill university requirements, please her parents, meet other history majors, or for any practical reason alone. She finds history interesting as history, though part of that interest lies exactly in the relationship of history to the present. It is much the same with aesthetic experience — we enjoy artworks as significant objects and part of their significance has to do with their complex relations with real life.

In the same way, we should not assume that talk about aesthetic experience implies an exclusiveness of motives. It might be doubted that we do, in fact, ever look at things only for the sake of their appearances. Isn't there always, we might ask, an element of some other interest — sexual, economic, religious — in any experience? We are in a sense back to the question raised by Hobbes. Can there ever be experience that is completely unconcerned with self? Perhaps not. In that case, there may be no pure instances of "aesthetic experience." But we can have a mixture of motives, and our experience will be aesthetic in character to the extent that it is shaped by an interest in appearances as such. To the extent that an experience is oriented to the qualities of appearance, it is to that extent aesthetic.

The discussion obviously is relevant to our previous account of the structure of the debate about the distinction between art and craft. We can define a work of art as an object that someone deliberately designed to be interesting to aesthetic attention. Unlike a pond, a painting is made for the primary purpose of provoking an aesthetic response. The artist creates it to have more interesting or more meaningful perceptual qualities. On the other hand, many craft objects are made with a dual purpose in mind: both to be enjoyed for their appearance and to be used for some practical purpose. The eighteenth-century philosophers considered these to be works not of art but of craft. We can see why. It was because they emphasized the negative point about attention, that one should not attend to practical matters, rather than the positive point, that one should attend to appearances for their own sake. They were afraid that the practical function of a work of craft would distract the viewer from the aesthetic one. If a pot has water in it, we may be more interested in drinking the water than in looking at the pot; and in that case it would not serve us as an aesthetic object. They also thought that practical constraints would limit the aesthetic possibilities open to the artist. The artist may imagine a thousand interesting forms, but if the pot is to be useful, it has to hold water. Hence it may be less interesting or less meaningful than something designed without practical restrictions. For these reasons they expected works of craft to be aesthetically less interesting than works of art and treated them as second-class citizens.

The distinction between arts and crafts is no longer a useful one and can no longer be defended on philosophical grounds. One has to remember that the eighteenth century had a different set of problems than we have. They were still consolidating the idea of aesthetic qualities or experience as being different from other kinds of qualities or experience. Before that time, all skillfully made objects were called works of art. This only meant that it took skill, attention, and knowledge to make them, not that their appearances were particularly significant. In the eighteenth century, people began to distinguish for the first time between the aesthetic and the nonaesthetic and so, for reasons explained above, between the fine and the useful arts. Later the useful arts were called crafts. We still have remnants of these older ways of speaking in our language. We still use "art" in the preeighteenth century way to mean simply something connected with skill. For instance, we speak of the art of blacksmithing or of administration and of *objets d'art*. And we still speak of the fine arts and the useful arts, meaning arts and crafts.

Today, when we are much clearer about what is aesthetic, we do not need to maintain a clear distinction between art and craft, and it has more or less been discredited. It is too general to be useful. It is a poor substitute for the much more fine-grained distinction between works that are aesthetically worthwhile and works that are not. There are so many kinds of objects and so many combinations of practical and aesthetic functions that no systematic distinction can work. Architecture has always presented a problem for the distinction. Many cultures make no distinction between arts and crafts and produce objects in which the aesthetic and the practical criteria merge easily. And today it is often hard to tell whether an object truly has a utilitarian purpose, or whether instead it just refers to a tradition of design for use. Many works are intended predominantly as aesthetic objects and yet carry the suggestion of practical use, a suggestion that enriches them rather than a necessity that distracts. An example is Susie Duncan's *Teapot Form* (fig. 6), which, we might say, rather than just being a teapot,

Figure 6. Susie Duncan, *Teapot Form*, 1988. The National Council on Education for the Ceramic Arts/Damien Johnson and Martina Schenal.

refers to the idea and uses of teapots as well. Our conclusion is that works of craft may be just as worthy of aesthetic enjoyment as anything else and that philosophy cannot defend the systematic use of the distinction between art and craft.

Summary

In this chapter we have defined aesthetics as the philosophy of art. We have described philosophy as consisting of both analyzing concepts and arguing about substantive general topics. For most people, we said, aesthetics begins with a problem, with something that puzzles us in an encounter either with artworks or with talk about art. This is a good way to teach it to students because the connection with their experience will make it more meaningful. It will also help them integrate the various disciplines of the study of art, even while distinguishing them. The methods of aesthetics cannot be reduced to rule but can be described as considering examples and counter-examples, making connections with what we already know, looking at language carefully, and considering the history of ideas. Finally, by way of example, we discussed the rather general concepts of art and of the aesthetic.

NOTES

1. Gene Beery, "NOTE: MAKE A PAINTING OF A NOTE AS A PAINTING," 1969 and Donald Burgy, Rock, Series #1," 1968.

2. Nelson Goodman, for example, tries to do just this in his *Languages of Art* (Indianapolis: Bobbs-Merrill, 1968). So too, from a different point of view, does Susanne Langer in her *Form and Feeling* (New York: Scribner, 1953).

3. Benedetto Croce, *Aesthetics*, trans. D. Ainslie (London: Macmillan, 1909) p. 90 ff.; Roger G. Collingwood, *The Principles of Art* (New York: Oxford University Press, 1958), p. 93 ff.

4. See, for example, the introductory essay in Arthur Danto, *Cindy Sherman: Untitled Film Stills* (New York: Rizzoli, 1990).

5. See Terry Barrett, *Criticizing Photographs: An Introduction to Understanding Images* (Mountain View, Calif.: Mayfield Publishing, 1990).

6. Linda Nochlin, "Seurat's *Grande Jatte:* An Anti-utopian Allegory," *The Art Institute of Chicago Museum Studies* 14:2 (1989).

7. See, for example, Sally Hagaman, "Philosophical Aesthetics in Art Education," *Art Education* (July 1990).

2

Art and Audience

The Need for Aesthetics in Art Education

Art education is today passing through an unusually difficult period. It is a time of intensive questioning and change, when being an art teacher is probably more interesting than ever before, a time to make one think of the proverbial Chinese curse: may you live in interesting times! The interest comes from the fact that our art education, and our world in general, is changing rapidly. Some of these changes lie within our schools, some in the world of art itself, others in our culture more broadly. And of course these three kinds of change are not really separable, for both school and art inevitably reflect the culture of which they are a part.

Our mainstream tradition of art has for a century been in a state of continuous change. It has consisted of a succession of movements and styles, accompanied by a value system that promotes change and results in the deliberate search for the new and the discontinuous. Change in our art world has now become so rapid that it is no longer a question of succession but of simultaneity of movements and styles. Where there was once a sense that art history was like a stream, moving in a direction that could be discerned at least in retrospect, it is now more like a mosaic or perhaps a jigsaw puzzle, colorful, multitudinous, difficult to understand as a whole. Increasingly, many of the traditional ways of thinking about the arts, in which most of us have been trained, are called into question. We are urged to abandon the old expectations of art, the old assumptions about art history, and the old criteria for artistic excellence. And yet among the many competing and often radical challenges that have appeared, no particular theory of art has been widely accepted. The result is the simultaneous advocacy of many theories of art, in the same way we have the simultaneous existence of art movements. These newer theories often have some elements in common, especially their criticism of what has gone before, and yet they differ among themselves a great deal. For the sake of convenience, we will call this kind of change in general "postmodernism" and these kinds of theories "postmodernisms."

A second kind of change is evident in our schools every day. Our students increasingly come from diverse cultural and ethnic backgrounds, and the demand grows for educational programs that are more responsive to those backgrounds. The demographic facts about schools in the United States are well known. By the year 2000, about fifty percent of the students will be from traditional "minority groups" in the U.S. The number of newer immigrant American groups is also growing fast and commonly results in situations where several different languages are spoken in one classroom. More importantly, we are becoming a pluralist society where the differences between cultural origins are publicly respected and fostered and where membership in a particular cultural group is a matter of pride. Sometimes progress in this respect seems to come slowly, but it is also inevitable. What is most significant is that our society has adopted multiculturalism as a goal and regards cultural diversity and understanding as desirable because it is a fulfillment of democracy and a national strength. We expect schools to help students to understand and be proud of their cultural backgrounds. We also expect schools to teach understanding across cultural differences, so that students will be able and willing to learn from each other. Moreover, the same thing is increasingly taken as desirable across national boundaries. Students should come to understand something of the cultures of other countries and peoples. The arguments for this are both practical and idealistic; the practical have to do with peace and world trade, and the idealistic with what we can learn from each other. Oversimplifying as we did before, we will label this kind of change "multiculturalism."

In this catalog of kinds of change, we must also mention the demand for equal treatment by groups other than ethnic groups. The most notable of these are women's and gay and lesbian groups. Women raise questions about whether our art tradition promotes respect for or understanding of women. Why are so few women artists represented in the traditional art canon? What is the image of women in traditional art? Have we systematically undervalued the kinds of art with which women have been most involved, arts that are often dismissed as being only crafts? What about quilting, for example? And do women have different values in art, more social and less individually oriented values? Gay and lesbian groups have raised questions about the social content and functions of art. The recent (1990) debates in the U.S. Senate about the National Endowment for the Arts have brought into focus questions about censorship and the relevance of subject-matter to judgments of art. There are questions, too, about the degree to which aesthetic values can be kept separate from social or religious values and how far art can be used in the service of social causes. Underneath some of this lies the question of how far women's groups, or gay and lesbian groups, can claim to represent a different culture. Does their art require a knowledge of particular cultural background material if we are to understand it? Is this kind of change a part of multiculturalism? The same question arises in connection with particular regions of the country. Is there an Appalachian art? A Cajun art? How many kinds of cultures and art forms are there that can lay claim to separate representation in school? How, in any case, do we decide when a culture is distinct from others?

In our view, the changes we have mentioned form the inescapable background to the major questions in both art education and aesthetics today. Among other things, they account for the increased interest in aesthetics, including the teaching of aesthetics in schools. Such changes create the need for a book of this kind, because they are what make us uncertain about what to count as art, how to think about it, and how to teach it. To take just one example, multiculturalism suggests that we should promote respect for artistic traditions of different cultural origins. This raises questions about the status and role of the canon of the Eurocentric art tradition. What is the canon and what is its relation to the culture and its politics? How do works become members of the canon and do they deserve their status? How far are we to demote or ignore the Eurocentric tradition? And how are we to make curriculum choices among all the other art traditions of the world? And which examples from those traditions shall we choose? Even more unsettling, is cross-cultural understanding really possible in school? How much will our students understand of art from cultures other than their own? How much, and what kind, of information should we supply students about cultural background? When does this cease to be a study of art and become a part of social studies? And so on. Every teacher is familiar with questions of this kind.

Notice that these questions are connected with issues in both aesthetics and in art education. For example, a major question in aesthetics is whether and how cross-cultural understanding of art is possible. A major question of art education is what cross-cultural goals to adopt and how to teach for them. Is the purpose somehow to preserve different traditions as they are, separate from each other, in their present integrity? Or is it to foster their amalgamation into one comprehensive, interacting art world? The boundaries of what we call art traditions are in any case very permeable, like the boundaries of the cultures in which they are found. Cultures and art traditions are always changing and influencing each other, always hybrid in one way or other. This makes it difficult to decide when we are dealing with a different cultural and artistic tradition. For instance, is there an African American aesthetic that is distinct from that of the mainstream? If we are to appreciate African American art, do we need to know a different history, a different set of values, and a different set of assumptions and conventions? The same question can be raised about the art of Japan or Russia. How important are the cultural and artistic differences? How much similarity is there? What is required to bridge the differences, if that is what we are trying to do? Urgent questions like these directly affect matters of curriculum and instruction. Providing answers for them is a task for the philosophy of art and of art education.

Art and Audience

How does social change raise questions about art and its audience? Imagine for a moment a traditional society that is *not* in the process of significant change. It has an ongoing and successful art tradition. Artists produce work according to established norms and there is an audience for their work that understands and appreciates it. There is no knowledge of art from other cultures. In such a society, much of what the average person needs to know about art may be learned in the ordinary processes of growing up and being socialized. People learn informally, through undirected experience, what kinds of things are artworks and what kinds of conventions and norms they conform to. There is no dispute about such things and people adopt definitions and values in the form of unnoticed assumptions while they are paying attention to particular artworks. In such a situation, there is little need for aesthetics in the schools. Aesthetics may be a small, specialized, branch of philosophy, but there would be no use for it among the art-loving citizens. Studio work and art criticism would have a place in schools, the latter being restricted to the criticism of individual works and artists. Art history would have a minimal educational role to play, and aesthetics none at all.

This situation is an imagination, of course, because there is no society that does not change. But change is a matter of degree, and the idea of an unchanging culture is useful because it allows us to see one of the essential conditions of a successful art tradition. The continued production of art requires a continuing understanding between artists and their audience about what kinds of things are artworks and about what makes them worthwhile. Art in this respect is like language: it exists only within a community of persons that understand it in approximately the same way. Its significance is sustained — and indeed created — by the mutual understanding of artist and audience that enables them to interpret it similarly. This community of artist and audience may be as large as an entire society, as we imagined above, or it may be a small group of persons within a larger social context. But in either case, the art is really a group creation, made possible only by the continuing communicative practices of the group and its grasp of the conventions and expectations that constitute art in that tradition.

In such a situation, the common conventions and expectations about art will seem to be natural and universal. People might even believe that all cultures share them and that they are valid for all art. We become aware of our own assumptions only when they are brought into doubt. Even if, in our imagined unchanging culture, there were a knowledge of the art of other cultures, it might still seem that the culture's own art was based on the only reasonable assumptions. The art of other cultures would be interpreted in light of those assumptions and conventions or dismissed as not worth knowing. And again there would be little need for aesthetics, because there would be no debate about what is to count as art or how it is to be interpreted.

In our imaginary unchanging society, the purposes of art education would be as unproblematic as the nature of art. It would be to ensure that the mutual understanding of artists and audience continues, so that art itself can continue. An ambitious educator might want to add the purpose of refining the audience's understanding of art, or of extending it further through the population, or even of improving the abilities of artists. But there would be no need for a debate about the basic purposes of art education or the nature of its curriculum, anymore than about the nature of art. In fact, art education might not be discussed at all, being more a matter of informal processes than of formal schooling, carried out by museums, churches, families, unplanned practices of different kinds. Art education itself might be taken for granted, because the continued understanding of artists and audience could be taken for granted.

Of course, our own situation is very different from this imaginary one. Change occurs in our society at an uncomfortably rapid pace and we are deluged with information from other cultures and traditions. The contrast helps clarify a basic fact about our society today: we are in danger of losing the community of understanding that makes the continuation of art possible. Artists and audiences do not automatically understand each other today. This determines for us the primary purpose of art education, which is to do what it can to promote that understanding. And since the pace of change has almost destroyed the informal mechanisms of common learning and the transfer of unnoticed assumptions and expectations that we used to rely on, art education has to become more reflective and philosophical. It has to bring to conscious awareness matters formerly passed on as unconscious assumptions. To do this, it has to include aesthetics.

Is Cross-Cultural Understanding of Art Possible?

How important is a knowledge of cultural context for understanding an artwork? Can we ever really understand artworks from other cultures? These questions have been pondered by many art educators. They are also topics in aesthetics. It used to be widely argued that we can and should appreciate an artwork in terms only of what can be directly seen in it, without knowing anything of its cultural origins. This view is less popular today. But then, what is the alternative? How much must we know of the cultural origins of a work if we are to appreciate it? Must we master everything that might be relevant in the original culture? This seems to be an impossible prescription, since it almost requires us to be a member of that culture. After all, is it inevitable that we look at the art of other cultures from our own perspective, understanding it only in the terms of our culture? And in that case is the search for cross-cultural or multicultural communication a mirage?

These questions may seem overwrought. On a first glance, with many works there may seem to be little problem. Often, art seems to speak directly and powerfully to us. At such times, there is no need for words or for thought of a deductive or intellectual kind. We feel no need to know anything of its background. The work has an immediate appeal for us, that is, an appeal that is not mediated by words or concepts, and it provides itself all the knowledge we need to have to understand it. We might say that it speaks a language more universal than words, and we are inclined to think that it will have the same appeal for anyone who sees it, regardless of their background. Words and further information seem beside the point. Such an experience is not uncommon with works from unfamiliar cultures. For example, the Bundu mask (fig. 7) is likely to strike most of us as quite beautiful, possessing a grace and serenity that is very appealing. In such cases, art seems accessible in a way that foreign languages are not. People can enjoy works of music and art that they have never studied, something obviously not possible with a foreign language. The directness with which some art speaks to us is an important fact about it.

Figure 7. Bundu mask, Mende Shande Society, Sierra Leone. Collection of Gene Blocker.

This directness, however, can be misleading and is often overstated. Art of other cultures can also leave us cold, be unintelligible, or seem merely grotesque. In such cases it seems obvious that we have to know something of its background to make any sense of it. In most cases, the art that speaks directly to us comes from our own traditions. Then, we want to say, the directness of our response rests on a set of expectations and conventions that we share with artists and their original audience and that lie beneath our conscious awareness. The immediacy of the appeal relies on intuitive understandings that we hardly notice. It is not that there are no intermediary interpretations; it is that we are not aware of them. All art, we would say, rests on expectations about its functions and how the audience should respond to it, and all art uses conventions that give shape to its structure and meaning. But in many cases these expectations and conventions have become habitual to us and have faded into transparency. This is an important psychological phenomenon. As we become familiar with expectations and conventions they fade from consciousness and move to the periphery of awareness, and there they seem more the products of nature than of culture. If we learned them as children, we may never have been aware of having acquired them at all. We may have absorbed them without noticing them, along with much else of our culture. In this respect, art may not be so different from language after all. We usually know the conventions of our own language only in an intuitive and not in an explicit way, and even its vocabulary can be transparent so that we notice not the words we use but the things we speak of. Yet when we encounter a foreign language, we often become aware of the conventions and the words themselves, and of the intermediate interpretative effort required to make sense. Something like this is true also of art, though the conventions are not so clearly formulable as are those of languages, and the vocabulary has much more to do with cultural ways of life in general.

The unconscious assimilation of ideas accounts for the immediate appeal of art from our own culture. But what about the apparently similar appeal of art from other cultures? This is more difficult to explain. Part of it may be due to some elements in art that are universally appealing — colors, lines, shapes, and combinations of colors, lines, and shapes that communicate at a primal, nonconventional level. After all, if there were no such inherently appealing sensory properties, it is hard to see how cultures could construct the conventions and expectations on which their art traditions rest. What would there be to build on? An analogy might be made from the case of sexual energies and their expression. Human societies channel sexual energies in many different and highly conventional cultural patterns, some of which are hard to appreciate cross-culturally; but this is only possible because there is a primary sexual energy in human nature to begin with. In the same way, there must be a primary aesthetic impulse oriented to the attractions of visual appearances.

This biological base alone will not explain much. Whatever elements in art are inherently appealing to human nature, their arrangement and combination into works of art is still highly conventional and culturally dependent. These combinations inevitably carry references to other works in the same art tradition and to other objects that are culturally significant. Art always carries overtones and nuances that are artistic, religious, and social in a particular society and not elsewhere. It is much the same with expectations of function and of what the audience is to do with the art object. There are perhaps some nonconventional elements with which we may understand some of the purposes of art objects. For instance, baskets are made to hold things and we can all appreciate the relation of a basket's form to this basic function. Similarly chairs are for sitting and clothes are for wearing. We may even say that some objects are for ornamentation and decoration and that we can all respond to that. But again the explanation does not take us very far. Clothes, for instance, are also for producing an impression, the more obviously so when they are thought of as aesthetic objects. That makes them culturally relative. A costume may be intended to produce the impression of a king, a god, or a solid citizen; but then everything will depend on what qualities are expected of a king, a god, or a solid citizen in the relevant society. The mask in figure 8, for instance, is thought to be the mask of a river god, and it was worn as a part of a complete costume. The way its original audience responded to it depended on their concept of the god and its powers and on the role it played in the dances and ceremonies that the costume was designed to be a part of. Even its visible aesthetic properties were dependent on these things. Does it look threatening, comic or kindly? Is it majestic and remote or familiar and intimate? The answers surely depend in part on whether the river god was thought of as threatening or protective, majestic or familiar. We cannot determine which of these qualities the mask has by only looking at it. One can get a sense of the original look of the work only if one has some knowledge of its cultural background.

One of the issues here is whether the aesthetic qualities of an object — that is, the way it looks — can be sharply distinguished from its religious or other qualities. If this distinction can be clearly made, it will be because artworks can be grasped directly in perception alone and

Figure 8. Tapa mask, Yoruba River God, Nigeria. Collection of Gene Blocker.

appreciated without being interpreted or understood. This is a view that we discuss more fully in our fifth chapter, under the title "formalism." Formalism was popular in the early part of this century but has lost credibility more recently. We have already suggested that we do not agree with it by arguing that we often need to know something of the culture of an artwork's origin. It is the frequent transparency of these assumptions and expectations that sometimes makes it plausible that perception does not require a knowledge of them. In fact most people nowadays recognize that an artwork calls for interpretation by the viewer, whether that interpretation is self-conscious or not, and that it is for that reason a symbolic object in some sense. Part of the reason for this increased recognition is our increased familiarity with works of other cultures and of the problems we have responding to them. Cases like those of the mask of the river god are increasingly common, where the object's aesthetic properties — the way it *looks* — seem to depend at least in part on its meanings and functions. Many times the reverse also is true: that the religious function is better fulfilled because it readily takes on a certain look. The mask is a better symbol of the river god if it is easily seen as having the qualities of the god, threatening or protective, majestic or familiar, as the case may be; if, in other words, its visual structures easily support the cultural interpretation.

We are currently witnessing a swing of opinion away from the Formalist position and toward a view, according to which, at its extreme, the properties of an artwork are determined almost wholly by its cultural background and the artwork itself determines little. This results in the claim that art does not really exist except as a part of a broad cultural context and its aesthetic qualities cannot be distinguished from its social, historical, religious, and political meanings. We reject this view also, for reasons discussed later. We think one can reasonably make some distinctions between aesthetic and other kinds of properties, without denying that one is dependent on the other.

The Incompleteness of Interpretations

The issue can be rephrased as an issue about how interpretation works. To respond to a work fully and relevantly we must interpret it. But can we ever interpret a work from another culture in a relevant way? One can lay out opinions on this question on much the same continuum, ranging between the same two extremes. At one extreme is the view that one can interpret any artwork, irrespective of its origins, if we approach it freshly, looking at it for its purely visual qualities and without worrying about context. In this view, interpretation is limited to noting the connections between the visual elements of the work and their visual effects, both as parts and wholes; and the aesthetic significance of the work can be sharply distinguished from its cultural or historical significance, because it depends wholly and only on the visual elements seen in this context-free way. In this view, the aesthetic qualities of the artwork – the way it looks and feels – will be universally available.

At the other end of the spectrum is the view that these qualities depend so heavily on the associations and connections of a work's visual elements with its cultural background that one cannot make sense of it without knowing a great deal of that cultural background. According to this extreme view, one should know all of the original cultural associations and connections if one is to interpret a work adequately. This amounts to saying that interpretation must aim at a grasp of the identical meanings the work had for the artist's contemporaries when it was made. But such a grasp may appear to be impossible, since it would require us not only to adopt the cultural associations and connections of another time or place but also to forget our own. This latter may seem to be beyond human ability. An interesting example might be made of the way Picasso and other European artists around the turn of the twentieth century initially interpreted traditional African artworks. They found those works uninhibited, individualistic, spontaneous, expressive, and they thought of them as highly original in form and expression. We now know, or think that we know, that much of that art was quite traditional in both form and expression and that it followed rather closely guidelines handed down from generation to generation. It seems to us now that the interpretation of Picasso's contemporaries was shaped mostly by the situation of art in Paris in their own time. They were struggling to create art that was individualistic, spontaneous, expressive, and original in form; they found what they were looking for in African art. Indeed, generalizing from such an example, we may be so impressed with the difficulty a viewer has in holding in abeyance her own cultural assumptions as to conclude that all interpretations will simply reflect the viewer's background. In that case, each interpretation will be different from others. We may conclude that interpretations cannot be compared with each other and that no one interpretation is any better than any other. This view, although extreme, is increasingly fashionable, and according to it there is no possibility of a reasonably accurate interpretation of artworks from other cultures.

This view also seems too extreme to us. It is an overreaction to the thought that we can never completely understand another culture. Although it may be true that we can never completely adopt the perspective of another culture, it is hasty to conclude that we can never interpret the art of another culture in some reasonable way. It is also true that we can never understand all of another person's mind and feelings, even a person from our own culture. At best all we can do is, through an act of imaginative sympathy, "put ourselves in someone else's shoes." Such an act involves a two-way and alternating interaction. In one direction, we try to see the world the way the other sees it, to relate it to her categories, assumptions, and history. This means, of course, trying to reconstruct for ourself what those categories, assumptions, and history are. We try to accommodate our understanding to match that of the other, putting our own preoccupations and categories aside so far as possible. But this latter putting aside of our own perspectives is only partially possible. Inevitably, we put things in our own terms of reference, translating them into categories and assumptions that we are familiar with and use to understand the world. There is, in the end, no way to avoid completely this assimilation of someone else's perspective into one's own, otherwise one would not be able to understand anything. The key point, though, is that we can do partially what we can't do completely: we can adopt the point of view of another to a degree and we can in part put aside our own point of view. Most of the time this seems to be enough to achieve what we call understanding. It seems that we can understand one another within a particular culture, or so we usually think. Such understanding happens all the time, and if it didn't, it is hard to see how societies would survive. It is rarely complete, but we call it understanding when, because of this two-way process of accommodation and assimilation of perspectives, we have a better grasp of the other person's meanings than we had before. To some extent we enlarge our own perspective to include that of the other, and to that extent we understand. To some extent also we distort the perspective of the other to match our own, and to that extent we do not understand. It follows that understanding is always partial, never complete, but usually worthwhile. It also follows that understanding other people, in all its partiality, is a matter of imagination and of trying, and can almost always be carried further.

It is not dissimilar, in principle, when we try to understand people or artworks from another culture. Our understanding will always be partial and will always be put in terms that fit our own perspective. We will always have a mixture of accommodation to the assumptions and categories of others and assimilation of their assumptions and categories to ours. What we try to do is to find the best combination and reconstruction of their categories and of ours, the one that will make most sense of what the artwork appears to be. This means that we never understand a work perfectly, that is, just as it was understood by its original audience. Indeed, if you could by some miracle do that — understand a work exactly as the people in some other culture understand it, which entails thinking exactly the way they think — then your understanding would be quite irrelevant to the people in your own society. They would then have the problem of understanding you in much the way they had the problem of understanding the work to begin with. Unless we make some connections with the art and interests of our times, and place the culturally different somehow within the orbit of our perspective and concerns, then we cannot talk to each other about it. More important, perhaps, we could learn nothing from it; it would make no difference to us since it could not affect our present understanding of the world.

So it seems that we can never perfectly understand something from another culture. But, on the other hand, this does not mean that we cannot understand its original meaning at all. Understanding is always partial, a matter of more and less. That is what we *mean* by understanding, whether of persons, artworks, or cultures. It would be foolish to deny that a person is tall just because she is not as tall as we can imagine a person being. In the same way, it is foolish to deny that someone understands something, just because one can imagine a better understanding. One can always imagine a taller person and a fuller understanding.

Moreover, notice that on this account a partial understanding has a definite value: one's total perspective grows as one comes to understand a work from another culture. The viewers' categories do not just change to become like those of the original audience; rather they grow to include them. Viewers do not abandon their previous understandings but make new connections with them, enlarging their total horizon of meaning. This is another way of saying that we cannot understand something exactly the way another culture did, for it will always be connected with elements in our own world, even as those connections enlarge our own world. To understand it as the original audience did would be to lose meaning rather than to gain it.

Notice, too, that an understanding can always be improved upon or corrected. We think of art as made by people and therefore "intentional" — that is, we try to approach it in terms of the way the original audience understood it. If archeologists find a handmade ceramic vessel, they will speculate on its original uses. If they think it was a ceremonial wine vessel used in religious ceremonies, this judgment will affect the way we look at it and understand its qualities. If later the archeologists decide that it was really a common pitcher used only for holding drinking water, we will change our understanding of it, and of the society it came from, too. We have already referred to another example of correction and improvement: early twentieth century European interpretations of African wood carvings. There is a longer history here that we can see as a history of progressively better understanding. The first Europeans saw African wood carvings as religious idols and destroyed as many as they could, thinking of them as objects of "devil worship." At the turn of the century, Europeans began to see them as artworks. They saw them first as unconventional and highly personal expressions of feeling, later as expressions of the unconscious mind. Still later, anthropologists insisted that they were parts of complex religious and social patterns and could be understood only in light of those patterns. In each case, the Europeans, trying to be accurate, nevertheless interpreted African artworks in terms of their own particular interests: from a missionary's concern with one religion, an artist's concern with expression, a critic's concern with symbolism, and finally an anthropologist's interest in social function. It is clear that none of these is the original understanding, but it is also clear that some are better than others and that there are reasons one can give for thinking so.

The point applies as much to the teaching of art history as it does to teaching the art of other cultures. Works remote in time may be as culturally foreign as works remote in place, and even where there is a demonstrable historical connectedness of tradition there will also be differences that require an imaginative effort of accommodation to understand. Historical differences are a form of cultural difference and the same kinds of principles apply. It is important to see that the purpose of art history is not to get students to understand ancient works exactly as they were understood by their original audience. It cannot be the purpose because it is not feasible. The purpose is to help students make as much sense of those works as they can, taking into account as much as they can of what we know about the works' origins. This means reinterpreting the past to better fit the present. The word "history" has a double meaning that illustrates the point. It can mean what historians study, the human past. It can also mean the sense we presently make of that past, the understanding that we have of it now. The latter is the inevitable result of studying the former. The natural goal of teaching history is to improve our present understanding of the past, not to replicate an original one.

It can be seen that there is a tension between the effort to understand a work the way it was understood by its original artist and audience and our need to connect it with our own concepts and experience. For the teacher, in practical terms, this is the tension between explaining the original significance of a work and making it relevant to students. This tension is nothing new, of course, though it may help to realize that it is not unique to children. It is a part of what we mean by understanding, a part of the structure of interpretation.

Modernism and Postmodernism

We turn now to the other major kind of change we spoke of earlier: change in the contemporary art world. We are living through a turbulent period in the art world that is often loosely referred to as "postmodern." It is characterized by a greatly increased variety of artforms and movements, by the simultaneous existence of theories and attitudes that would previously have been thought incompatible, and by various kinds of protesting and alternative voices wanting to redefine our concepts of art and artists. Postmodernism is not a single theory but a loose collection of different views and movements. It has been said that postmodernism is only the view that all these other views may coexist side by side without contradicting each other. It has much in common with what we have called *multiculturalism* and has an equal importance for the teaching of art. Because it is so diffuse, postmodernism is difficult to discuss in any detail, but we will say some general things about it for the sake of perspective. We will do this by comparing it with its presumed precursor, "modernism."

Modernism itself is a vast and complex phenomenon that covers many tendencies and takes different shapes in different art forms. Broadly speaking, however, we can say that modernism contains a set of central assumptions about art that achieved dominance between about 1870 and 1970. A partial list of these assumptions would include the following: art history as progress; the role of art in social progress; a traditional canon; objectivity and universality; and the autonomy of the artwork. We will briefly describe each of these assumptions.

Art History as Progress

Modernism assumes an evolving art tradition in which each generation of artists builds on the work of its predecessors. "Building on" implies both using and going beyond; that is, it implies learning from the previous generation and also taking one's predecessors' work a little further than they did. This latter point in turn implies a common direction: one can only "go further" if there is a direction involved. An artist learns from what has gone before to sense the direction in which history is moving and then tries to move further in that direction. This means that the significance of individual works and artists is very much tied up with their place in art history. Picasso's *Demoiselles d'Avignon*, for example, is an important work because of its transitional character: it points the way toward cubism and represents a historical advance. Painted earlier, it would have been meaningless; painted later, trivial. Importance of this kind is only possible in the context of assumptions about a direction in history.

Part of the work of modernist critics and theorists was to articulate the direction of the artistic tradition and to identify the point that current work had reached. There are many minor variants in these stories, but there have been perhaps two major ones. One was the story according to which art moved toward increasingly naturalistic representations of the world. This story is told, for instance, by Gombrich.[1] The development of naturalism in our tradition had two beginnings, once with the ancient Greeks, and once with the Renaissance. From Giotto in the Italian Renaissance onward, one can tell the history of Western art as the gradual movement toward greater naturalism. The other story has to do with the development of abstraction in art. It tells of a movement toward greater purity with respect to the use of the medium, in which artists gradually refined their sense of the essence of their medium. In painting, for example, they progressively abandoned the appeal of narrative, of illustration, of reference to the real world, of the illusion of depth, the rectangular picture frame, each time revealing and exploiting more purely the character of the medium itself. This is the story told, for instance, by Greenberg.[2] An analysis of contemporary attempts to create alternative stories is contained in Carrier.[3]

The importance of thinking that there is a direction in art history is that it allows us to make overall sense of the art world, a sense within which there is a place for interpretations and judgments of individual works and artists. For one thing, it enables us to distinguish between serious or "high" art and other kinds. "High" art is the art that participates in determining the direction of art history. There are many other kinds of art, notably folk art, regional art, and the art of other cultures. In the modernist view, these may be important to the people who create and enjoy them, but they are less important to the tradition because they usually do not affect its movement in a direction. This is a way of saying that they do not reinterpret the contemporary world to us in the way that contemporary high art does.

The Role of Art in Social Progress

Modernism assumes that art has an important role in the evolution of society generally. Social change, we could say, consists of change in material respects, largely because of advances in technology, and also of changes of social norms and values. Obviously, these two kinds of change influence each other. The role of art is to articulate the evolving social norms and values to make them fit the emerging society. Kandinsky, the early twentieth-century Russian painter, expressed this view very clearly. Before social norms and values can be stated logically, enacted legally, or even recognized by the majority, they must be intuited and explored by a few people. This is the role of the artist. In Kandinsky's famous image of the triangle of social change,[4] the artist is first alone at the apex of the triangle, developing a personal vision of the state of the changing society and of the human consequences of its changes. If the artist is successful, her art is gradually accepted, first by artists and critics and others in the art world. This creates a wider base of the triangle. If the art continues to be successful (and by this time it may be an art movement), it is accepted by a wider audience, widening the triangle, until it comes to influence virtually the whole of the society. By that time, no doubt, some other artist is already developing the personal vision that will build on the now successful one.

Thus modernism gives art an enormously important role to play in both individual development and in social change. In this view, art provides a mirror in which we can see and understand our future as individuals and as a society. The assumption is that society is constantly changing and that value choices have to be made in light of the human consequences of change. Art is our way of exploring those choices most sensitively.

Traditional Canon

A corollary of this is that there is a group of widely acclaimed artworks in the tradition. There is a highly selective list of great works, or "masterpieces" — a word that is characteristic of modernism. These are the works that have been most influential in shaping our social norms and values and have determined the direction of art history. Together they form a "canon" that is familiar to all educated modernists. It is largely by studying this canon that the new generation of artists develop their sense of the direction of history and the needs of the times. They work by intuition, internalizing this traditional canon, adopting or criticizing its values, fostering or changing its directions. Something similar happens in the education of citizens in general, though at a lower level of intensity. Citizens also study masterpieces of the tradition, acquiring through them a sense of their own times and of the values that best fit them. Study of art at this level, at the thickest part of Kandinsky's triangle, is important because of its role in the formation of social values. It helps citizens not only to share similar values but also to keep their values up to date with other changes in society. Hence art education has both a conservative and a progressive role to play in the processes of social coherence and change.

Objectivity and Universality

Modernism assumes that, in spite of all the variation in art and taste, it is possible in principle for us to reach agreement in our interpretations and judgments of artworks. We may not *actually* reach this agreement in particular cases because it may not be worth the extended discussion that agreement would require. But in principle and in the important cases we could reach agreement. This is because, according to modernism, some of the reasons we give each other for our interpretations and judgments are relevant and others are not. The relevant reasons focus on the artwork itself and especially on its visual appearance, including its expressive qualities. Because we can be clear about the character of appropriate reasons, we have a kind of objectivity in our arguments and in the observations and inquiries that lie behind them. If we care enough about a particular work, we can continue to look at it and respond to it and to tell each other what we see. We will in the end presumably come to see the same things because they are the things that are objectively there to be seen. This suggests the possibility of a universal, cross-cultural kind of rationality that will solve aesthetic disputes among individuals, groups, and cultures.

Behind this picture of rational discussion and possible agreement in art lie a number of assumptions. Modernism assumes that our common human nature provides a solid foundation for a potentially common response to art. Something in our human nature accounts for our need both to create and to respond to art, though we may not be clear exactly what that something is. An aesthetic foundation is common to humankind and it largely determines the way we respond to art. This assumption motivated the eighteenth- and nineteenth-century search to articulate a universal aesthetic dimension to the human psyche. The view relied a great deal on the thought that we all respond similarly to the visual elements of art — to particular hues and shades, to lines and shapes and volumes, and to particular arrangements and combinations of these. To the extent to which these kinds of elements determine or heavily influence our aesthetic response, to that extent we can say that there is a common foundation that art builds on and that enables us to discuss art across different backgrounds and cultures.

This approach downplays the role of cultural conventions and expectations in determining response but it does not totally ignore it. Modernists are usually quite willing to agree, even to insist, that the viewer needs an appropriate background and training to make interpretations of artworks. The notion of the "ideal viewer" has played an important role in modernist discussions. Certainly the ideal viewer has an awareness of the artistic conventions involved. The idea of a possible universal agreement can include a recognition of the need for an appropriate education and a knowledge of the cultural background of the work. In this case, the claim about universality really amounts to the claim that agreement about artworks is possible within the group of people who know enough of the culture of origin to understand the artworks well. Once the artistic conventions have been learned, they become "internalized" and largely unconscious. Usually, therefore, the emphasis is on a response to the purely visual aspects of art worlds, though guided by a knowledge of artistic conventions that does not extensively involve things cultural.

The Autonomy of the Artwork

The assumption that interpretations can be objective is related to another assumption: that the artwork itself remains the same regardless of who is looking at it. Even if interpretations of the work do vary with different viewers, the work itself does not. The notion of the objectivity of interpretations assumes that we can judge the adequacy of different interpretations by comparing them with the work itself. If the interpretation fits the artwork, it is adequate, relevant, and truthful. If, on the other hand, it attributes to the work some qualities that it does not really have, it is inadequate, irrelevant, and misleading. The assumption here is obviously that we each have access to the same work and it is supported by the commonsense idea that an artwork is after all basically a physical object. Paintings and sculptures seem obviously to be physical objects and in the case of music and literature there are texts that we can all consult. Of course, artworks can age, deteriorate, be lost or destroyed, but these are accidental matters. Unless there are accidents, modernists assume that the same artwork is available to different people, different groups, even different cultures. The important part of this assumption is that changing the context of an artwork will not change what the artwork *is*. The work can be approached in itself, on its own terms, regardless of context, and an adequate aesthetic response will take account only of it and not of other things. In short, what is aesthetically relevant about the work is determined by the work itself and not by the context.

Postmodernism

Within aesthetics, "postmodernism" is a term frequently mentioned but seldom explicitly defined and defended. It is often mostly a reaction to, a criticism of, or a rejection of, many of the longstanding assumptions of the modernist tradition, and it is rarely a clearly articulated and argued theory itself. In other words, it is usually a matter of negative rather than positive claims. This is due in part to the fact that the theoretical underpinnings of postmodernism have arisen outside Anglo-American philosophical traditions, within continental European traditions that American and British aestheticians are often not familiar with. The main elements in the pedigree of postmodernism include French semiotics (e.g., Saussure); French structuralists (e.g., Lévi-Strauss); German phenomenologists (especially Heidegger); French deconstructionists (e.g., Derrida); American followers of Derrida (the Yale group: de Man, Spanos, J. Hillis Miller, Bloom); German hermeneutics (especially Gadamer and Habermas); Foucault and his followers; Marxists (e.g., Althuser); Freudians (e.g., Lacan).[5] Much of this work is formidable to read and is alien to American and British philosophical traditions. To understand de Man, for instance, one would have to have read Derrida and Heidegger, and to understand these one would have to know something of phenomenology (Husserl) and the structuralists (Saussure, Lévi-Strauss). Without such a preparation, virtually every sentence of de Man is incomprehensible and is written in a style that is hard to penetrate. Nevertheless, there are popular introductions and accounts (Culler, Leitch[6]), and we can understand something of postmodernism by contrasting it with the assumptions of modernism.

The Plurality of Art Histories

Postmodernism denies that we can make good sense of art history by attributing a direction to it. It assumes instead that there are many kinds and traditions of art, each existing in its own cultural context. Each of these has its own history to tell and so the very idea that there is *one* art history is misleading. Moreover, these many kinds of art can exist side by side in the same society, especially in a society as complex as ours. The question which is more advanced, avant-garde, or relevant to the future is not one that makes much sense, since there is no reason to prefer one art history over another. This means that distinctions of value between kinds of art also make little sense; in particular, the distinction between "high" or main-stream art and folk art is to be distrusted. There is no good reason to think that contemporary art in New York is any better than folk art in the Appalachian mountains. Indeed, the question of "better" makes no sense here. Is English a better language than Spanish? Is one culture better than another? Is an apple better than an orange? What could these questions mean? Comparisons between art traditions are equally meaningless. It makes little sense to ask which of the many art histories is truer. They do not compete with or deny each other; they coexist. Postmodernism therefore substitutes simultaneity for direction in art history.

Art History as Politics

We might ask, then, how are we to account for the success that the dominant view of our art history and art tradition has had? Postmodernism interprets that success politically. Successful interpretations of art history are not more true than others; they are simply more persuasive. They are the ones that have been accepted by a particular group at a particular time. Of course, one can ask why one view of art history is accepted and another not. The postmodern answer to this question is not that it is truer or closer to the facts, but that it satisfies the interests of the dominant group. The dominant account of art history supports the beliefs and upholds the social values of the dominant social group. This dominance is usually achieved at the expense of other social groups. Our standard Eurocentric art history supports the group that has been in power so long—wealthy white males—and suppresses the interests of other groups. For one thing, it ignores the artworks of other groups and their histories. For another, the story it tells reflects a more general story that flatters the dominant group. This is the story of progress in general, the idea that things have gotten better with each generation. The supposed direction of art history derives from this supposed direction of our civilization itself, and both stories serve to maintain the privileges of those in power.

Of course, with the same logic we could say the same thing about any other art history that might take the place of our received history. If, as a result of protest and persuasion, some other more radical account of art history becomes the received view, it will not be because it is a truer or better account; it will simply support a different social group that has somehow gained power. A feminist art history, for example, would be no more true than what we have now; it would represent simply a decision to support a different social group. For postmodernism, then, the choice between art histories is a political and not an aesthetic choice. In this same way, most questions of value in art are interpreted as matters not of aesthetics but of power.

The Traditional Art Canon as Social Dominance

It follows, then, that the modernist idea of the canon of masterpieces from which we may all learn is just a part of the dominant ideology. The traditional canon symbolizes the values of a Eurocentric male elite. There are many alternative canons one could construct and we could also get rid of the idea of masterpieces altogether. This is the revolutionary side of postmodernism, which encourages all the "marginalized" groups to demand a greater share of attention. All the customary distinctions are politicized: high and low art, masterpiece and minor work, classical and folk, art and craft, great and popular.

One way to understand this is to see postmodernism as removing the conceptual boundaries we have used to keep art separate from other aspects of society — economics, politics, religion, social class, and so on. The earliest dream of the modernists was to be able to interpret an artwork in itself without regard to context or history. Recent discussion of art has increasingly insisted on the importance of context and history and has gradually enlarged the scope of the context in which art should be interpreted. Arthur Danto[7] and others consider the context of the "art world," which includes the entire institutional and intellectual structure of the art establishment — galleries, museums, art schools, art funding agencies, art journals, and the concepts and criteria they use. Postmodernism asks us to expand our contextual horizon still further to include the rest of society, including its politics and economics. Traditionally we have not paid much attention to these broader contexts, and to do so is often referred to as a "historicist" interpretation of art. "Historicist" is the opposite of "universalist." It means that the meaning of a work occurs at a certain time in the history of a culture and keeps changing over time.

This line of thought complicates the already difficult curriculum question for schools. Which artworks should we study in the classroom? In retrospect, the traditional canon made that question relatively easy. Now it has become a difficult intellectual issue and also a political one. In some respects, postmodernism reinforces the effect of what we called multiculturalism on this issue. It supports plurality and weakens the claims of the traditional canon. It sympathizes with the notion that there are many art forms, many styles, many art histories, each with as much right as others to be studied in school. It also favors making student or community relevance a more important criterion than is the customary importance accorded a work by the standard art history books.

But there are differences with multiculturalism too. Most revisionists champion their revisions to art history on the grounds that they are more true than the received version. Many feminists, for example, want to see more women in art history because women actually did produce valuable works that have been ignored. Most cultural pluralists want to see works from other cultures in the curriculum because they are valuable as artworks and are therefore worthy of study. They do not want trivial or worthless pieces to be chosen just because they are from a particular culture. They want the canon enlarged to represent the best of many cultures, rather than just that of the dominant elite. These attitudes do not fit well with some versions of postmodernism, for they presuppose that we can make some judgments as to what is aesthetically worthwhile, and *that* presupposes that aesthetic questions can be distinguished from political ones. From a revisionist point of view, it is demeaning to suggest that the inclusion of works from marginalized groups is wholly a political decision and not an aesthetic one. It implies that their artworks will be studied for political reasons, no matter what their quality, which leads to the worst kind of tokenism in the curriculum.

Objectivity and Individual Meaning

Underlying these issues are more fundamental ones about objectivity. We saw that foundational to modernism is the idea that there is in principle a way to secure agreement about the truth of a claim about art or art history. Postmodernism asserts that this is an illusion. On this view we cannot compare a claim about the way things are with the things themselves; hence we cannot see how far the claim corresponds with reality. The reason is that we can never get outside of our language in order to see whether the language matches reality. There is no direct access to reality independent of language and the way we describe the world determines the way we experience it. We have only experience to rely on and that is linguistically shaped. It follows that there is no way to make our judgments any more objective than they now are, because we can never get out of the linguistic boundaries of understanding. Nor can we have a trustworthy way of reaching an agreement when two persons disagree in interpretation, for each interpretation simply reflects the linguistic background of each person. Any agreement that is reached is more a matter of persuasion or power than of increased truth.

Some postmodernists try to show that the idea of an external and linguistically independent reality is a myth by "deconstructing" the language. Deconstruction shows how language has constructed what we call reality and then deconstructs those constructions. It tries to show that what we took for reality is really just a way of speaking. When it is successful, it exposes linguistic constructions as myths — some favorite myths are the myth of truth as correspondence with reality, of rationality as universal, of science as neutral and value-free. There is a Zen Buddhist saying (borrowed from earlier Taoist philosophers): when you point to the moon, don't mistake the finger for the moon. Postmodernists say something similar about art, except that they think there is no real moon to begin with. There is *something*, of course, but it is not the same thing for all people. If there is something real out there that people point at, moon or artwork, it is a mistake to suppose that we can get behind our way of speaking to the thing itself.

This is not an entirely new idea. Philosophers have long been aware of the gap between theory and reality and many have accepted the idea that there is no direct, linguistically uncontaminated contact with reality. And there have always been sceptics and relativists who, in different ways, have despaired of getting to the direct and unconstructed truth about external reality. But in spite of a long history of scepticism and relativism, the main traditions of philosophy have rejected a radical subjectivism and have instead sought ways of modifying or overcoming it. In the history of philosophy, sceptical positions appear mostly as challenges to be answered; they seldom represent major traditions themselves. Postmodernism is more radical than past philosophy because it rejects the attempt to overcome sceptical and relativist positions and instead embraces them. It does not try to defend the idea of objectivity from the subjectivist impulse; it attacks the idea of objectivity in the cause of subjectivism. This is a change of attitude as much as of new ideas.

There are too many versions of postmodernism to discuss individually, but there is a distinction between kinds that is worth considering. There are those that emphasize the social and collective character of the limitations on objectivity and those that emphasize the personal and individual. The social variants are much less radical. Their basic argument is that we can never get outside language to the objective reality. Why not? Because "language" is the whole set of concepts and assumptions that we use to make sense of the world, including expectations and behaviors of which we may not be wholly aware. Language is eminently a social and collective construction, a repository and conveyor of the culture of a group. And therefore the linguistic limits on objectivity are also cultural limits. Persons within the same linguistic or cultural community can offer each other reasons that are good reasons within that community, and so they can come to a reasoned agreement about the truth. It will be, not just an agreement, but the truth for persons in that community, though not for persons in another.

An example may help. Suppose someone says that Picasso's *Guernica* is a powerful and impassioned cry of outrage against the inhumanity of war and someone else says they cannot understand it. A similar case might have to do with the African carving we saw in figure 8. Someone might say that in its original context it conveyed powerfully the attitude that a person should take toward a particular river god. To explicate and justify either claim would be to examine the work, its parts and their relationships, against the background of the relevant culture. In the case of the Picasso, this would require enough knowledge of our standard art history to understand the composition and the distortions of the figures as deliberate and meaningful, something of the twentieth-century reaction to naturalism and perhaps also of Spanish mural painting and of the work of Goya. It would also take a wider set of concepts that we usually take for granted: of paintings as expressions of attitudes, of surrealism, of the idea that war *can* be outrageous, perhaps even of the idea of war itself. These ideas connect with others in many ways, though within the culture we don't have to learn them deliberately. The idea that some acts of war can be outrageous, for instance, requires some knowledge of our history of war and of our changing attitudes and theories about it, of the idea of human rights, of human sympathy, of what we mean by outrage and how we justify it. If we have this background of understanding, which comes with the "language," particular claims about the *Guernica* will make sense to us and we can agree or disagree in light of the arguments offered. It will be true within the language community that the *Guernica* is a powerful expression of outrage. It will not be "universally" true, that is, true regardless of language and culture, because its truth is dependent on language and culture. In that sense, truth is socially constructed. This is as close to objectivity as we can come.

The same sorts of things will be true of the claim about the figure of the river god in figure 8, except that in this case we (that is, we the authors) cannot presently spell out the set of understandings that would be necessary. Presumably they would include a knowledge not only of the particular art tradition to which the work belongs but also of the god and the kinds of attributes it has, and of the pantheon and the theology in which the god has its place, and of the sorts of attitudes a reasonable supplicant to the god should have. Given our lack of such knowledge, we cannot understand the claim except by using our generic

knowledge of gods and pantheons. In that case, the figure can be understood only in the thinnest — though still not a negligible — way.

What we said about the Picasso-claim can be said of claims about
democracy, abortion, atomic physics, the psychology of depression,
or whether God exists. These are only meaningful topics within a framework of concepts that are culturally dependent. Within that framework
one can argue about them reasonably and make meaningful judgments
about the truth of claims. But one cannot get outside of that framework
to judge those claims because they have no meaning outside it. The
Guernica has no meaning outside of the cultural framework since it
is constituted as an artwork only within that framework. In another
culture, the same physical object might exist but it would not be the
artwork *Guernica*. Similarly we may say that the object in figure 8
exists today but the original artwork does not exist. Artworks and the
truth of claims about them are both socially constructed, as is the
framework of concepts embodied in the language that makes them
possible. And so we can say that truth is possible, but it is culturally
relative.

This version of postmodernism is not as radical as the personal and
individual versions because it does allow that a work exists, that truth
claims can be meaningful, and that a form of objectivity is possible.
It is not so difficult for traditional philosophers to accept since many
of them had already come to similar conclusions within the Anglo-
American tradition. John Dewey, for example, and Wittgenstein[8] have
written extensively about the linguistic and cultural limits to meaning
and have reached very similar conclusions about the nature of meaning
and the possibility of truth.

The Artwork as the Reader's Construction

Individualist versions of postmodernism are more radical. One of
the notions that they "deconstruct" is that of the artwork as an independently existing piece of reality. We have already mentioned the
modernist assumption that there is one artwork, even though there
may be many different interpretations of it, and even though we may
have no access to the work except through an interpretation. This
assumption allows us to compare interpretations with each other, to
correct one with the aid of another and to ask which is the more accurate. The social variants of postmodernism allow us to say that there
is one artwork *within a culture*. Things change considerably if we drop
this assumption. If we say that each interpretation creates the work,
then for each interpretation there will be a different work created by
it. Each work is then uniquely linked to an interpretation and the

question of the faithfulness of interpretations cannot arise. Imagine watching some people target shooting. If some shots are described as close and others as way off, we imagine there is a target that can be identified independently of where the shots land. But if all shots were said to be equally accurate, or if there were no target at all, then the question of accuracy would be meaningless. It is somewhat like this with the individualist versions of postmodernism.

Postmodernism of this sort gives much greater importance to the viewer. In effect it makes the viewer the creator of the work rather than the *artist*, or, we could say, it makes the viewer an artist. The viewer has always had an important place in aesthetics; in chapter 1 we saw that the aesthetic point of view is traditionally identified as the point of view of the individual person responding to something as an artwork. But in the traditional account the viewer was expected to look at the work as a generic human being — not as a particular one, man or woman, black or white, rich or poor. It was assumed that the viewer would conform to various conventions governing art and would have enough knowledge of the relevant art history and cultural context. In other words, traditionally there was a normative account of a viewer who adopted the aesthetic point of view and was traditionally educated. Postmodernists delight in exposing the assumptions behind this normative account. These assumptions were, for example, that the viewer knew at least the outlines of the Eurocentric art history and tradition, was detached in attitude, had emotional associations that were normal, was politically neutral, and knew how to behave in museums. The philosophical tradition compared real viewers with this ideal viewer, just as it compared interpretations with the real artwork. Postmodernists deny that the ideal viewer exists anymore than the real artwork does. Nor will they accept either as a useful fiction.

If we cannot use the notion of an ideal viewer, then the interpretations of actual viewers all have equal validity. Interpretations, or "readings," become more important than the work, which no longer really exists except in the plural form of its readings. There *are* only readings. This means that art criticism has ceased to be an activity subsidiary to artworks, serving primarily to highlight their qualities; it has itself become a creative art form, generating its own linguistic artifacts. And of course the works of the art critic are no more stable and independently existing than are the works of the artist. They also dissolve into various readings, which are then interpretations of interpretations of artworks. We cannot assess the accuracy of these readings any more than we can assess the accuracy of interpretations of artworks, and all are equally valid. This makes it hard to establish agreements that will allow communication about art to take place, except those agreements that are a matter of early socialization and cultural expectation. But these latter are only habits and cannot be rationally justified. The moment they are questioned or ignored, they lose their validity. The price of emphasizing to this extreme the freedom of individual interpretation appears to be the loss of those conventions and institutions that make possible communication between members of a society or art world. Most philosophers today remain unwilling to pay that price.

Art Education and Postmodernism

For most of us, postmodernisms are both attractive and disturbing. On the one hand, many of the teachers we talk with agree that contemporary art is eclectic, pluralistic, and not moving in a single direction. They welcome the opening of the art world and of art education to disenfranchised traditions and groups and the richness they bring. And they approve an emphasis on what makes art most meaningful to each student in our classes. Art traditions have often been too elitist, too exclusive, and too remote from students' experience. Art educators have often paid little attention to their students' interpretations and to the connections the students make between the artworks they study and the concrete realities of their lives.

On the other hand, however, most of us want to retain the idea of art traditions that shape the meanings of works and are important for students to understand. It seems hard to deny that there are established conventions and expectations of art that help one make sense of many individual works and that therefore students should know them. And most of us think that art tells us something about ourselves individually and collectively and want our students to learn something of its insights. In short, we want *both* for our students to approach art individually and to love it freely *and* also to understand art and to learn what is valuable in it. The problem for most of us, therefore, is not whether to accept modernism or postmodernism, but how to strike the right balance between those approaches and to take from them what is most valuable to us.

When new movements challenge established positions, it often happens that initially the genuine differences are exaggerated. There is a tendency for those who embrace new positions to be more concerned with dissociating themselves from the old views than with explaining the new. This contributes to a sense of an unbridgeable gulf between the two. Each side feels that its views are simplified and caricatured by the other and genuine debate becomes difficult. Certainly, there has been plenty of confrontational writing in the postmodernist debates, writing oriented more to attacking and defending than to achieving clearer understandings. But when we look at the situation rather generally, it appears that many of the differences between modernism and postmodernism are in fact not unbridgeable. When we look at the work of actual modernists we see many anticipations of postmodernism and it seems that the more sophisticated modernists have been evolving for years in that direction. And when we look at the actual analyses of artworks by postmodernists we see that they retain some very traditional elements of modernist analysis.

An important example has to do with the postmodernist denial that there is a real (i.e., absolute) difference between facts and interpretations. This is often presented by postmodernists as a black and white issue. But we can happily accept this denial without abandoning the *relative* use of the distinction as a heuristic device. That is in fact what most of us do in our ordinary affairs. We speak in one context about "facts" that are given various "interpretations" and yet understand that in another context those same facts might be treated as interpretations. For example, it may be a "fact" that Jones committed suicide by jumping out of a fifteen-story window, and we look for interpretations of the fact; why did he do it? Only if the fact is later called into question by new evidence will we treat it as an interpretation. Perhaps new evidence suggests he may have been murdered. Then the fact is that he fell from a fifteen-story window, and the interpretive question is whether he was murdered or committed suicide. In this relative use of the distinction, a fact is simply what is not disputed by a group of people at a particular time and an interpretation is what *is* disputed. Understood in this way, it is still a very useful distinction, though not an absolute one, because it enables us to discuss issues in a reasonable way. We can discuss the adequacy of particular interpretations just because we can, at least temporarily, treat other features of the case as facts. When we interpret an artwork, it is usually possible to establish some facts about it. That is to say, at any given time there are usually some reasonably established conventions and expectations that help us reach a range of agreements about the work and these agreements help us to identify and discuss the issues on which we don't agree. If there were no "facts" at all to begin with, it is hard to see how we could discuss anything at all.

The same sort of point can be made about the claim that we have no direct knowledge of reality and that all knowledge involves a subjective and linguistically mediated point of view. This also is often presented as an all-or-nothing issue. But in fact we can regard the distinction between reality and appearance as useful and even as necessary, even though it is not ultimate. We call things real when we are relatively sure we know what they are; we call them appearances when we are unsure. Suppose we disagree who that person is standing over there on the corner. I say it is Mary; you say it is Taiwo. We approach more closely and see that it is Taiwo. I was "wrong," you were right. Relative to the situation, we can distinguish reality from appearance and truth from falsity, although the distinction is not absolute if that means that it removes all possibility of error. Later it may turn out that it was Taiwo's twin sister, or a holograph of Taiwo, or an artwork by Duane Hanson. But if we do find out that one of these latter possibilities is the case, it will be because we have new evidence, and then in the context of that evidence we will again be able to distinguish the reality from appearance, though again not without possibility of error. The point is that, so long as we do not call the same thing both true and false *in the same context*, it is useful to distinguish truth from falsity and reality from appearance. We can talk with each other about the same work, or tradition, or culture. This is so, even if at the same time we know that interpretations of the work, tradition, or culture, have varied over the centuries and that we have no knowledge of it except through these interpretations. In short, the distinction between reality and appearance is useful, though not ultimate, because it enables us to compare interpretations and to learn from their variety. Modernists and some postmodernists can agree on this.

And finally, the same sort of point seems to apply to the question of objectivity. It is true that no knowledge is completely free of subjective bias and all knowledge must be interpreted through particular conceptual frameworks that embody particular interests. But it is still useful to distinguish between objectivity and bias, between history and propaganda. We can today recognize biases in the history of art that only recently were unchallenged: the Eurocentric bias, for example, or the male bias. It is because of arguments that we can recognize these biases. Multiculturalism and feminism are not merely advertising campaigns but have objective arguments to make; and we have not merely changed our minds but have come to see that we really did have a bias. These arguments are based on the assumption that we can distinguish between bias and objectivity and they have been successful because we can recognize the distinction. But again this does not mean that we assume that we now are operating in a *fully* objective fashion and have no more biases that we are yet unaware of. We assume only that we are more objective, relatively, now that we have recognized some of our biases. In this way, we can make good sense of the relative, though not ultimate, use of the distinction between objectivity and bias.

The conclusion is that we should learn from postmodernisms a measure of modesty about our claims and a sense of the historical character of our understanding. They can help us be more aware of power and political relations than we were. At the same time we should be sceptical of the more extreme claims about the failure of basic distinctions and should continue to do what makes sense to us, not absolutely in all times and places but in our own time and place. Art traditions and conventions have elements of continuity as well as of change, and it is the former that allows us to make sense of the latter. Teaching has always been the attempt to pass on our best understanding of the present so that our students will make sense of the future. Postmodernism shows us how important and difficult that task has become.

NOTES

1. E. H. Gombrich, *Art and Illusion* (Princeton, 1961).

2. Clement Greenberg, *Art and Culture* (Boston, 1961).

3. David Carrier, *Artwriting* (Amherst: University of Massachusetts Press, 1987).

4. Wassily Kandinsky, *On the Spiritual in Art*, trans. Hilla Rebay (New York: Witt, 1946).

5. For a discussion of major topics in postmodernism, see Ferdinand de Saussure, *Course in General Linguistics*, ed. Charles Bally and Albert Sechehaye, trans. Wade Baskin (New York: Philosophical Library, 1959); Claude Lévi-Strauss, *Structural Anthropology*, trans. Claire Jacobsen and Brooke Schoepf (New York: Basic Books, 1963); Martin Heidegger, *Poetry, Language, Thought*, trans. Albert Hofstadter (New York: Harper and Row, 1971); Jacques Derrida, *Speech and Phenomena*, trans. David Allison (Evanston, Ill.: Northwest University Press, 1973); Paul de Man, *Blindness and Insight* (New York: Oxford University Press, 1971); Hans-Georg Gadamer, *Philosophical Hermeneutics*, trans. David Linge (Berkeley: University of California Press, 1976); Jürgen Habermas, *Theory of Communicative Action*, trans. Thomas McCarthy (Boston: Beacon Press, 1984); Michel Foucault, *The Archeology of Knowledge*, trans. A. Sheridan Smith (New York: Harper and Row, 1972); Louis Althuser, *Lenin and Philosophy and Other Essays*, trans. Ben Brewster (London: New Left Books, 1971); Jacques Lacan, *The Four Fundemental Concepts of Psychoanalysis*, ed. Jacques Miller, trans. Alan Sheridan (New York: Norton, 1978).

6. Jonathan Culler, *The Pursuit of Signs: Semiotics, Literature, Deconstruction* (Ithaca, N.Y.: Cornell University Press, 1981); Vincent B. Leitch, *Deconstructive Criticism* (New York: Columbia University Press, 1983).

7. Arthur Danto, "The Artworld," *Journal of Philosophy* 6 (1964).

8. John Dewey, *Art as Experience* (New York: Putnam, 1962); Ludwig Wittgenstein, *Philosophical Investigations*, trans. G. Anscombe (New York: Macmillan, 1953).

3

Art, and the World
It Represents

Theories and the Relations of Artworks

Artworks relate to their surroundings in many ways. A number of these relations provide grounds for attributing meanings to the works and our interpretations will vary as we emphasize one relation over another. In general, we can group art theories according to which kind of relation they emphasize.

In this book, we group the many relations of artworks into four kinds. We have already considered one kind: the relations artworks have with their audience. The audience can be either the original one, those people belonging to the artists' own time and culture who were intended to see it, or it can be the present one, people existing now in our culture. A second kind of relation is that of artworks with the world they represent, whether that world is actual or imaginary. A third kind connects artworks with the individual artists that make them. And lastly there are the relations of artworks with the culture of its origin, including especially the art world of that culture; that is, especially their relations with other artworks, with art institutions and with theories of art. There are also the relations of the elements and forms of a work not with something external to the work but to each other.

If we look at the standard theories in aesthetics, we can say that each tries to interpret art in terms of one of these kinds of relations. Postmodernist aesthetic theories pay most attention to the relations artworks have with their audience; representational theories thematize their relations with the world they represent; expressionist and intentionalist theories, their relations with individual artists; institutionalist theories, the art world relations of artworks; and formalist theories, the internal relations of elements and forms with each other. We find this to be a helpful category system and have organized our chapters in terms of it. In this chapter we discuss theories that stress the relations artworks have with the world they represent.

Before we begin, though, it might be asked why we discuss the standard theories of aesthetics at all. We have already discussed our view that, if aesthetics is to be taught meaningfully in school, it should be problem oriented and linked to the students' own opinions and experiences with artworks. It follows that we do not suggest that theories in aesthetics be used as material for class lectures and discussions. And we do not think that students in school should study these theories as theories or that they should focus on what Plato or Arthur Danto said.

Why, then, discuss the standard theories here? Why not just give a list of problems and cases that can be used in class?[1] For one thing, the standard theories are convenient ways of organizing and remembering the problems, topics, arguments and concepts of aesthetics. They are also ways of understanding the connections between various points and ultimately the significance of the issues involved. It is not that one needs to choose between these theories, as if one of them is true and the others are not. They all contain insights. It is better to think of them, at least at first, as laying out the ground that philosophers contest, the material that they do not agree on but find worth arguing about. The theories then serve as a kind of road map to help one find one's way around the territory of aesthetics.

Underneath this lies a more basic point. Teachers need to know more of their subject than what they teach to students. This is true of teaching any subject, whether it be mathematics, social science, or art. A teacher needs a good sense of how the subject works and feels, of its major topics and problems, and of at least a few extended examples. Only with a good roadmap can one make good choices about where to take the students. Teaching requires many decisions, monthly, weekly, daily, about what is most worth studying with a particular class. It also requires decisions in the classroom about how to answer a question, in which direction to lead a discussion, what is important about a topic, and when to move on to another activity. These decisions are the heart of good teaching. They require of the teacher a good general understanding of the subject. A good roadmap enables one to locate students' concerns in the aesthetic domain and to point them in the right direction. Otherwise student activities may too easily become trivial or irrelevant.

Emphasizing the need for a sense of direction is not inconsistent with urging that teaching should begin with students' experience and problems. Teaching requires one to guide students from where they are to where they might be. A knowledge of both the beginning and the destination are necessary if there is to be a journey. One requires an understanding of the student's thinking, the other of the subject matter. Teachers need to relate the one to the other, the subject matter to the students' experience. We think that, in the case of aesthetics, the best way to do that is from a sense of the standard theories.

Art as Representation

In this chapter we discuss theories of representation. Much visual art depicts or represents some piece of the world, real or imaginary. We will call what an artwork pictures its subject matter. The subject matter, then, is for most people its most immediate aspect. What a work represents is often so dominant an aspect that we naturally use it to identify and interpret the work. This is a picture of plum blossoms, we say; that is an image of a king; even, pointing to a painting, this *is* a plum blossom, that *is* a king. For this reason, the subject matter has been the most persistent theme in Western thinking about art, dominating philosophy and criticism for over two thousand years. It has often been the basis of theories of art. The central question has been, simply: What is the relationship of artworks to the world they represent? For example, can an artwork in some sense tell us the truth (visual or other) about the world?

In what follows we will use the term "representation" as a neutral word for the relation of an artwork to the world. "Representation" is a general term, for there are many ways of representing. To say art represents is to be neutral between various accounts of how it represents. More specific terms, like "imitation" and "interpretation" are used in connection with more particular theories of how art represents. We begin by considering imitation.

Art as Imitation

The most obvious way to think about representation is to think of it as imitation. Art imitates reality. The earliest and most persistent Western theory says that art represents the world by giving us a faithful copy of some piece of it. If this is so, it gives us a way to identify and interpret artworks and perhaps to evaluate them as well.

It is helpful to compare the idea of imitation with that of resemblance. Notice that imitation is not the same thing as resemblance, because it requires intention. If a stone on the beach resembles Fidel Castro, it does not follow that the stone is imitating Fidel, or that Fidel is imitating the stone. On the other hand, imitation does presuppose resemblance of some sort. Imitation is the deliberate attempt to resemble something. It is something people try to accomplish and can succeed or fail at. This is not true of resemblance, conceptually. Two things may not look much alike but there is no question of a failure or a success of resemblance. There is no reason why they *should* look alike, unless we think of one of them as an imitation. Resemblance goes in two directions; imitation in only one. If I resemble Fidel Castro, then he resembles me. But if I imitate Fidel, he is not thereby imitating me. This is another way of saying that imitation has an aim — to look exactly like some real thing — and because it is an aim it can provide a standard by which to judge the imitation.

Sometimes it is assumed that the aim of imitation is not only to resemble but also to deceive; in other words, to create the illusion that the imitation is not a copy at all but is actually the original. This is usually the objective with imitation furs and leather, where the best imitation is one that will be mistaken for real. It is sometimes, but not always, a goal of art. Duane Hanson's work would be a good example. But though deception is sometimes thought to be the inevitable goal of realism in art, it does not have to be. One might be quite content with exact imitation, if one thought it could give one some truth concerning reality.

Plato and the Mirror of Nature

The history of art from the time of the ancient Greeks is full of stories of people and animals mistaking artworks for the objects they depict. It is clear that those stories were meant as compliments. For example, according to the Roman historian Pliny the Elder,[2] Appelles painted a horse so lifelike that real horses tried to communicate with it by neighing. Pliny also says that, in a contest with Parrhasius, Zeuxis painted grapes so realistically that birds tried to eat them; but when Zeuxis went to pull the curtain from Parrhasius's painting, he discovered the curtain was only painted on the canvas, and so the prize went to Parrhasius! It is a greater achievement, Zeuxis said, to deceive a man than a bird.[3]

There is a famous passage in the *Iliad* where admiration for imitation in art is clearly expressed. In describing a pastoral scene embossed in gold on Achilles's shield, Homer writes, "And the field looked black and seemed as though it had been ploughed although it was made of gold, for this was the great marvel of the work."[4]

It was just prior to Plato's generation that Greek naturalism in painting and sculpture reached its high point and on all accounts it was a magnificent achievement in the history of art. It is not surprising, then, that the Greeks began the long history of imitation theories of art. We will give a brief account of Plato's, perhaps the most famous.

In *The Republic* Plato examined the assumptions behind the developments in the art of his time. As a philosopher, he tried to articulate these assumptions clearly and to think through their consequences. This is, incidentally, a good example of the way philosophy is often a response to current developments in art. What assumptions did Plato find in a theory of imitation?

Plato imagines an artist who paints a realistic picture of a bed. The first point he makes about this work is that, no matter how well it pictures the bed, it is not something you can sleep on. Even the most realistic imitation is only *like* the thing it imitates and never a genuine substitute. For it lacks reality. It is all appearance and no reality. How can a two-dimensional object like a painting have the reality of a three-dimensional object like a bed? Even if, like Rauschenberg, we take a real bed, paint colors on it, hang it on the wall, and call it a work of art, we still don't have something we can sleep on. Rauschenberg's *Bed* is an artwork. It would be a mistake to sleep on it because we do not sleep on artworks. And if, by mistake, we did sleep on it, we would be treating it as a real bed and not as an artwork.

Plato here fastens on the fact that an imitation of any object is a pseudo-object. Its qualities and value depend wholly on the original object and yet it cannot have what is most important about the original — its reality. The imitation has no value of its own. If it has qualities that derive uniquely from the medium or the artist, then they are blemishes or imperfections. This is a conceptual point. If the work is an imitation, it should not have qualities that the original does not have.

Secondly, what can a picture of a bed tell us about the bed? Nothing of its real nature. Knowledge of the bed's real nature is available only to those who understand the idea of a bed and can define it correctly. Although the carpenter may not have a good understanding of the idea, we expect at least a practical knowledge of the thing. But the artists — all they know and all they can convey in a work of art is what the bed looks like. Artists can reveal no more about reality than everyday opinion about what it *seems* like. This second point is a reflection of the intellectualist bias in Plato, the bias that the best grasp of the nature of things comes through intellectual means — definitions, arguments, proof — very similar to a contemporary scientific bias. Given such a bias, of course, the artist comes last in terms of helping us understand reality.

Plato criticized artists for presenting a sham reality that is always defective and for not helping us understand reality. He also criticized them for making mistakes within the terms of the idea of imigation itself. Not only were painted saddles fake so that no one could ride them but they also were often inaccurately done — missing a strap here, a latch there. If painters are going to produce imitation saddles, Plato thought, they ought at least to get them right. But artists cannot know everything about all the things they imitate. They cannot know as much about saddles as the saddlemaker does and about beds as the bedmaker does. We might ask, then, why artists should be expected to know such things? The answer is that art has a deceptive power and leads us to believe that what the artist portrays is accurate. If we see a movie that involves homeless people, or the drug trade, or one that is set in Iraq, we tend to believe that the conditions portrayed actually are so, whereas, of course, the artist may have invented them for the needs of the plot. Documentary films and television news notoriously have great power to shape the beliefs of the audience. In short, we can say that the idea of art as imitation implies that the things imitated in art are presented as they exist in real life.

The heart of this criticism is that, if you start with the view that art is an imitation of reality, you wind up with the view that it must be worth less than what it imitates. The original must always be better than the copy — first because it is real and second because the copy is inevitably inaccurate at some level of detail. Furthermore, there is no room in this view for values that are uniquely aesthetic. Neither the medium nor the artist can add anything valuable to the imitation. So it could not, in principle, be worth as much as the original. If you have the choice, why not look at the original?

Plato summed up much of this discussion in a comparison of the artist to a person holding a mirror up to reality. A famous passage runs:

> Now what name would you give to a craftsman who can produce all the things made by every sort of workman? . . . For besides producing any kind of artificial thing, this same craftsman can create all plants and animals, himself included, and earth and sky and gods and the heavenly bodies and all the things under the earth. . . . That sounds like a miraculous fact of virtuosity. . . . There is no difficulty; in fact there are several ways in which the thing can be done quickly. The quickest perhaps would be to take a mirror and turn it round in all directions. In a very short time you could produce sun and stars and earth yourself and all the other animals and plants and lifeless objects which we mentioned just now.[5]

This image of the artist as someone turning a mirror round in all directions conveys the essentials of the theory and its problems. The work of art is, at its best, an unreal image of the world. The most it can possibly present is no more than we already see with normal vision. It follows that the value of art is very limited. It seems to be limited to those circumstances in which the original is inaccessible to us. We can use pictures to give us an idea of what things look like that we have never seen. When we are separated from our loved ones we carry around their likenesses, but when we have access to the originals our interest in the pictures declines.

The only other value Plato could find for art is its value to moral education. In this regard art is a powerful but double-edged instrument. The idea that art is imitation seems to imply that whatever has a beneficial effect on the development of moral character will have a similar effect when imitated in art; and, conversely, whatever has a bad effect will have a bad effect when imitated in art. For Plato, these latter were such things as scenes of debauchery, violent passion, cowardice, and treachery; and he concluded that the arts should be censored by the State. Many people hold a similar view today. They think that it is harmful, at least for children, to see violence on TV. They believe that pornography has an undesirable effect on people's behavior. As we write this, the newspapers are full of debates about the works of Robert Mapplethorpe (whether they should be shown in public by the Cincinnati Art Museum) and the role of the National Endowment of the Arts. These kinds of questions make best sense in light of the imitation theory. It seems probable that most supporters of censorship hold at least some of the views about art that Plato held.

The strength of Plato's views on censorship in the arts, unpleasant as they are today, is that they make clear the assumptions behind the imitation view of art and its logical consequences. Plato's tough attitude in *The Republic*, depreciating art and censoring artists, follows directly from the imitation theory. The result is what Bernard Bosanquet[6] calls an *argumentum ad absurdum* for the theory. It takes the theory quite strictly and shows that its logical consequences are unacceptable. Plato's analysis shows us that art is either more limited and less valuable than we had supposed, or that there is something seriously wrong with the idea that art is imitation. We must either accept Plato's conclusion or reexamine the basic assumptions. And since most of us are unwilling to accept his conclusion, he has set us a philosophical task.

Children and the Imitation Theory

Children are often drawn to the imitation theory because many of their responses to art are in line with it. For example, children usually focus mostly on the subject matter of artworks. Their first concern is often what is pictured, and sometimes it is their only concern. They interpret a work in terms of its subject matter and, if they can't tell what it pictures, they may be quite baffled to respond. One child, Angela, nine years old, was unusually aware of this. She liked most art, she said, but only when she understood it. How did she understand it? In terms of what it pictures. She said: "Well, I like most things. Sometimes, if I see a painting far away, it looks kind of weird and stuff; but then I get up close and I look at it. I sit down, or turn my head around, and I look at it, and I figure out the figure in the painting. I look straight at it, and I figure out what it is, and then I like it."[7] It is as if Angela assumes that the function of a work is to show her something and her role as viewer is to figure out what that something is. Angela assumes that the purpose of art is to reveal the world. She is always interested in looking at pictures and likes to see what they show her about the world. If a work pictures an insect, she is interested in what the insect looks like; if it is a picture of a battle, she is interested in what the battle was like. For her, the interest of the picture is much the same as the interest of the object pictured, as if there is little distinction between art and illustration, portrait and snapshot. For this reason, imitation theories will make intuitive sense to her.

Children are also inclined to admire realism in art. This admiration is so common that it appears to be part of a typical developmental pattern, one that most art teachers are aware of. The young child, at the beginning of elementary school, is at a stage that has been called "schematic realism."[8] Such a child attempts to produce, in her own art, the symbolic equivalent of the subject matter. This means that she tries to represent the important features of the subject; a face must have two eyes, a nose, a mouth, and so on. She also looks at the art of others with a similar interest. For instance, Betty, 5½ years old, was asked what she thought of the hands of the Picasso's *Weeping Woman* (see fig. 2). She said, after counting, that the hands are fine, because they have the right number of fingers:

> *What do you think about the hands?*
> He's got all the fingers on. I think it's good, because he's even got fingernails on each one.

As children grow older during the elementary years, they become more aware of the exact visual appearances of things and more appreciative of the realism with which appearances are imitated. This appreciation grows gradually, because this awareness grows gradually. It reaches a peak toward the end of elementary school and in the junior high school years, when children are often so conscious of the difficulties of achieving realism that they become discouraged in producing work of their own. It also influences their evaluation of other people's works.

For example, Cynthia, eleven years old, found the hands of the *Weeping Woman* unrealistic, because of their gesture. She said:

What do you think about the hands?
Well, they have five fingers and everything, but they definitely don't
look like hands.

What should he do to make them better?
Just make them look like real hands. He even put the fingernails on the
wrong side.

This developmental pattern is well known to art teachers. A significant part of their task is to guide children's development so that, on the one hand, their growing admiration of realism is acknowledged as legitimate, and, on the other hand, it does not swamp an interest in other aspects of artworks. Teachers usually do this by making sure the curriculum contains the practice and discussion of a wide variety of styles, including various kinds of realistic and nonrealistic works. Aesthetics can also help in this regard by discussing the issue directly. The best help may be to talk explicitly about the assumptions and values of realism, because that gives children greater awareness of the basis of their own choices and of alternatives.

Most children abandon a consistent reliance on imitationist views at some point, though often without a good understanding of what the problems are or of the alternatives. Sometimes, however, imitation continues to make such good intuitive sense to them that they seem locked into it and, as they become a little older, they are able to spell out its consequences rather well. Here, for instance, is part of a conversation with Derek, twelve years old, about subject matter:

Are there any subjects that are not good for art?
Oh, I don't know, I don't think so. I think most things are art. The one
thing I don't like, personally, I don't like just scribble for a painting,
like Modern Art.

You don't like Modern Art?
No, I think they scribble all over the painting, things like that. In other
pictures, they take longer and the person who does it has to really
think like a real artist, not just someone scribbling on a paper. . . .
Sometimes art is I don't think art.

What kinds are they?
Well, like I said, Modern Art. All it is is just splattering paint on a piece of
board or scribbling with a pencil. I mean, anyone can do it. And
there's no artistic form.

Tell me about that a little.
It's not like you have to draw a human being or something that actually
requires skill. I mean, like, in Modern Art they don't say: "Well, I'm
going to draw a person with a table . . . sitting in a chair doing this."
They just sort of say: "Oh well, let's just scribble."
They just sort of scribble, huh?
Yeah, it's just whatever comes out. Now I know some people like that
sort of art, but I personally don't.

The usual way to try to help Derek appreciate a wider range of
artworks is to introduce him to a variety of nonrealistic works and
to discuss them in class. But the conclusion seems almost inevitable
that at some point he should have an overt discussion of his assumptions
about the nature of art. This seems to us a more direct approach in
this case. There are several points of entry in what Derek says in this
one passage. There is, for instance, the notion of thinking "like a real
artist." One could very well develop the question of how artists think.
Derek apparently means drawing skillfully from life and one could
easily ask what other kinds of thinking an artist might engage in. What
about thinking creatively, for instance — whatever that is to mean? What
about using an eye for color or a knowledge of history; are these not
forms of thinking? And does thinking include having or brooding on
strong feelings?

The general point is that Derek has, however unclearly, a set of
theoretical assumptions that guide his responses. He is quite articulate
about them and seems to have invested enough emotion in them that
further discussion of them could be quite motivating. Moreover, these
assumptions are by no means unique to Derek but are rather what
philosophers have been exploring since Plato. It would be helpful to
him to realize that and to realize that there are many questions to ask
about them. The topic of representation, and especially of imitation,
is usually appropriate to students around Derek's age.

Five Assumptions of the Imitation Theory

The idea that art should imitate reality is still alive today, and among
more than schoolchildren. Spokesmen for New Realism and Super
Realism usually adopt it and assert that the imitative aspects of art
are its most valuable. Robbe-Grillet, for example, a leader of New
Realist writing, deplores those who give us images that are already
made significant by the artist, thereby clouding the objective reality
of things. He praises instead artists who present things as they are
without interpretation:

Instead of this universe of signification (psychological, social, functional), we must try then to construct a world both more solid and more immediate. Let it be first of all by their presence that objects and gestures establish themselves. . . . The world is neither significant nor absurd. It *is*, quite simply. . . . And suddenly the obviousness of this strikes us with irresistible force. All at once the whole splendid construction collapses, opening our eyes unexpectedly (to) . . . the shock of the stubborn reality we were pretending to have mastered. Around us, defying the noisy pack of our animistic or protective adjectives, things are there.[9]

And he says that ideally in art: "The world around us turns back into a smooth surface, without significance, without soul, without values . . . we find ourselves once again facing things."

The ideal art, according to this view of art, is an art that reveals reality, that enables the perceiver directly to grasp things as they are. It is an art in which images have the presence of uninterpreted reality, seen for itself, unaccommodated to human needs and ideas. Anything that gets in the way of this direct presentation of reality is a distortion, a projection of wishful thinking on to things as they are.

Behind this view are several assumptions, which, for the purposes of exposition, we will divide into five, as follows.

1. With respect to the medium of art: the artwork is a transparent opening onto the subject matter, like a clear window that has no dirt on it.
2. With respect to the artist: the artist does not affect the character of the reality represented.
3. The artwork itself tells us nothing beyond what the pictured items tell us.
4. Art criticism is tied to realistic standards: accuracy of the picture or interest of the subject matter.
5. Our response to the artwork is of the same kind as our response to the piece of reality that is pictured.

It is worthwhile looking at these assumptions one by one. In what follows, we will present arguments against each of one of them. Similarly, it would be possible to discuss any one of them separately in class, if one wished, collecting examples, counter-examples, arguments about it. But it is also true that the five assumptions overlap considerably and are closely related to one another. It is not always desirable to separate them and imitation can also be discussed as one single idea.

The Medium as Language

The first assumption is that the artwork should ideally be a kind of transparent opening, giving us a view of the subject in the way a window does. This means that the medium of the work should not be noticeable in itself. That is, it should not intrude itself on our attention. If there are smears and scratches on a window, they will distract us from full attention on what lies beyond the window. They are blemishes. It is somewhat the same with aspects of the medium that draw attention to themselves. The medium should be invisible to the casual observer so that he can see the subject matter without distortion. The skill of the artist is then thought to lie largely in making the medium invisible. This shapes the common idea of skill, the one that Derek presupposed, that it is a mastery of the medium, the ability to make the medium do what one wants it to do. Lovers of realism, in fact, often praise the degree of transparency the artist has been able to give the medium, and, in a curious way, this makes the qualities of the medium actually an important part of the art.

Many people, including Rudolf Arnheim[10] and E. H. Gombrich,[11] have argued that this expectation is simply illusory. It cannot be that the medium of a work does not affect the subject matter. On the contrary, they assert, any portrayal of reality is a translation of the reality into a particular medium, and the translation is necessarily affected by that medium and by the conventions adopted within it.

According to Arnheim, there is no conceivable realistic style that can exactly reproduce the original reality. Because an artwork is always created within a medium of some kind, it cannot be a faithful duplication of reality. It must be a translation into the terms of the medium and the character of the medium will necessarily add something to the qualities of the original. As Gombrich says, we must "translate, not transcribe," "transpose, not copy." Arnheim puts it this way: "Representation produces not a replica of the object but its structural equivalent in a given medium."[12] Therefore the medium must affect the character of the representation. There are always smears on the window, except that in the case of art we must reconceive them as positive potential sources of aesthetic value.

It is not uncommon to make this point by drawing an analogy between the medium of an artwork and a natural language. Just as the general sense of a statement can be expressed in English, German, and Japanese, so you can represent volume in different media: with pencil lines on paper, with wire sculpture, or with ink wash. The analogy reminds us that different representations of volume are translations and not exact duplications. Just as no translation from one language to another is absolutely equivalent in all shades and grades of meaning, so the same scene done with oil paint can never express quite the same thing as a water color. And just as some effects are more readily expressed in one language than another, so some things, like volume, are better conveyed with oil paint than with pen and ink. The analogy also suggests that the visual arts have a vocabulary as a natural language does and a syntax that allows us to combine and recombine the vocabulary in indefinitely many ways. There is some truth to these suggestions, especially if we do not assume that the vocabulary and syntax are based on conventions that must be learned, as with languages like English or Japanese.

An example may help. Objects in the real world do not have the lines around them that we often find in a drawing. A house has its own outline or silhouette or shape, but there is no dark line which traces out this shape — the brick ends and the sky begins at a certain point — that's all. The boundary between red brick and blue sky may be translated in a drawing into a thin black line separating the two areas that represent the house the sky. This line is an elementary part of the artist's "vocabulary"; this same convention is used to indicate all kinds of boundaries — the boundaries of a tree, or a chair, or a person.

Moreover, lines can be used to represent many kinds of things. Look at the face in figure 9. There, lines represent (1) outlines, for example, head and eyes; (2) single entities, for example, hair, eyebrows, mouth; (3) contour, for example, nose and cheeks. The same item could be represented in different ways; that is, the mouth could be represented either as an outline or a single entity (as above), and the nose either as outline (in profile), as contour (as above), or as single line-entity. A line may also represent (4) a slit, gash, or crease, as in the brow furrow on the face or the mouth slit, if we interpret the line above not as representing the total mouth but only the crease between the lips. Lines may also represent (5) shadow. If we see a number of parallel lines very close together, we do not take them to mean that the object has been sliced up, but that this part of the object is in shadow.

The point is that there is no necessity that the lines be read in any particular one of these ways. Imagine someone who knew only water-color paintings, in which there are no lines. Such a person would not understand what was meant by the lines in a drawing and might object that the picture was inaccurate since objects are not bounded by fine black lines nor are their surfaces sliced up in that way. If such a viewer did understand, she would at least be very aware of the conventional character of the meanings of the lines.

Figure 9. Candice Blocker, *Dema*, 1990.Collection of Candice Blocker.

Note that the fact that these are conventions does not mean that particular lines are arbitrary. Once the convention is established that lines represent the outlines of objects, then we can objectively test the accuracy of a drawing within that convention; for example, an oval will be a more accurate drawing of an eye than will a square. Nor is the conventional character of such cases denied by the fact we are often oblivious of having learned the conventions. Some conventions are so basic and are learned so early that they seem natural rather than conventional. According to this line of thought, all ways of representing are based on conventions about how to use the medium and therefore there can be no "natural" way to imitate reality.

One important difference between artistic representation and a natural language is the ease with which we can "read" drawings once we understand the conventions. Knowing the word "cat" doesn't help me understand what "dog" means, but once I understand a line drawing of a cat I can, without additional tutoring, understand a line drawing of a dog. In this sense we don't read pictures, we look at them; there is a visual correlation between pictures and reality that does not exist between words and reality. Linguistic representation, we can say, is almost wholly conventional, artistic representation only partially so. But because it is partly conventional, there can never be a wholly objective artistic representation of the world.

Each society has its own set of conventions for representing reality, in terms of which it finds its own interpretations of reality natural and other versions conventional and stylized. For we tend not to notice our own conventions but to be very aware of those of other societies. This explains the fact that when we look at the art that the Renaissance thought to be so impressively realistic we do not today find it so. Judged against the paintings themselves, the sorts of stories told about them seem exaggerated. The works themselves look quite highly stylized, and in a number of styles. Yet at the time of their origin, they were taken as paradigms of realism. In short, realism itself seems to be culturally relative.

The Contribution of the Artist

What about our second assumption, that the artist does not come between the reality represented and the viewer? There are equally good reasons for thinking this false.

Ludwig Richter relates an experience he had as a young man.[13] He and three friends decided they would draw the same view of a river as accurately as they possibly could. They all worked from the same place on the same day. "We fell in love with every blade of grass," says Richter, "every tiny twig, and refused to let anything escape us. Everyone tried to render the motif as objectively as possible." The result was four quite different renderings of the scene, each one reflecting the temperament of its maker. One of the four, for example, who Richter says was of a rather somber and even gloomy disposition, "straightened the exuberant contours and emphasized the blue tinges." Each representation of the scene was different because it reflected the four different personalities. Richter concluded that no representation is ever completely objective because it must reflect the point of view of the artists. Inevitably artists give us something not there in the reality: a glimpse of the way things look and feel to them. Whether they want to or not, artists cannot avoid revealing something of their personalities when they represent reality. This would be true even of photographers as well as painters.

The general name for this phenomenon is style. It is pervasive in the arts. Most of us identify the works of our favorite artists by their style. There is a large enterprise of connoisseurship that has grown up around the practice of identifying individual styles in the most difficult of cases. One of the fundamental concepts of art history has been the individual style and the tracking of its growth and development one of its major preoccupations. And many philosophers have concluded that style is in many ways like personality, a parallel in art to what we take for granted in people. Arthur Danto, for example, says:

> The structure of a style is like the structure of a personality. And learning to recognize a style is not a simple taxonomic exercise. Learning to recognize a style is like learning to recognize a person's touch or his character. In attributing a work to a person, we are doing something (like) attributing an act to a person when we are uncertain of his authorship. We have to ask whether it would have been consistent with his character, as we have to ask whether it would have been consistent with his corpus.[14]

There is also the phenomenon of group and period style. Even a beginner in art can probably sort artworks into different stylistic groupings, such as African, Egyptian, Greek, and Renaissance and modern French paintings. The concept of style, it seems, can cover a very wide range. A style can be very particular and individual, as with the style of, for instance, the blue period of Picasso; and it can be very broad, as with the style of, for instance, Archaic Greek or traditional Yoruba art. This situation has fascinated many art historians and psychologists who have labored to get clear what exactly makes up what we call style, what it is that we often easily recognize but find so hard to articulate. It seems that within any style there must be certain common features, or family resemblances, however different among themselves the works in that style may be. Some of these reflect differences of personality; others reflect the artistic practices, conventions, or even mood, of the time. Style reflects in part the artists' culture and in part their idiosyncratic personalities. In both respects, style inevitably comes between the reality represented and the viewer, making the dream of imitation impossible.

Representation as Aboutness

We turn now to consider a different sense of representation; of representation not as imitation but as something more like the interpretation of the reality it represents. According to this line of thought, art says something about what it represents. It draws our attention to some aspects of the world rather than to others and so; in a manner of speaking, it makes comments on the world. It has "aboutness," a sense of significance. In exploring this thought we will encounter the remaining assumptions of the imitation view spelled out earlier.

Artistic representations often lend a sense of significance to their subject matter. They are read as pictures not only of individuals but also of types — as showing an old man, for example, a stormy day, life in rural China, or young love. This may be so even when we are familiar with the individual persons or places represented; even more so when we are not. Many philosophers have thought that this general significance is the essential difference between an ordinary picture and an artwork, between, for example, a snapshot that is part of the family album and a photograph that is an artwork. In the family album, it will be "sister Ann, aged six;" in the photograph, it will be "A Young Girl." In art the object is represented according to some general idea.

A good example would be the photographs of Cindy Sherman (fig. 4). Terry Barrett, an art educator and a photography critic, discusses what these photographs are about:

> Most of these photographs are self-portraits, so in one sense her subject-matter is herself. But she titles the black and white self-portraits made between 1977 and 1980 "Untitled Film Stills." In them she pictures herself, but as a woman in a wide variety of guises from hitchhiker to housewife. Moreover, these pictures look like stills from old movies. In 1981 she did a series of "centerfolds" for which she posed clothed and in the manner of soft-porn photographs. So what is the subject-matter of these pictures? . . . They are pictures of Cindy Sherman and pictures of Cindy Sherman disguised as others; they are also pictures of women as women are represented in cultural artifacts such as movies and magazines, especially as pictured by male producers, directors, editors, and photographers. To simply identify them as "portraits" or "portraits of women" or "self-portraits" or "self-portraits of Cindy Sherman" would be to misidentify them.[15]

Barrett is saying here that it would be a mistake to think of these photographs as simply pictures of Cindy Sherman, as the imitationist view would have us do. They are significant because we read them according to a general idea like "male stereotypes of women."

Artists and philosophers have long been aware of this generalizing character of artistic representation. In fact, the long history of representational theories has shifted back and forth between two poles, one stressing the particular and the other the general character of what is represented. The particular emphasis, such as Plato's, belongs to the imitation view, and winds up, as we have seen, with the complaint that the artwork can be only an inadequate copy of the original. Aristotle, Plato's former student, was the first to argue for the emphasis on the general idea, according to which the particular items represented in an artwork signify some truth about a type of thing.[16] For this reason, the representation can deviate from the exact details of the particular item represented in order to suggest the type more accurately, just as Cindy Sherman dressed, posed and developed her photographs for the sake of her idea. Aristotle said that the historian represents the things that actually happened but the artist represents "a kind of thing that might happen, i.e., what is possible as being what is probable or necessary." He held that for this reason art is more insightful than history. It grasps the nature of things better because history must record what actually happens whereas art can represent what typically happens. An actual case is often bizarre or uncharacteristic. If artists take their material from actual cases, they are artists only insofar as they select and rearrange, making changes that reveal the significance of what actually happened.

Notice that this account in effect denies the third assumption of the imitation view, which was that the artwork can tell us nothing beyond what the actual thing pictured could tell us. On the contrary, on this account, artistic representations give us insights that actual things do not. They have "aboutness," which of course actual things do not; that is to say, artworks interpret the things that they represent by portraying them according to some general idea. They are more like symbols, "vessels of spirit," as Arthur Danto calls it,[17] than like actual objects.

We have also encountered reasons for denying the fourth assumption, which was that art criticism is necessarily tied to realistic standards. This assumption proceeds, of course, from the notion that the artwork will have nothing of value apart from its imitation of some actual objects. In this case the value of the artwork seems limited to the interest of the subject matter or perhaps the faithfulness with which it is represented. This leaves no room for ascribing any independently artistic value to the artwork. But, in reviewing and rejecting the first three assumptions, we have uncovered three different sources of potential value. There is the medium, if we accept that the work is a translation into a medium of the subject matter. There is the artist, if we accept that the work may be an expression of personality. And there is aboutness, if we accept that the artwork presents its subject matter in some significant light. In all three cases, there is a potential source of value that the critic might consider. The critic is not limited to the external demands of the actual, either to the interest of the objects represented or to the faithfulness of the representation. Instead, we can judge the work significant if it displays the qualities of the medium to advantage, expresses the artist significantly, or conveys some insight about the subject matter.

Beauty

The fifth assumption of the imitation view that we identified was that we respond in much the same way to an artwork as we would to the reality that it pictures. The interest of the artwork is much the same as the interest of the actual object that it pictures. This assumption is most plausible when we think of the way we look at much of nature. For example, we often look at landscapes, mountains, the sea, sunsets, for their beauty, and it is not implausible that we look at pictures of landscapes, mountains, and so on, in just the same way. The same might be said of pictures of attractive or imposing people. This view, in other words, which assimilates artworks with natural things, is most plausible when we focus on beauty as the quality we look for in art.

Beauty has a special place in our thinking about art. Indeed, until quite recently it was a central topic in aesthetics. The discussion was thought to be basically about not artworks and their significance but the aesthetic and its qualities. The aesthetic was any object, natural or artifact, that we look at for its visual qualities, and the chief of these qualities was beauty. Beauty was assumed to be a natural goal for art and the analysis of beauty a major topic in aesthetics. This way of thinking about art and beauty remains influential among many people, if not among artists and philosophers. It is a part of our popular culture. Many people think that beauty is the chief virtue of art and there are plenty of paintings of mountain lakes and sunsets still being made. Naturally, children are affected by this and the topic is an almost inevitable one in a school program of aesthetics.

On the other hand, the discussion of beauty has become relatively rare in contemporary aesthetics. Philosophers often prefer to speak of the meaningfulness of art rather than the beauty of the aesthetic. Besides, art in modern times has sought many values other than beauty, demanding to be appreciated in quite other terms, and at times deliberately avoiding the beautiful. Think of all the ways we praise art today: we can call it powerful, moving, expressive, radical, witty, original, insightful; even tough, ambiguous, unsettling, outraged, anxious, horrific. Much of the most powerful and significant art is not, and has not been, beautiful. The consequence is that, for philosophers and sophisticated adults today, beauty may not be an important topic.

Beauty, in the sense that is relevant here, has to do with the pleasing visual qualities of the subject matter. There are many pictures of things that people find pleasing to look at in real life. A fine landscape, a beautiful person, colorful flowers, are all pleasing to see in reality and are popular themes in art. Subjects like these seem strongly to suggest the fifth assumption of the imitation view, that we respond to the representations in much the same way that we respond to the actual things. The natural assumption is that if we like to look at the originals then we will like to look at the pictures. And if the subject is beautiful then the picture will be beautiful.

This assumption is common among children. It is not hard to list the kinds of subjects that they think are beautiful subjects for art. A teacher might well try getting students to make such a list. Examples we have often heard mentioned by elementary schoolchildren include beautiful women, cute children, animals, flowers, trees, landscapes, and sunsets. Older children gradually add to the list. They might add things that are sublime, such as mountains and oceans; stylish, such as fast cars and airplanes; nostalgic, such as empty houses and old barns; and even the safely threatening, such as tigers and armies in uniform. All these things are beautiful, impressive, or charming, in their own right, and therefore make good subjects for art.

It might be worthwhile pointing out that this idea of beauty is different from another that is also often used in connection with artworks. This other idea of beauty has to do with the qualities of the medium and its form. Beauty in this sense belongs to the qualities of the medium, the lines, colors, shapes, textures, and to its form, the combinations of lines, colors, shapes and textures. There seems no doubt that, quite apart from the appeal of the subject matter, we find certain qualities and certain combinations of qualities of the medium pleasing to look at. The appeal of the world's greatest art comes in part from the way in which it takes advantage of the qualities of the medium. Some philosophers have thought that this kind of beauty is the most purely aesthetic, because it exists strictly within the artwork itself and not in the qualities of things that have their home outside of the work. Roughly, this is the view of formalism. The point at the moment is that this is a different idea of beauty from the one we are presently discussing, where beauty belongs primarily to natural objects and only secondarily to the artworks that picture them.

The beauty of an artwork, in the sense we are now discussing, derives from the beauty of things in the real world. This means that the primary question about beauty does not have to do with art at all; it is the question what makes things beautiful in real life. There is secondarily the question whether, or in what conditions, the picture of a beautiful thing will also be beautiful. These are questions that children are usually very ready to discuss.

Then what can we say about the beauty of actual things in the world? It seems that we call them beautiful when they look like good specimens of their kind. A landscape will be beautiful if it looks rich and fertile; an animal if it looks healthy and well developed; an automobile if it looks fast and well maintained. The same is true of people, who constitute perhaps the primary cases of beauty. The difference is that in the case of people our notion of what constitutes a good specimen is much more complicated. Beautiful people usually look healthy and well maintained, certainly, but they must also have elements of ideal character about them. For example, they might look compassionate, or sexy, or honest, or brave, or intelligent. Of course, just what is considered ideal in people will vary with particular cultures and periods of history and so will what is found beautiful in people.

A closely related topic is ugliness. Ugliness, we can say, is the reverse of beauty. In the case of people, it is the suggestion of failure to meet ideals. Children respond variously to ugliness in art, finding it sometimes fascinating and sometimes revolting. Sometimes they are very interested and sometimes will hardly bear to look at it. Which of these reactions will occur seems to depend on just which work and which child interact in which context. The interest of ugliness is often an interest in information. A picture of a dead person can show what corpses are like and a battle scene can show how battles are fought. In their own art, many children like to draw scenes of battle with plenty of violence and death in them.

Nevertheless, there is also often the expectation that art will be beautiful and ugliness may bring rejection. This often occurs, for example, with Albright's *Into the World Came a Soul Called Ida* (fig. 1). For example, Debbie, thirteen years old, had a negative reaction to it. She said:

What do you see in this painting?
There's a lady sitting in a chair with her legs exposed. They're bare and they're really ugly. They've got bumps all over them and she's sitting there with a powder-puff in one hand and a mirror in the other. . . . She sort of looks like a witch.

What's the feeling in this painting?
I don't know. It's just that the legs are getting on my nerves.

Why do you suppose the painter painted it?
He was angry with his mother-in-law (laughs). I don't know. He just felt like it. He saw some lady going down the street and he said: "That looks sickening," and so he decided to paint her. He was angry at her for some reason.

There are several things one could say about this reaction of Debbie's. One is that, although her revulsion from ugliness is the dominant tone, there is also a suggestion of its more positive interest. Debbie imagines that the artist saw Ida "going down the street," thought she was ugly, and painted her for that reason. This suggests that ugliness has its interest. Later in the same discussion Debbie said: "Like, I won't look at a painting like that — well, I will, because it's so disgusting — but I'll pass it up and go look at a woman in a boat or something."

These remarks suggest that the power of the work is almost enough to get past Debbie's expectations about art being beautiful and that Debbie is almost — but not quite — aware of the implied conflict in her experience. On the one hand, she expects art to be about beautiful things and is repelled when it is about ugly ones; on the other hand, she finds the work powerful, interesting, disturbing. One could easily imagine spending a quarter's work with Debbie's class exploring and exploiting this ambivalence. One might get students to collect and categorize images of people and things that they think are beautiful and ugly and that have been thought beautiful and ugly in the past.

One theme that would emerge from such an activity is the cultural variability of notions of beauty and ugliness. Debbie of course is a child of our culture and has adopted its attitudes toward the beauty of women. She seems to have learned these attitudes from the popular culture, from magazine covers, television, advertising and the like, rather than from the feminist movement. Her response to Ida embodies expectations about what women should look like that are still dominant in our culture and that Albright might have shared: oversimplifying, beauty in women means thin, young, sexy, happy. These expectations, it is fair to say, are found oppressively narrow and offensive by many people today. It would help Debbie to become aware of the extent to which her expectations are a product of a particular time and culture. One way to do this is to have students collect a range of contemporary pictures of people that are intended to be beautiful and to compare them with those of a generation earlier. Such pictures can come from magazines, yearbooks, posters, movies, and so on. The point of the discussion would be to identify the kinds of ideal virtues suggested by the pictures and to have students realize the extent to which ideals change and how they are communicated through visual images. Similarly, it is useful to have them collect and talk about images of the contemporary young people whom they themselves think beautiful, or cool, or worth imitating and make the same analysis of the visual qualities they possess and the human virtues they suggest. One could ask what kinds of attributes, according to these images, we find attractive in people. What character ideals do the images suggest? How are they different for men and women? Where do they come from? How have these things been different at other times?

There is another way of speaking about Debbie's lack of awareness of her own expectations. It is to notice that when Debbie speaks of Ida's ugliness, she speaks as if she is reporting facts rather than making judgments. She speaks as if she expects no disagreement because what she says is purely descriptive. She is unaware of her own role in constructing the judgment that Ida is ugly and implies that she has made no contribution to the situation. It is as if beauty and ugliness are facts to be seen rather than expectations to be met. She takes her norms to be objective, the properties of objects to be seen rather than the standards of judgment to be met. This is a way of saying that she has learned her standards from the culture and has not yet become aware of them. Being unaware of them, she cannot deal with them — that is, explain, make allowances for, criticize or change them. One goal of teaching aesthetics would be to help students distinguish norms from facts and to be able to identify the norms they have adopted. This would make their judgments more reflective and more tolerant.

Another theme that might emerge from categorizing images of beautiful people, or from Debbie's reaction to the Albright, is more specifically about beauty in images. The question here is: Do the beauty and ugliness of the pictured object always coincide with the beauty and ugliness of the image? Or can a beautiful painting picture an ugly object? This is the point at which theories of representation become crucial again. If one adopts the imitation view, then the beauty and ugliness of the image are simply borrowed from the beauty and ugliness of the thing imitated. But if representation requires interpretation, then beauty and ugliness will be matters of interpretation, too (they will also weigh less heavily in our thinking about art). One could make this point with Debbie and her classmates by getting them to see that *Ida* the painting is not an ugly work, though Ida the person may be. Students can be brought to read the painting as a sympathetic interpretation of Ida's state of mind. Ida's suffering is brought rather forcefully to our attention and is thereby made significant, and what the viewer should be preoccupied with is Ida's sense of loss of youth and attractiveness and hence dejection and hopelessness. This is a view of the work that will often strike students quite powerfully and will transform their response to it.[18]

A third theme that might emerge has to do with the connections between aesthetic and moral judgments. This is a complicated theme because connections between art and morality occur in many ways and it would be foolhardy for anyone to say that they always know how to separate the two. But there are some simple distinctions between the aesthetic and the moral, and it is useful to introduce the question because students may never have considered it. For example, we can make a simple distinction something like this: aesthetic judgments are about how people and things look and moral judgments are about what people do. Most children will not find this initial distinction puzzling and they will be able to think of examples of the difference readily enough. It would be a good discussion that resulted in a list of examples of moral and of aesthetic judgments that exemplify this distinction and a formulation of the basic difference between them. This would help the class before they discuss more complex cases of the connections between the aesthetic and the moral, such as may at times be found in their responses to artworks.

Some of this complexity readily emerges in students' responses to the Albright and similar works. For example, Eric, fourteen years old, had a response not unlike Debbie's:

Why did the artist paint this?
To show what people are like. People do this all the time. And they just sit around and vegetate and dwindle away. And they look in the mirror and wonder why. "Oh, I'm so depressed! Look at me now!" You know. She should fight it. It wouldn't be a bad time to start. She's not dead yet. Let me tell you, my mom goes to a health spa. So when I see a fat person like this, it really makes me squirm . . .

Clearly there are moral elements in this judgment. Eric is discussing the person pictured as much as the painting and he is responding not only to her appearance but to the character that the appearance suggests. He deplores her character and, it seems consequently, he rejects the painting as ugly — as something that no one would want to look at. He seems to be confusing ugliness with bad moral character. His judgment is made almost as much on moral as on aesthetic grounds and the emotional character of his response is suffused with moral indignation. Moreover, this moral feeling seems to get in the way of his seeing the painting clearly. The same thing is true of Debbie, who imagined that the artist was angry with Ida and found her "sickening." Such an adjective also suggests, though less clearly, that her judgment of the painting contains elements of moral disapproval of the character represented in it.

Such combinations of moral and aesthetic elements often occur in connection with judgments of beauty because, as we have said, the idea of beauty is used in talking about people as much as in talking about art. We also said that the idea of beauty implies a sense of the ideal, and, used of people, this is often an ideal of character. For though we can say that beauty has to do with outward appearances, nevertheless the appearances are appearances of something: in the case of persons usually the appearances of something inner. A beautiful person is to be admired for some aspect of character that is hinted at subtly in a facial expression, displayed boldly by some clothing, or suggested by the context. This connection with ideal character necessarily invites a connection with moral judgment.

A philosophical discussion with Eric combined with a closer look at the Albright might enable him to become more aware of the moral component of his response. We might ask him what the difference is between judging Ida the real person and *Ida* the painting? Only on the imitation version of representation might there be no difference. On the interpretive version there is a difference and it will be the difference between a moral and an aesthetic judgment. We might also ask whether the painting is a moral commentary on Ida, portrayed as a type of the lazy, defeated person that Eric disapproves of. In that case, maybe Eric's moral indignation is an appropriate response. But it might be that the artist's intention was to get people to empathize with Ida, to focus more on what she is feeling than on how she looks? She might represent a type of victim of disease and our society's neglect of such people, in which case Eric's indignation should be turned toward society.

The point of such a discussion would be both to understand the Albright better and also to become aware of the mixture in Eric's response of aesthetic and moral elements. It is not to teach that there is an easy disjunction to be made between the aesthetic and the moral, because, as we have seen, whether moral indignation is an appropriate response to the Albright depends on how we interpret it. Sometimes moral concerns are important in art and sometimes they are not and it is not always easy to sort out which is which. But it is important to understand that a distinction between art and morality can often be made and to be aware of the moral elements in one's response. Such awareness would give Eric greater control of his response, for it does appear that his indignation here controls him and does not allow him to reflect on it. This is clearly a case where raising the question is more important than answering it.

A more complicated example of the way moral judgments may become part of aesthetic response is the work of Cindy Sherman. We have seen that each of the photographs in her *Movie Stills* series is intended to suggest a slightly different aspect of the character of Everywoman, or at least of Every American Woman of a certain period. The complication is that this ideal of character is both suggested and also brought into question by the photograph. This moral connection gives the work its interest and power and it is not untypical of much contemporary political art.

At this point we are back to the moral concerns of Plato and the question of censorship. Remember that Plato thought that, when we disapprove strongly enough of the character of the persons represented by a work, we have reason to censor it. The question is as salient today as it ever was, as is evidenced by the current furor over the photographs of Robert Mapplethorpe. It seems to us that, if you adopt the imitation view of representation as Plato did, then you do have to be willing to censor artistic representations rather often. If, on the other hand, you adopt the interpretive view, then there is more room for debate. Each case will be different and some may be very difficult. But one can defend art from censorship on the general ground that, because artworks interpret their subject matter, our response to the works can be quite different from our response to the actual things represented. This also allows us to acknowledge that art sometimes has a role to play in what we could call moral guidance. As we saw in the case of the Cindy Sherman work, art may call for interpretations that include the recognition of moral judgments. This would not be possible on the imitation view.

Summary

In this chapter we have reviewed issues related to the way in which artworks represent the things that they picture. This is a theme that has a long history in the philosophy of art because it is a dominant fact about so many artworks that they picture objects. The simplest way to conceive of pictorial representation is to think that art imitates objects in the real (or imagined) world: that is, it tries to present things without distortion, as they are in themselves. This is a view that Plato first explored and that is still attractive to many people.

We identified five assumptions of the imitation view and discussed each of them. In each case we found reasons for doubting the assumption. We found that art inevitably translates its subject matter in terms of its medium, expresses something of the personality of the artist and imputes some general significance to what it pictures. Therefore, we concluded, art criticism can find values in representations beyond the interest of the items pictured and the degree of realism achieved. We also concluded that our response to a work can be different from our response to the actual items represented.

The imitation and interpretation views of representation differ in their implications for censorship and for the connection between works of nature and works of art. The imitation view tends to favor censorship in relevant cases because it holds that the artwork is a substitute for actual things. The interpretation view tends not to support censorship because it allows that art may comment, and comment morally, on what it represents. Similarly, the imitation view tends to assimilate our responses to nature and to art, making the philosophy of art the philosophy of the aesthetic qualities possessed by both natural and artistic objects. Beauty has historically been one important such quality. The interpretive view tends to distinguish art from nature, understanding artworks to have a meaning that works of nature do not.

NOTES

1. A good collection of cases and problems for discussion is Margeret P. Battin, John Fisher, Ronald Moore, and Anita Silvers, *Puzzles about Art: An Aesthetics Casebook* (New York: St. Martin's Press, 1989).

2. Pliny the Elder, *Natural History*, 35 vols. trans. H. Rackham (Loeb Classical Library), 9:331.

3. Ibid. p. 305.

4. Homer, *The Iliad*, trans. Richard Lattimore (Chicago: University of Chicago Press, 1951), xviii, 548–49.

5. Plato, *The Republic*, trans. F. M. Cornford (London: Oxford University Press), pp. 325 ff.

6. Bernard Bosanquet, *History of Aesthetics* (London, 1910).

7. This quotation, and others from children in this book, is taken from recorded interviews with individual children discussing particular artworks. The interviews are discussed more fully in Michael Parsons, *How We Understand Art: A Cognitive Developmental Account of Aesthetic Experience* (New York: Cambridge University Press, 1987).

8. The phrase, and the most influential account of children's development in making art, comes from Victor Lowenfeld and William Brittain's *Creative and Mental Growth*, 5th ed. (New York: Macmillan, 1970). A useful summary account can be found in Elliot Eisner, "What We Know about Children's Art," in *The Arts, Human Development and Education*, ed. E. Eisner (Berkeley, Calif.: McCutchan Publishing, 1976).

9. Alain Robbe-Grillet, *For a New Novel*, trans. Richard Howard (New York: Grove Press, 1965).

10. Rudolph Arnheim, *Art and Visual Perception* (Berkeley, Calif.: University of California Press, 1954).

11. E. H. Gombrich, *Art and Illusion* (London: Phaidon Press, 1960).

12. Rudolph Arnheim, *Art and Visual Perception*, pp. 120–25.

13. Ludwig Richter, in Heinrich Wölfflin, *Principles of Art History*, trans. M. D. Hottinger (New York: Dover Publications, 1950); and in E. H. Gombrich, *Art and Illusion*, p. 55.

14. Arthur C. Danto, *The Transfiguration of the Commonplace: A Philosophy of Art* (Cambridge: Harvard University Press, 1981), p. 207.

15. Terry Barrett, *Criticizing Photographs: An Introduction to Understanding Images* (Mountain View, Calif.: Mayfield Publishing Co., 1990), pp. 20–22.

16. Aristotle, *The Poetics*, trans. Ingram Bywater (London: Oxford University Press, 1920).

17. Arthur Danto, "The Basket Folk and the Pot People," in *Art/Artifact: African Art in Anthropology Collections*, ed. Susan Vogel (New York: Te Neues Publishing, 1990).

18. See Marilyn Johnston and Michael Parsons, "Ugliness and Expression: Two Views of Ida," in *Curriculum Issues in Arts Education*, ed. Malcolm Ross (London: Pergamon Press, 1987).

4

Art and the Artist

In this chapter we will look at the relations between artworks and artists. It may seem obvious that artists express themselves in their works and that this relation should affect our interpretations of the works, even that we can determine the meaning of works by reference to the artist or to the artist's intentions. We usually take some connection like this for granted. In ordinary conversation we often speak in a way that takes the importance of the artist for granted. For example, we might ask: "Why did Klee paint his *Head of a Man* (fig. 5) with a frontal view? Was he thinking of it as a kind of mask?" Much of art history discusses the artist's opinions, character, circumstances, influences and historical context, especially the artist's style, all with the assumption that these things can be related to the meanings of the artworks.

But in fact philosophers have debated whether artists can be said to express themselves in their works, whether their intentions are relevant, and in just what ways the works' meanings are dependent on their makers. For one thing, it is not clear just what we mean when we say that artists put their thoughts or feelings into their artworks. This difficulty has seemed insuperable to many. Nor is it obvious that we need to know anything at all about the artist in order to understand the artwork. The work, after all, is an object that appears to exist independently of whoever made it. The question about the Klee work might easily be phrased without reference to the artist. We could simply say: "What is the effect of the frontal view in *Head of a Man?* Is it a kind of mask, or related somehow to the idea of masks?" In this formulation the question does not ask about Klee at all. Nor, if we do decide to talk about him, is it clear just what kind of information about Klee we need, if our primary interest is to understand the work. Do we need to know about Klee's conscious thoughts about this work, his attitudes toward people in general, the conventions of his art world, or what? In short, it is disputed what kind of information would best help us to interpret artworks. Should art history focus on the artist's emotions and opinions or on more objective matters, such as the art world of the time or stylistic relationships between artworks?

In the literature of aesthetics, there are two major foci of discussion here. One has to do with the idea that artists express their emotions or points of view in artworks and that we understand the works by grasping those emotions or points of view. This idea is usually called expressionism, and theories that depend on it are called expressionist theories. The second discussion approaches the topic from the other end and is about what viewers need to know of the artist's mind if they are to understand the work. This is usually called the problem of the artist's intention. We will discuss these two topics in sequence because they arose historically at somewhat different times and in different contexts, though they circle around the same issue.

Students are usually interested in these topics because they like to know something about particular artists, and they assume, as do most of us, that this knowledge affects the meanings of the artists' works. Older students are also usually quite affected by the expressiveness of some works and are eager to discuss it.

It may be worth saying again that our reason for reviewing these topics is primarily to help readers identify some standard topics and arguments in aesthetics and to examine the assumptions that they themselves make about these topics and to raise some questions in a way that will help them think about the topics more clearly. It is not that they should learn arguments and theories by heart in order later to reproduce them in class as arguments and theories. Rather we hope that the points made during the discussion will illuminate the readers' own way of thinking about these topics and will in that way affect their teaching. In our view, that mirrors the reason for teaching aesthetics in school in the first place. Only if the points made are illuminating to the teacher are they likely later to prove useful in teaching, as situations are encountered (or constructed) in the classroom that are relevant to the students.

Expression in Art

We begin with the basic idea of expressionism: that art is essentially the expression of the artist's mind. Although the idea has forerunners in antiquity and can be traced to isolated statements throughout the Renaissance and medieval period, it held little interest for philosophers until the latter part of the nineteenth century. Just as the theory of representation is tied historically to the representational art of Greece and the Renaissance and to the academic period of the seventeenth and eighteenth centuries, so the expression theory is linked with the romantic art of the nineteenth and twentieth centuries. In general, while representational theories try to account for art in terms of the external, objective world represented in works of art, expressionist theories direct attention to the inner, subjective world of the artist.

To many people it seems obvious that art is connected with human feeling. When they talk about an artwork, they frequently use a vocabulary that derives from the world of subjective experience. For example, they might say that Goya's *Lo Mismo* (fig. 3) expresses outrage at the horrors of war or that Picasso's *Weeping Woman* (fig. 2) conveys a strong sense of grief. Similarly, Chagall's La Grande Cirque has been described as expressing a combination of a naive delight in simple events that seem enchanted as in a dream and also a rather repetitive attitude and a lack of close attention to details. There are several things to notice about these statements, whether or not they are defensible in detail. They are about feelings or states of mind expressed in the works; these feelings or states of mind are attributed to the artist; and the resultant expressive qualities are key to the interpretation of the works. For many people these kinds of qualities are so important that they are what makes the works worth attending to in the first place and even what makes them art.

However, it is often unclear just what this kind of expressive vocabulary implies, even to the people who are inclined to use it. For example, it is not easy to say just what kinds of things these subjective states are nor where to locate them. "Feelings" is a term commonly used, along with "emotions," but there are many others: ideas, moods, attitudes, points of view, and so on. It is instructive to listen to a high school student talk about the Goya etching (fig. 3). Here is part of an interview with Amy, who was seventeen years old at the time:

What do you think art should do?
I think it should put a point across, and I think you should have a feeling about it.

A feeling?
Yeah. There should be an aura about it, something, a feeling that permeates it, a mood overall.

When you say "put a point across," what do you mean?
I think it should be almost didactic. It's so different, because there's so many different kinds of art or painting, like portraits. There are kinds that don't teach you or have a point to them, like people wandering in a meadow or something. There should be an overall subject . . . In this painting you can see what's going to happen next. It's tense.

You say that some paintings teach us something. Is this a painting like that?

Well, not even teach. I think a more appropriate way of saying it is to put across something. For people who've never been close to anything violent, it's really dramatic, this painting, I mean.

So what is it putting across?

An emotion, an idea. It's obvious what it's putting across. It's just what it is: death, people dying and about to be killed. In the man that's standing up, you can read the fatigue in his face. There's an essence about the picture.

In this passage, Amy uses a variety of words for what is important to her about a painting: a point, a feeling, an aura, a mood, something didactic, an overall subject, something put across, an emotion, an idea, an essence. These are all phrases for the work's expressive quality. And this expressive quality, she says, is obvious, meaning that she has a direct experience of it. In fact, the reason she does not feel it necessary to choose her words carefully seems to be that the quality is, for her, a matter of direct experience and she thinks it will not be affected by the language she uses. In what follows we will use the generic term "emotions" for what works are said to express. Later we will say more about what emotions are, since we think much of the difficulty of expressionist theories lies in the failure to get this clear. The assumptions involved, about what kinds of things emotions and, later, intentions are, will turn out to be responsible for the difficulties of much expressionist thinking. It is already clear, though, that Amy does not want to exclude a cognitive element from "emotions," since she also speaks of an "idea" and a "point" that the artist wants to put across.

Amy's experience of art like the Goya, and her way of speaking about it, are common, especially among older students. She has experienced the expressive power of art and she talks about it in what we might call expressionist ways. She has not thought much about those ways of talking but we can say that expressionist theories are the result of following through the implications of talking the way Amy talks. This means that these theories can illuminate many of the assumptions students make and make their meanings more intelligible when they talk this way. In discussing these topics, therefore, students may come to understand their own assumptions and their experience of art better.

The Expressionist Problem

Amy's experience gives rise to this central question: How can something that is private and subjective like an emotion appear to be

part of a public and physical object such as a painting? A work of
visual art is made of canvas, paint, wood, stone, metal, and so on.
The feeling that the work expresses, on the other hand, is a private
experience, the sort of thing that goes on inside people's heads. It is
a state of mind, subjective and intangible. How, then, can it be part
of a physical object? How can a physical object "express" a mental state
like an emotion? What can "express" mean in such a case?

When we put it like this, it may seem impossible that an artwork
could express feelings and yet we know from experience that it can.
This apparent contradiction is a sure sign of a philosophical problem.
To deal with it, we will need to keep in mind the distinction between
the experience itself and the theory that attempts to explain the difficulties raised by the experience. This is a commonsense distinction. There
is, on the one hand, the actual experience of the artwork, such as Amy's,
during which attention is on the object, its qualities and complexities.
On the other hand, there is our description of and reflection on the
experience we have had, which occurs at a second level of thought.
At this second level, we try to describe to ourselves and others what
the experience was like. We may also try to analyze the situation into
its component parts — for instance, we may say there is the artwork,
the viewer, and the artist — and we may try to explain it with a theory
of some kind. At the first level, we think about the artwork; at the
second level, we think about the first level. This means, of course,
that if there were no first level there could be no second level. The
first level is called "direct experience" because it makes contact with
the artwork in a way that appears unmediated by the concepts and
theories developed at the second level.

One must remember that the distinction is only an approximation
and is made only for analytic purposes. Certainly, our actual experience
does not fall cleanly into one or other of these two levels. In actuality,
the two levels of experience merge with each other and importantly
affect each another. In particular, the words and concepts that are
developed at the second level of reflection affect the character of
experience that occurs at the first level and in this way it is not really
"direct" after all. Nevertheless, the distinction can be a useful one. Of
course, when we *use* the distinction we are thinking at the second,
reflective, level.

On first thought, it seems that the direct experience of a work cannot
reasonably be doubted. If the Goya, for example, speaks to you, as
it does to Amy, directly of death, of horror, of violence and of revulsion from violence, then it is hard to doubt that these emotions exist
somewhere and somehow in the situation. It is hard to doubt what

one sees and feels. It is true that the emotions felt on looking at the Goya are not exactly the same as the emotions one would feel if one were looking at the actual fighting represented there. They are, for example, not as strongly felt, somehow more distanced. But, notice, already in saying this we are beginning to reflect on the experience instead of simply having it. The main point is that the emotions — actual emotions of a marked and particular character — are seen and felt to be *there* in the work. The evidence is right there, in one's own experience, apparently incontestable.

In short, expressionism begins with the common experience of the emotional power of art. Notice that this, so far, is not a theory but a statement about our experience. As the expressionist R. G. Collingwood put it:

> Since the artist proper has something to do with emotion . . . what is it that he does? . . . nothing could be more entirely commonplace than to say he expresses them. The idea is familiar to every artist, and to everyone else who has any acquaintance with the arts. To state it is not to state a philosophical theory or definition of art; it is to state a fact or supposed fact about which, when we have sufficiently identified it, we shall have later to theorize philosophically. For the present . . . we have to decide what it is that people are saying when they use the phrase. Later on, we shall have to see whether it will fit into a coherent theory.[1]

Expressionist theories, then, begin with a certain kind of experience of art and a way of talking about it in terms of emotions, ideas and states of mind. The problem is that as soon as we start thinking about this experience and way of talking we seem committed to views that are hard to explain, such as that the artwork actually has the emotions. A chief difficulty is to explain how the emotions, which seem private and subjective, can be connected with the work, which seems public and physical.

The Importance of Experience

What we have said about the relation of reflection to experience points to the importance of students' personal experience in education. It suggests that students should have some experience at the first level to reflect on when they are asked to do philosophy. They should have some good examples at hand when they are trying to make sense of the way we talk and the puzzles it gives rise to. We have already said that good philosophy uses examples and often discusses them at length. This is also true of good teaching. In the case of the discussion of expressionism, students should have some recent experience with works that are likely to move them emotionally. It would be helpful to have students study a small number of highly expressive works, covering a range of moods and attitudes, as a preparation for thinking about expressionism. It would also be helpful to have them discuss these works in groups and notice the way they spontaneously talk about them. Their experience of these works and their ways of talking can then provide examples for subsequent discussion.

This, by the way, is a natural opportunity for the integration of aesthetics with art criticism and history. With older students, for example, one might take works like the Goya or the Albright, which they are likely to find emotionally powerful, and study them in class critically and historically. Nor does this study of artworks all have to be done first and the philosophy second, for the two kinds of discussion can alternate helpfully in an interactive way. The important thing, for our present purposes, is that students have some actual examples to talk about when they discuss expressionism, examples of particular works, of their experience of the works, and of the ways they and their peers talk about both.

Consider, for example, what Betty, a seventeen-year-old student, said about the Albright (fig. 1):

What is the subject of this painting?
It tries to put across the thing with beauty and it's all so superficial. You get old, and it's putting across the pointlessness of the whole looks thing, the obsession with beauty . . .

What do you think was the artist's feeling?
It's hard to say. Maybe he was mad at a woman and painted her looking like that! No. The fact that there's money and crystal — it's materialistic but it's not a good picture of materialistic things. It's something that downgrades them and makes them seem less important. It shows the degree of their importance in the artist's opinion. So I think he feels that people are all too concerned with superficial materialistic values.

Is that why he did this?
I don't know. That's what I see in it, and also you see the pointlessness of it too because if you end up looking like that . . . I like it a lot, I really do.

Why?
It's depressing but that's also something that I'm obsessed with, the fact that people are so superficial and materialistic. And I'm not exempt from that. But I catch myself being that way and it frustrates me and this just illustrates it again . . .

Such a passage suggests that Betty would be quite motivated to discuss her experience of the work. There is also plenty of material for discussion in what she says. For one thing, she claims to see feelings and opinions in the work and it would be worthwhile asking her to spell these out in more detail, pointing to aspects of the work that justify what she says. For another thing, she attributes these feelings and opinions to the artist. But can she be sure these were the feelings and opinions of the artist? What, as a matter of fact, does historical research tell us about the artist? Moreover, Betty speaks as if the emotions belong simultaneously to the artist, the work and herself. Which of these does she really mean? Are they all the same? How could Betty have the same feelings as the artist had or the same as some other viewer has? How could we compare them? Is it possible for feelings to be passed somehow from the artist to the viewer?

The extract just quoted was from a one-on-one interview and it could be used in class to raise philosophical questions as just suggested. But it is probably more useful to have discussions of particular works in small groups or with a class as a whole. Such discussions are likely to be more lively and varied. They are likely to help more students to see more in the work and also to give them some common examples of expressiveness in art to refer to later. It helps if some kind of record is kept — the notes of a group secretary, individual writing, a tape recording — so that the teacher can at times remind the group of what they felt and said. "Do you remember that half of you agreed with Betty that Albright wanted to put across his sense of the vanity of people and of how superficial they can be?" Such tactics greatly increase the chance that philosophical discussions will remain meaningful to students.

For students to look closely at their experiences of art, and at the way they talk about them and at the concepts lying behind their talk, is already to think philosophically, although such thinking is not yet about philosophical theories. It is the activity that Collingwood called "sufficiently identifying the fact or supposed fact" of experience. As he suggested, it is helpful to examine the supposed facts first if we want to do good theorizing, because they provide examples for reflection and motivate our thinking.

Children's Awareness of Expressiveness

In the afore-cited passage, Collingwood claims that everyone "who has any acquaintance with the arts" is familiar with the idea that artworks have "something to do with emotion." Perhaps this claim is right. But what about the students in our schools, most of whom

Collingwood would think have little serious "acquaintance with the arts." Is it obvious to them that art has something to do with emotion?

Most children of elementary school age interpret the expressiveness of artworks in terms of what the works picture. They look, for example, at faces for the kind of emotional states they suggest. They read emotion in gestures, events and activities. They attribute any feelings so identified to persons represented in the painting rather than to the artist and they may invent stories that explain why so-and-so has those feelings. A painting of a girl with a dog, for example, will be called happy because she is smiling and playing with her dog. Where persons or events are not pictured, they find it hard to identify feelings. And, perhaps most importantly, few elementary school-age children spontaneously look for expressiveness in art or think that art has something important to do with emotion.

Nevertheless, by the end of elementary school most children learn to talk about art in terms of the expression of emotion and to make reference to the artist's state of mind. They may, and may not, still understand this way of talking in terms of what the artworks picture. The following is an example of someone who does, from a conversation with Dunstan, twelve years old:

What do you mean by expression?
It gets out their feelings.

Gets out their feelings?
Yeah, in a way. If they're feeling sad and unhappy, they could make a picture of a sad and unhappy person. The reason they are unhappy, they will just sort of express it and that will help to get it out. And then another reason is that, like, if they're happy, they enjoy painting. So they like to paint certain subjects and certain things. . . . because I know I draw pictures — just drawings — but it's usually the mood that I'm in that I draw the picture, like. Unless someone asks me to draw something. If you would ask me to draw an elephant's head, if I could, then I'd draw an elephant's head. But sometimes, if I'm mad and angry, I draw a dragon. If I'm happy, I'll draw a meadow with some flowers and all sorts of things.

The point to notice here is that, on the one hand, Dunstan has the idea that art has something to do with artists' emotions; as he says, it "gets out their feelings." On the other hand, his understanding of that idea is still in terms of subject matter. He understands the expression of feelings primarily in terms of what artworks picture: "if I'm mad and angry, I draw a dragon. If I'm happy, then I'll draw a meadow with some flowers and all sorts of things." It may, and may not, be hard to get Dunstan to see that the subject matter does not wholly determine the emotional expression of a work, because one can draw happy dragons as well as angry ones and sad meadows as well as happy ones. One could perhaps make the point with a set of slides of paintings with different moods but picturing the same subject. At that point, Dunstan might question just how it is that artists "get their feelings out" and how he can tell what those feelings are.

More abstractly, one might ask a younger class to list the kinds of things that can be pictured and the kinds of things that can't. Is there a difference in this respect between a smile and a feeling of happiness? Can one smile without feeling happy? Can one draw a smile without portraying happiness? One might ask them to identify the different ways one person can convey states of mind to another: by naming them, for example, by grimacing and gesturing, by telling a story, with conventional symbols (black for mourning), and so on. Which of these is art most like? How many of these things can paintings do or use?

Older students are often more impressed with the expressive character of art and, at an intuitive level, more aware of the problems it suggests. We can see this in the struggle they often engage in when pressed to explain how art expresses emotions. For example, consider what Frank, who was eighteen years old, said when he was asked what he meant by "expression." "When you have strong feelings on a subject, to express it would be to paint a painting to portray your feelings just the way you want them to be portrayed, straightforward, yet disguised in a way, so you have to look at it to see what he wants. He puts it down so other people can look at it and see part of him."

Frank is aware that to "portray feelings" is different from portraying objects. Their portrayal, he says, is "straightforward, yet disguised in a way," a phrase that seems to acknowledge that emotions can't be pictured in the way apples can. The phrase "you have to look at it to see what he wants" seems to rule out Dunstan's suggestion that emotions can be attached one-to-one to particular subject matters, so that you can tell what an artist feels simply by knowing what the subject is. ("If I'm happy, then I'll draw a meadow with some flowers.") And Frank also spontaneously suggests that when you do look at the work, you will see "part of him" — that is, of the artist. It would be worthwhile getting students to identify the implications of what Frank says for they lead us toward expressionist theories.

Expression as Illusion

We go back to the philosophical problem we identified earlier. We have had the experience of an emotionally powerful work; we have come to see that our natural way of talking about it raises problems. How can the artist's subjective state of mind be made visible in a work made of wood, stone, canvas, or paint? This is the first stage of philosophical reflection. Now we want to move on to clarify our initial intuitions and to construct a sensible account from them.

One common response is to doubt that the emotions are really there in the artwork as they appear to be. They only appear to be in the work, we may say, but actually they are in the viewer. For on reflection it seems that they must be in the viewer. After all, emotions are subjective things, they must be privately experienced and are not themselves visible. So they must really belong to the viewer and not to the artwork. It is an illusion that they are in the work.

Monroe Beardsley, a major contemporary American aesthetician who does not agree with this conclusion, nevertheless makes the point this way:

Consider, to begin with, the three following statements which are drawn from a large class: "Some passages of Byron's *Don Juan* are funny." "This Moorish interior by Matisse is cheerful." "The slow movement of Debussy's string quartet is very sad." These statements all purport to be statements about the qualities of aesthetic objects, but, on second glance, it may seem that they cannot be. For example, some philosophers would hold that when I call *Don Juan* "Funny" I am really saying something like "It makes me laugh," or "I feel amused when I read it."[2]

One of the philosophers Beardsley refers to here is George Santayana. Santayana made an early, classic statement of the view that the emotion is in the viewer, not the work. He first identified two elements in the situation, the emotion and the artwork, and he described their difference: "In all expression we may thus distinguish two terms; the first is the object actually presented, the word, the image, the expressive thing; the second is the object suggested, the further thought, emotion, or image evoked, the thing expressed."[3]

Santayana thought that on reflection we can always distinguish these two different components of artistic expression: the object presented to perception and the feelings suggested. On the other hand, he said, we always experience the two not separately but together as one:

These lie together in the mind, and their union constitutes expression. . . . Expression depends upon the union of two terms. . . . Not until I confound the impressions, and suffuse the symbols themselves with the emotions they arouse, and find joy and sweetness in the very words I hear, will the expressiveness constitute a beauty. . . .The value of the second term must be incorporated in the first; for the beauty of expression is . . . inherent in the object. . . . Expressiveness becomes an aesthetic value, that is, becomes expression, when the values involved in the associations thus awakened are incorporated in the present object.[4]

According to Santayana, then, in our experience the emotions appear to be in the work itself, as part of the object. But when we reflect on the situation, logic compels us to conclude that the emotion is within us and is not part of the object. The problem is how to reconcile these two different accounts.

One suggested solution is that the two accounts arise from two different levels of experience, what we earlier called the first and the second levels. Another philosopher, Henry Marshall, put it this way: "All of us, whether ignorant or highly sophisticated, naturally think of beauty as something residing in these objects in the world about us. Beauty seems to be beyond us in space, in the object we are observing. But when we come to consider the matter carefully we see that this habitual naive mode of thought is scarcely warranted."[5]

Our ordinary, or "naive" experience is thus corrected by a more "considered" or "careful" way of looking at things.

The Causal Theory

So far, though, this looks more like a restatement of the problem than a solution to it. The difficulty of reconciling physical objects like paintings with subjective ones like feelings has been restated in terms of the difficulty of reconciling the different reports of two different levels of experience. But we still have no explanation of the difficulty. Why do reports from the two levels conflict so routinely?

At this point, many are inclined toward a causal theory of expression. The basic idea is that an artist has a certain emotion inside and that this emotion has such force that it overflows into the work. Something like this may have been what Dunstan had in mind when he said: "It gets out their feelings." As the emotion overflows, it causes the work to have certain qualities and these qualities in turn cause the same emotion to rise in the viewer. This idea seems to be supported by the etymology of the word "expression": ex-press: to press out, squeeze out, as one might squeeze toothpaste out of a tube. First the toothpaste or the emotion is inside, then it is pressed out, ex-pressed onto the canvas.

This causal sense of "expression" has tended to dominate expressionist theories of art. Many late romantics talked about art as the overflow, venting, pouring forth of human emotion and the idea was also popular among philosophers and psychologists at the turn of the century. But the idea of causality here presents a problem. It seems to be similar to the idea we have when we think of pain causing behavior. We might say, for instance, that a pain *causes* someone to shout "Ouch!" We might also say that the shout "Ouch!" expresses the pain. Or the pain may cause a person to grimace or writhe, in which case we can say that the gesture expresses the pain. In a similar way, according to this view, an emotion causes an artist to create a work and the work expresses the emotion. The pain behaviors — shouting, grimacing, writhing — may also cause similar feelings, empathetic pain of some kind, in those who observe them. And again in the same way, seeing a painting causes the viewer to have empathetically the artist's feeling.

One unfortunate consequence of this idea is that the emotion expressed in a work is made to seem not really a part of the work. The emotion occurs within the artist; the visual qualities of the work belong to the work but are not the emotion itself; they merely serve to make manifest that which is elsewhere. The work of art is one thing; what it expresses is something else. More generally, we can say that causes are always distinct from their effects. As one writer put it: "It is Chardin himself whom we admire in his representation of a glass of water. We admire the genius of Rembrandt in the profound and individual character which he imparted to every head that posed before him."[6]

The same thing is true of the viewer's feelings. We can say that the work causes an emotion in the viewer and that this emotion is the essence of the work, though still no actual part of it. It belongs to the viewer, not the work. And of course you can combine these two ideas, bringing the emotions of the artist and the viewer together. In this fuller version of the theory, the emotion caused in the viewer is the same emotion as that of the artist when he created the work. The work becomes a kind of communication device for the emotion, something that makes possible its transfer from the artist to the viewer without ever itself having the emotion.

There are other difficulties with the causal theory of expression. Above all, it is not clear how the causality works. It is not clear *how* an artist's state of mind can cause an artwork to have certain qualities nor how an artwork can cause viewers to have certain emotions. But unless a causal theory provides an explanation, it has only redescribed the situation with the word "cause." It has added no further understanding.

A number of people have tried to explain the causality involved in the effect of a work on a viewer. It has many times been claimed that particular colors, shapes, lines, formal arrangements cause particular feelings in people; for example, jagged lines make people excited, gentle curves make them feel calm. In the late nineteenth century several people tried to explain the causality involved with a theory of Empathy — often known by its German name as Einfühlung.[7] According to this theory, we unconsciously imitate the gesture of an artwork within our body. So, for instance, we tense our body when looking at jagged lines and relax it when looking at gentle curves. This tenseness or relaxation produces a mental counterpart in the form of excited or calm emotions. Of course, we have to imagine the causes and the effects being much more complex and subtle than this.

One of the assumptions of such a view is that the cause-and-effect connections involved apply to everyone — that they are in effect universal and ahistorical. This seems required by the notion of cause itself. In this way, the theory of Empathy is related to the kind of universal formalism that we reviewed in the second chapter, where we found the evidence for it very shaky. But for our part, we would argue that such cause-and-effect chains are highly dependent on their historical and cultural context and hence could not provide the kind of explanation the theory seems to call for.

It seems that the emotional character of aesthetic response is dependent on the cultural background of the viewer. As we said earlier, inevitably we see the world through our own forms of thought. This includes our emotions. We see the world in emotional terms that we have learned from our culture. The sky looks menacing, the thunder sounds frightening, the lake looks serene. We rarely experience the world as if it were free of emotion, a collection of bare physical objects, but rather as a set of objects already meaningful, that we already have categories for — sky, thunder, lake — and that we already see as menacing, frightening, calm. Furthermore, each culture has its own way of identifying and conceiving emotions and the objects in the world that they respond to. By first grade a child is already looking at artworks with culturally structured emotions. This fact seems incompatible with the universalism required by the causal version of expressionism.

In addition, the causal theory implies some things about experience that are simply false. It implies, for example, that a person could create a sad work only while actually feeling sad and that a person could recognize the work as being sad only if he were feeling sad at that moment. This is explicitly claimed by Tolstoy, for example, who says in a famous passage: "A boy, having experienced fear on encountering a wolf, relates that encounter, and . . . this — if only the boy when telling the story again experiences the feelings he had lived through, and infects the hearers and compels them to feel what he had experienced — is art."[8]

In other words, Tolstoy says it is not enough that an artist tells a story that is emotional. In addition, the story must be true and the emotions must be felt by both the artist in telling and the listener in hearing about them. But these implications run counter to fact in many instances. It seems just untrue to common experience both that an artist feels the particular emotions while working on the painting and also that the viewer actually feels them while looking at it. A little introspection will provide examples. The causal theory also implies an oversimplified view of artistic creation, as though all one had to do to create an angry work of art is to get so angry one cannot restrain the anger.

Underneath all these objections, the main problem with the causal theory is the dualistic model of mind and body that it presupposes. This is the model that Santayana's argument began with. According to this model, there are two quite different kinds of things in the world. There are physical objects, which we can touch, see, move about, and which exist in time and space; and there are mental objects, such as thoughts, emotions, moods, which cannot be touched, seen, or moved, and which do not exist in time and space. Our bodies are physical objects, of course, and so are paintings and sculptures. Emotions, on the other hand, are mental. This is a natural-seeming way to think of the world for most of us, at least for those of us who have been brought up in Western cultures.

This way of thinking is called "dualistic" because it holds that there are two fundamental kinds of things, the physical and the mental. Most of us have grown up with this idea, and we use it to think about the world and explain our experience. Naturally, then, when we describe our experience of emotional expressiveness in art, we do so in terms of this dualistic idea. There, in one category, is the paint, canvas, wood, stone, and so on, and there, in another category, are the emotions, ideas, and so on. This dualism dictates both the problem and the failure of attempts to solve it because it implies that by definition — or really in most cases by unexamined assumption — we will never bring the two kinds of things together. The problem is unsolvable until we challenge the dualistic picture of the world that gives rise to them. We return to this point shortly.

Another Theory: The Clarification of Emotion

It is a common observation that emotions aroused by artworks are not exactly the same as their real life counterpart. When we look at works like the Goya (fig. 3) or go to horror movies, we don't experience real life feelings of horror or fear.[9] Otherwise we would not voluntarily look at such things. Our emotions are somehow more reflective than that, and more rewarding. Embodied as they are in an artwork, they can be savored and thought about—even the unpleasant ones—rather than merely suffered through.

This thought provides the basis for a different explanation of expression. On this view, art expresses emotion more in the way words express meaning than in the way a cider press expresses juice. Instead of getting rid of an emotion in art, the artist articulates it and in so doing transforms it into something that can be contemplated. In a not dissimilar way, there is sometimes value in talking about our emotions with a sympathetic friend. By putting them into words, we may be able to get some distance on our emotions and somehow grasp them better. Collingwood analyzed the phenomenon this way:

> When a man is said to express emotion, what is being said about him comes to this. At first, he is conscious of having an emotion, but not conscious of what this emotion is. All he is conscious of is a perturbation or excitement, which he feels going on within him, but of whose nature he is ignorant. While in this state, all he can say about his emotion is: "I feel . . . I don't know what I feel." From this helpless and oppressed condition he extricates himself by doing something which we call expressing himself. This is an activity which has something to do with the thing we call language: he expresses himself by speaking. It has also something to do with consciousness: the emotion expressed is an emotion of whose nature the person who feels it is no longer unconscious. It has also something to do with the way in which he feels the emotion. As unexpressed, he feels it in what we have called a helpless and oppressed way; as expressed, he feels it in a way from which this sense of oppression has vanished. His mind is somehow lightened and eased.[10]

Artistic expression, interpreted this way, means the transformation of an emotional state from something that is oppressive to something that is more nearly understood. We do this by articulating the emotion in an image that can be seen. The motivation is not, as the causal theory suggests, to get rid of our emotion but is rather to grasp it, to come closer to understanding it. This makes creation more difficult than the causal theory suggests. It is not enough to get angry and then "let it all go." That might create a scene but not a work of art. Creation requires careful scrutiny of the work as it develops, scrupulous awareness of how one feels when contemplating what one has so far accomplished, sensitive adjustment of the work to fit one's intuitive experience, until one feels that one has grasped something one didn't grasp before.

Under critical scrutiny, then, the causal theory of expression begins to give way to a hermeneutic theory, that is, a theory that has to do with meanings. Artworks have meanings rather than feelings. As Collingwood put it: "The characteristic mark of expression . . . is lucidity or intelligibility; a person who expresses something becomes conscious of what it is that he is expressing and enables others to become conscious of it."[11]

On this account, the emotion that is the origin of a work of art is not exactly what is finally expressed. It is transformed in some respects by the art activity. It is this transformation that the causal theory of expression seems to ignore, just as the imitation theory of representation ignored the transformation of subject matter.

This transformation of emotion is one of the differences between actively looking at the visual environment or actively listening to music and being passively influenced by them. There are many reasons we might have for decorating a room or for playing some music. Sometimes it is to get us in the right mood for other activities, such as talking with friends, doing homework or having a party. We all know that a color scheme or some background music can make one relaxed or edgy. This looks like a case that fits the causal theory well. But it is exactly a case when we are not attending to paintings or music as art; instead we are using them as background for other activities that have our attention. Ironically then, the causal theory seems to be most plausible in just those cases when we are not looking or listening aesthetically.

The Public Character of Emotions

This theory of art as the clarification of emotions also needs a theory of emotions. Just as we said that the causal theory needed to explain how the causality worked, so this clarification theory needs to explain how emotions can be clarified and understood. We will briefly indicate how this explanation usually proceeds.

The explanation makes the assumption, for the purposes of analysis, that we already suggested: that there are several levels to our consciousness. The first level where we experience our emotions as inarticulate sensations and feelings. This is the level at which we encounter our emotions most directly, where they are most strongly felt and least clearly grasped. Collingwood says that at this level emotions are frequently felt as oppressive and uncontrolled.

The next level is where emotions are articulated in artistic images. At this level, emotions acquire more stability and clarity. Their character can be grasped by intuition and contemplated. This does not mean they can be easily named and talked about, for they remain highly contextual and individual. They retain much of their power to move us. There is also a third level, at which emotions have names and can be generalized in language. At this level we can put their names into sentences and say things about them, such as what we think caused them. At a still further level we can theorize about and explain emotions in general. A particular emotion may travel across these four levels, beginning as an undigested and unidentified turmoil, becoming an emotion expressed in an artistic image, then being named by the word "anger," and finally analyzed as a response to a childhood spent with Father.

It is important to see that, at points like these, the philosophy of art moves inescapably into the philosophy of mind and into epistemology. This move is both typical and inescapable. It is not possible to provide an account that links art with artists without having a general theory of mind. And just as the causal theory assumed that emotions are private and subjective, a clarification theory needs to explain how emotions are not so. In fact, the view that emotions are partly public and objective is not limited to proponents of this theory of expression. It is much more widespread because there is a general rejection in philosophy of the dualistic mind-and-body picture mentioned earlier. We will briefly explain this view, though we will not follow it very far.

If we look at our experience without prejudgment, we find a wide range of phenomena that are neither wholly private nor wholly public. These include emotions: for example, menacing sky or frightening thunder, where the menace or the fear must be felt internally but is experienced also as external, as part of what is seen or heard. One way to describe this situation is to say that emotions are usually about something. To be afraid means to perceive something — the sky or the thunder — as threatening. Similarly, to be angry is to be angry at something perceived as annoying and to be delighted is to feel delight over something pleasant. It would not, in normal cases, make sense to say we are afraid, angry, or delighted but do not know what we are afraid of, angry at, or delighted with.

It follows that we can communicate what our emotions are by discussing what they are about. We can try to describe the look of the sky, the sound of the thunder. In this way, we make our emotions public in the sense that other people can see what we are reacting to and understand our reaction. They may even have an empathetic sharing of the emotion. In such cases we can say that our emotions have an internal and private component — what we experience, and perhaps also what our listeners empathetically experience — and an external and public component — what we can all see, hear, and attend to.

According to the clarification version of the expressive theory, emotions are made public — that is, communicated — through art. There are many cultural influences that help shape our emotions, including myth, morality, religion and science, but art is the most important. Artists help us to interpret our own emotions by articulating images of them and of the items in the world they are about. Such images, when powerful enough, become part of the common culture and serve to celebrate and communicate that culture to its new members. For this reason much of our emotional life is quite traditional; we learned it from the stock of common images of our culture. Much of our life consists of having feelings and thoughts that people have had before, reexperiencing the inner life made possible by our culture. The theory is also compatible with the modernist, avant-garde view of the artist as a kind of emotional pioneer who constantly challenges the cliches of the time. We met this view in chapter 2, where we saw Wassily Kandinsky praise the artist as one who teaches his culture how to respond to a changing world.

Knowing Your Own Mind

The important thing to notice is that in this view, whether the emotions are traditional or avant-garde, art teaches us to have them more clearly and precisely. Expressionist philosophers, notably including Benedetto Croce[12] and R. G. Collingwood,[13] have argued that we cannot have a clear idea or emotion, even a perception, unless we articulate it in some medium. Nothing, they argue, is simply *given* in perception. If you are to see something, you must look attentively at it and track its detail with your eye. It is not much of an exaggeration to translate the point by saying: you can't see what you can't draw or paint. In this sense, any perception is an achievement, not something that happens automatically.

In the same way, our emotional life is not transparent to us, to be understood simply by undergoing it. Rather, we must actively attend to our emotions and give them shape in terms of some medium. Collingwood says, "Until a man has expressed his emotion he does not yet know what emotion it is." And the same is true of ideas. Until we have given an idea some shape, there is no clear idea. If you are given an assignment to write an essay, you cannot think about what you are going to say until you have begun to put it into words, concepts, and arguments. And once you have an articulated idea of what you want to express, it has already been formulated in terms of the means you will use to express it — in words, color arrangements, and the like. You do not first think to yourself what you are going to express and then decide on how you will express it.

Part of what the expressionists are debunking is the common temptation to believe that we have within us great, sensitive, and profound thoughts which we haven't expressed yet but could if we wanted to. Croce in particular comes down hard on this. If you truly have such thoughts, he argues, they must be expressed, verbally, visually, or in some other way. Otherwise you don't know what they are and hence you don't really have them. If people really had the thoughts they sometimes suppose they have, he says, "they would already have coined them into beautiful, ringing words, and thus expressed them." In short, the crucial test for a good thought is to say: "speak, or here's a pencil, draw it."[14]

This idea is opposed to the popular view that art simply dresses up an already existing idea in a pleasant form — "What oft was thought, but ne'er so well expressed," as the eighteenth-century poet Alexander Pope put it. An English critic, A. C. Bradley, said: "Poetry is not the decoration of a preconceived and clearly defined matter; it springs from the creative impulse of a vague imaginative mass pressing for development and definition. If the poet already knew exactly what he meant to say, why should he write the poem? . . . Only its completion can reveal, even to him, exactly what he wanted."[15]

Of course, there is a sense in which artists can express ideas in words. They can try to say, before they begin painting, what kind of works they are trying to create. In fact artists often talk about their intentions. Critics, too, after the creation of a work, often try to formulate in words its meaning or content, and this can help us see things in the work we might not otherwise see. This is common experience.

But the expressionists insist that an artist has only a very general and approximate intention until the work is finished. Nor do they believe that an idea expressed in one medium can be translated exactly into another. Form and content are inseparable. Change the form of expression and you change the content. Artworks therefore are untranslatable except in very approximate ways.

This theory provides an answer to our original problem about how an emotion can be found in something public like an artwork. The answer is that emotions, perceptions, and thoughts as well, can be grasped only when they are articulated in a medium through the activity of art and at that point they have become public and communicable. The relation of emotions to artworks is not a causal one but something more like the relation of a word to its meaning or, more generally, of a symbol to its significance.

The Intentional Fallacy

We turn now to the question of the artist's intention and whether it is relevant to our interpretation of a work. This raises some of the same issues from a slightly different point of view. We already touched on the question when we discussed whether artists can say, before creating a work, what their intentions for it are. The Croce-Collingwood expressionist line of thought, we said, is that the artist's idea is expressed adequately only in the artwork itself. Any talk about it, by the artist or by anyone else, can only be a general approximation of, and poor substitute for, what the work expresses.

It will be seen that this line of thought tends to depreciate the value of art history. It suggests that when we want to understand a work, all we need is the work itself and additional information from or about the artist will not help. Either the intention is fulfilled in the work, in which case we can find it by attending to the work, or the intention is not relevant. Either way, we do not really need art historical information.

But in practice we often appeal to the artist's intentions or to various facts about the artist when trying to make sense of a work. It is natural, when we're not sure what a work means, to ask what the artist was trying to do. When archeologists find an object of fired clay, they ask themselves what the intention of its maker was in order to decide what it was. If they decide that it was an oil lamp, that would mean that it was made with the intention of being used as a lamp. In other words, the object was a lamp if that was what the maker had in mind. Art historians also spend a lot of their time studying what it was that particular artists intended to make, studying, that is, their lives, their times, their practices, what they said and did, trying to ascertain what kinds of attitudes, thoughts, ambitions, states of mind they had when they made their art. All this is done in order to shed light on the meaning of individual works. The assumption seems to be that a knowledge of both specific intentions and also of the general character and life of the artist, can affect our understanding of a work. Art historians, for example, tell us about Van Gogh's tortured states of mind and unhappy end because they assume that that knowledge will affect the way we look at his work. Much common practice makes the same assumption.

However, Monroe Beardsley, a major recent figure in the philosophy of art, has argued that this is a false assumption. It is, he says, a mistake to use the intentions of the artist to help decide the meaning of a work.

He called the appeal to the artist's intentions the "intentional fallacy," a title that has become well known.[16] Beardsley was the major philosopher of the New Criticism movement and was arguing against prior practices of romanticizing the artist and confusing the interesting life of the artist with the significance of the works.

Beardsley's argument is that we should not have to deduce the meaning of a work from sources external to the work. The meaning should be in the work itself and we should be able to grasp it by looking at the work. The evidence we need should be provided by the work itself and not by extraneous investigations. Beardsley is arguing against having to find out about the artist's intentions from sources external to the work, such as letters written by the artist or stories told by the artist's friends or conjectures of art historians. He believes that when we interpret the work we should consider only the evidence that can be found in the work itself.

His reason is that the artist may have failed to fulfill the intention for a work. The artist may have intended a work to be morally serious but in fact it comes over as melodramatic; or what was intended to be heroically expressive may turn out to be bombastic and empty. In general, whenever a work fails in some respect, it will not help to learn that the artist did not intend the failure but something else instead. The work is still what it is, in Beardsley's view, unchanged by whatever we learn about the artist or the intentions. Even if the work is successful, it may not be successful in exactly the way the artist intended. Perhaps the artist intended one thing and did something different, and the something different was better than what was intended. In such a case, again, what is important is the work itself and not a knowledge of what was originally intended. And, of course, there may be cases where the artist's intentions are perfectly fulfilled. In these cases, Beardsley continues, we have all the evidence we need to interpret the work right there in the work itself, and it will not be helpful to add external evidence about intentions.

This argument has become so well known and has had so much influence that it is worthwhile noticing what Beardsley does *not* argue against. He is not against talking about the work in terms of the artist's intentions. He is concerned about the source of evidence used for such talk; the only evidence he would allow for determining what the intentions were is the evidence to be found in the work itself. Notice too that his argument is about the interpretation, not the identification, of works. When it comes to identifying artworks, that is, to determining whether an item is an artwork rather than a natural object or an ordinary artifact, he thinks that artists' intentions are required. Beardsley thinks that artworks must have been intended by the artist to be artworks, that is, to be looked at aesthetically. So he does not count driftwood cases as art, nor chimpanzee paintings, nor even ready-mades. Such things may be aesthetic objects in his view but, lacking an artist's intention, are not artworks.[17]

˜ It will be seen that Beardsley's view about the irrelevance of artist's intentions to interpretation is consistent with the expressionist views of Croce and Collingwood that we discussed. The expressionists insist that it is only after the work is done that artists know exactly what their intentions are anyway, because the work just is the exact articulation of those intentions. Anything else that the artists might say about the work will inevitably be less precise, more general, and maybe different than what the work itself says. Artworks cannot be translated exactly. And so again, it will be at best a waste of time looking for evidence outside the work, and at worst it will be misleading. The expressionists' view and Beardsley's are two sides of the same coin. The first argues that artists do express their states of mind exactly in their artworks; the second argues that when we look at their artworks, we have all we need to read the artists' states of mind.

The Revival of Intentionalism

Recently we have seen the reemergence of an intentionalist approach to interpretation among philosophers of art and with it a number of attacks on the "intentional fallacy." This development is connected with a growing general concern for the way in which the meaning of a work is affected by the historical context of its creation.[18] In fact, one of the issues that frequently occurs in this connection is the degree to which the artist's life and intentions are separable from the historical art world and culture.

These philosophers argue that there are many cases where the intentions of the artist are part of what determines the artistic properties of the work. The most obvious are cases such as irony, allusion, symbolism and membership in a genre. These are essentially intentional, for if the artist did not intend something to be ironic, allusive, symbolic or in a particular genre, it would not be so. Even if it appeared ironic, allusive, and so on, it would not be so unless the artist intended it. Of course, the appearance and the intention usually coincide and so we can usually tell from the work itself whether an item is ironic, and so on. But often there are subtler differences. For example, one might guess, without knowing anything of the artist's religious beliefs, that the young bull in Potter's *Young Bull* represents the divine power. The work has visual properties, a certain majesty and glow, we may say, that suggest that much to any viewer. But the exact character of these visual properties depends on just what kind of divine power Potter believed in, whether he was a pantheist, say, or believed in blood sacrifices, or was a Christian. This shows that the very properties of the work we see may be affected by the artist's intentions and that therefore we need to know some things about him.

The same thing is true even of representational properties for, as we noticed in chapter 3, similarity is not enough to establish representation. There has to be an intention to represent as well, though most of the time we can take it for granted. But if, for example, without knowing anything about what is intended, we were to look at Bruegel's *Fall of Icarus* (fig. 10), we would see a peaceful scene of rural life on the edge of the sea. It is only when we know that this painting is intended to represent the fall of Icarus that we can see that the tiny far-off splash in the sea is a boy falling from the sky. When we see this, the character of the work changes entirely. What was unimportant becomes crucial, what was peaceful becomes ironic, what was simple becomes complex.

Arthur Danto has produced some particularly influential examples of the centrality of intentions in his writings. He has been especially impressed by the problem of "indiscernibles," that is, artworks which look exactly like some other objects that are not artworks.[19] The *Brillo Boxes* of Warhol are a favorite example because Danto believes that the exhibition of this work was a key event in the twentieth-century history of artists challenging our idea of art. In 1964 Warhol made some boxes from plywood, painted them to look exactly like the commercially available Brillo boxes, and stacked them in a gallery the way they might be stacked in a supermarket. A number of critics were impressed, though others, of course, were not, and *Brillo Boxes* has usually been accepted as an artwork in the history books. Danto understands this work to rephrase the question What is art? into the form, which he thinks central to the philosophy of art: What makes this an artwork when the look-alike, commercially available Brillo boxes are not? The answer obviously cannot be found in the visual qualities of the artwork because it has exactly the same visual qualities as the ordinary Brillo boxes. The same question applies to most readymades and for the innumerable works that have used the Brillo Box strategy since Warhol's invention and, Danto argues, by extension to all works. In Danto's view, this situation allows us to discount visual appearances almost by definition when we ask the question What makes something an artwork? The answer, he argues, must have something

Figure 10. Pieter Bruegel the Elder, *Landscape with the Fall of Icarus*, Royal Museums of Fine Arts, Brussels. Giraudon/Art Resource, New York.

to do with the historical circumstances in which the work was created, including importantly the intentions of the artist.

Another example of Danto's, one that has become famous as a philosophical example, is imaginary in character. It is what philosophers sometimes call a "thought experiment," a case deliberately imagined to pose a question as clearly as possible. Danto imagines seven squares of canvas, each painted red, each looking identically like the other.[20] Some of these are artworks, some are not. Of those that are artworks, each is a different work. For example, one is by a Danish portraitist and is called *Kierkegaard's Mood*; another is by "an embittered disciple of Matisse" and is called *Red Tablecloth*; a third is called *The Israelites Crossing the Red Sea*, where the Israelites have already crossed over and the Egyptians have been drowned; and a fourth is a Minimalist work simply titled *Red Square*. Of the nonartworks, one is a canvas primed by Giorgione, intended as a ground for a painting that he never began, and another is just a square of canvas with paint on it. Danto's question about this spectacular imaginary display of red squares is: What makes each artwork the artwork that it is and what prevents those items that are not artworks from being so? He has imagined these cases carefully just in order that the answer cannot lie in their visual qualities.

His answer is that the difference has to do with the artist's intentions. For example, the follower of Matisse intended to picture a table cloth and that is what her work does; this makes her painting different from that of the Danish portrait painter, whose work is a portrait of a person just for the reason that she intended it so. The reason that two of the squares are not artworks is that there is no appropriate intention by the artist, even though one of them was painted by an artist (Giorgione). The point is not that, when interpreting these works, we can ignore their visual properties, anymore than we can ignore the visual properties of *The Fall of Icarus* when we interpret it. It is that we must bear the artists' intentions in mind when we look to see what the properties of the works are. *Kierkegaard's Mood*, for example, has a strong emotional character, whereas *Red Tablecloth* does not; *The Israelites Crossing the Red Sea* has three dimensional depth whereas the Minimalist *Red Square* does not.

This line of thought raises a question about the distinction between evidence for interpretation that is internal to a work and evidence that is external to it, a distinction that earlier we took for granted. Those who support the "Intentional Fallacy" often seem to suppose without argument that we can tell by inspection what is internal to the work and what is external to it (though Monroe Beardsley does discuss this issue in his original article). Internal evidence, they suppose, is what we get just by looking at the work itself, because it is part of the visual properties of the work. External evidence is what comes from consulting some other source, such as a knowledge of what the artist did, or said, or the context in which she worked, the sort of knowledge that is often found in art history books. But in fact, it turns out, the difference is not that clear. It is often unclear whether a property is internal or external. For example, the tiny splash that represents Daedalus can be seen in the painting by anyone, but it can be seen *as* Daedalus only by those who know that the artist intended it so. And only those who see it as Daedalus will see it as important. The same thing is true of the property of representing-a-red-tablecloth of the *Red Tablecloth*: it is a visual property of the work that we can see, but we can see it only after we know what the artist intended. Again the same sort of thing is true of ironic, allusive, symbolic, genre and representational properties in general. The conclusion is that often the visual properties of a work, which are supposed to be internal, are dependent on knowledge about the artist, which is supposed to be external.

In this way, the distinction between internal and external evidence breaks down. A more useful distinction, in our opinion, has to do with how much knowledge an ordinary viewer brings to a particular work.

The viewer always needs to know something to interpret a work relevantly. Sometimes we know enough already and we can interpret the work just by looking at it attentively, without a need for further information. In other cases we do not know enough and we have to consult some other source of information to see the work completely and to make a relevant interpretation. The difference then lies in how much the viewer knows already rather than in the work itself or in what kind of evidence (internal or external) is relevant. Naturally there will be large differences between viewers in this respect, depending on which work is in question.

There is a similar conceptual point to be made about the notion of artists' intentions. The idea of the artist's intention is not as simple as it might seem. An intention is rarely the unambiguous and easily formulated purpose of the artist we may have supposed. For one thing, at any one time a person has a variety of desires, some of which are relatively transient wishes, others are long-sustained motives, and many lie between these extremes. These desires may be in conflict with each other and they certainly will not all be carefully thought through and articulated. Some of them may never have been formulated at all, the artist may be quite unaware of them and yet they are the most important: anger at Father, for instance. Collingwood's view, after all, was that we never know exactly what our emotions or desires are until we have articulated them in art. It follows that, if we want to find out what the artists' intentions were, we may be forced to interpret whatever they wrote or said in the same way we must interpret the artworks themselves — that is, in light of whatever evidence is available about the artist's life and states of mind, her friends and influences, and the culture of her time.

This is to say that the artist's intentions were shaped by the historical context in which they were adopted, so that establishing just what those intentions were requires art historical study. Intentions are complex and are shaped by culture, so that what is wished for, desired, feared, aspired to, mocked, is in part a function of culture. For example, ideational frameworks, such as Christianity, humanism, democracy, feminism, provide a good deal of structure to intentions. So, for artists, do art movements. In fact, intentionalist philosophers usually argue that a large part of the relevant intentions of an artist amount to varying, taking further, or repudiating the work of previous artists and art movements.[21] At least a part of an artist's intention, in other words, is formed in light of the history of art itself; it is related to the artist's understanding of previous art and attitudes toward it. The artist intends to produce work of a certain kind understood in light of, and also limited by, the art of the time. One could not intend to be, for example, an abstract expressionist until the 1940s, because that intention required a set of ideas that were not available before then. By the 1960s it was a common intention.

There are also art-specific conventions and procedures that shape an artist's intentions and that also restrict their range. For example, there are notions of genre, such as altarpieces, landscape, history painting, portraits that at certain times have been quite influential and at other times not. To do a history painting, for example, required one to work in a certain way and to imitate, or have the ambition of outdoing, certain predecessors. It required one to work in oils, to use a rectangular canvas, to allude to a certain set of historical or literary characters, to be realistic in particular ways, and so on. Such things would form part of the artist's intentions, though we might just as easily think of them as the conventions and expectations of the time. Because artists' intentions are inevitably influenced by the art practices of their time, it is often difficult to distinguish discussions of individual artists from discussions of the art world they participated in. At this point, the intentionalist approach becomes close to the institutional one, which we discuss in the next chapter. The heart of this convergence is the idea that, in talking about the meaning of a work, we may find helpful a knowledge both of the artist's individual life and of the art world of the time.

A simple example comes from Grant Woods's *American Gothic*. We can assume that the loose strand of the woman's hair is intended by the artist to suggest a slight but significant softening of the moral rigidity suggested by the rest of the painting. This assumption is justified not so much by a knowledge of what Grant Woods actually thought as by understanding the conventions of the genre. If this were a photograph, the inference would not be justified: the loose strand of hair might have been accidental. In a painting like this, we know everything is expected to be significant. The stray hair, painted so carefully, could not but be meaningful.

Consider, too, that in the case of Danto's imaginary gallery of red squares, the artists are anonymous. We know very little about any of them, but that little seems enough. We know, for example, that the painter of *Red Tablecloth* was a follower of Matisse, which seems enough to explain her intentions for the work. The case of the Danish portraitist is a little more complicated. If we wanted to understand this work better we would probably not want to learn about the artist's psychological state but more about Kierkegaard, or perhaps more exactly, more about what the artist thought about Kierkegaard. This would be the part of her intention that is relevant for our interpretation.

Notice, too, that we learn a lot about the artists' intentions from the titles of the works, which are another kind of convention. Perhaps we should regard the titles as actually part of the works. After all, they are a part of what the artist presents. Even a title like *Untitled* tells us quite a lot: that the work is intended as a finished artwork, that it is not a representation of something, and that it is influenced by ideas that reject particular titles. Of course, it takes an acquaintance with some twentieth-century ideas about art to make sense of such a title and hence of the intentions behind a work that would have such a title. In fact, the point Danto was trying to make with his imaginary red squares had as much to do with artistic ideas as with artists' intentions. He wanted to show that objects can only be interpreted as artworks against the background of particular ideas about what art is and can do. Artworks only exist, he wanted to say, in "an atmosphere of theory." The most striking case is the Minimalist *Red Square*, which is intelligible only because of the Minimalist movement and the ideas that shaped it. Otherwise it cannot be interpreted as art and is about nothing at all, as in fact a Minimalist would claim it is. But, according to Danto, the very fact that the Minimalist painter shows the work as an artwork and claims that it defies interpretation reveals that in fact it is at least about the defiance of interpretation, and in that way it is different from the red squares that are not artworks, which truly are not about anything.

The general conclusion from this line of argument is that, on the one hand, it is often important for interpretation that we know something of what the artist intended; and, on the other hand, determining the intentions of an artist may be as much a social or institutional investigation as it is a personal one.

Summary

In this chapter we have considered the relationship of artworks with the artists that made them. We have asked whether an artwork can be thought to express the mind of the artist and, conversely, whether we need to know something of the mind of the artist to interpret the artwork. This discussion has required us to discuss a number of related ideas, including the idea of expression, the relevance of art history to interpretation, and the individual/social nature of emotions and intentions.

The idea that artworks express the mind of the artist has been a major one in the philosophy of art, responding to the importance of expressiveness in Western art. Students in school are likely to be affected by the expressiveness of particular works and hence it is also a major topic for them. They are also likely to be interested in general about how the personalities of artists are reflected in their artworks. We first identified the general problem of expression, which is that artworks, consisting in physical objects, seem to exist independently of whatever the artist may have thought or felt. We explored the causal notion of expression, according to which the feelings of the artist cause the work to have particular visual qualities and those qualities in turn cause the viewer to have the feelings that the artist had. This notion conflicts with many facts about art and in the end remains mysterious. It is also a view that makes art history irrelevant. A more adequate account of expression conceives an artwork as the articulation of feelings such that they can be more adequately grasped by both the artist and the viewer.

The philosophers considered in this chapter all agree that artworks are intentional objects; that is, they are shaped by the intentions of the artist. But they disagree about whether we need to consult more than the evidence of the artwork itself in order to interpret its meaning. Some, including many expressionists and also Monroe Beardsley, have felt that it is sufficient to consider only the visual properties of the work. If the work is successful, they argue, it will reveal the artist's intentions; if it is not, knowing about the failed intentions will not help interpret the work. Others argue that the visual properties of the work may depend on a knowledge of the artist's intentions. They argue that what is internal and what external to the work cannot be easily decided in advance of investigation and that therefore art historical studies are crucial for interpretation of artworks. This conclusion suggests that it will be helpful to teach students about the cultural context in which a work originated, the conventions and practices of the time, and relevant parts of the life of the artist.

Lastly, the expressionist and the intentionalist views both require us to understand the artist's mind, whether consisting in emotions or in intentions, as being socially constructed as well as individually experienced. What the artist expressed or intended is to be understood in light of the public practice of the time as well as by subjective determination. What can be expressed or intended by individual artists is shaped by — that is, both made possible and also restricted by — the historical context.

NOTES

1. R. G. Collingwood, *The Principles of Art* (New York: Oxford University Press, 1958), p. 109.

2. Monroe Beardsley, *Aesthetics* (New York: Harcourt Brace Jovanovich, 1958), p. 35.

3. George Santayana, *The Sense of Beauty* (New York: Dover Publications, 1955), p. 186.

4. Ibid., p. 188.

5. Henry P. Marshall, *The Beautiful* (London: Macmillan, 1924), p. 27.

6. Fritz Bürger, quoted in Eugene Véron, *Aesthetics*, trans. W. Armstrong (London: Oxford University Press, 1878).

7. Vernon Lee, *The Beautiful* (Cambridge: Cambridge University Press, 1913), chs. 5, 9.

8. Leo Tolstoy, *What is Art?* trans. Aylmer Maude (London: Oxford University Press, 1896), p. 62.

9. See Noel Carroll, *Mystifying Movies: Fads and Fallacies in Contemporary Film* (New York: Columbia University Press, 1988), for an account of our response to horror movies.

10. Collingwood, *The Principles of Art*, pp. 109-10.

11. Ibid., p.122.

12. Benedetto Croce, *Aesthetics*, trans. D. Ainslie (London: MacMillan, 1909).

13. Collingwood, *The Principles of Art*.

14. Benedetto Croce, *Aesthetics*, pp. 90, 100.

15. A. C. Bradley, "Poetry for Poetry's Sake," *Oxford Lectures on Poetry* (London: Macmillan, 1909).

16. William K. Wimsatt and Monroe C. Beardsley, "The Intentional Fallacy," *The Sewanee Review* 54 (1946): 486-88; widely anthologized and discussed. See also Monroe C. Beardsley, "Intentions and Interpretations," in *The Aesthetic Point of View*, ed. Michael J. Wren and Donald M. Callen (Ithaca, N.Y.: Cornell University Press, 1982).

17. See Stephen Davies, *Definitions of Art* (Ithaca, N.Y.: Cornell University Press, 1991), ch. 3, for a clear and interesting discussion of Beardsley's views.

18. See, for example, Noel Carroll, "Art, Practice and Narrative," *The Monist* 71 (1988): 140-56; and Jerrold Levinson, "Defining Art Historically," *Music, Art and Metaphysics* (Ithaca, N.Y.: Cornell University Press, 1990).

19. Arthur C. Danto, *The Transfiguration of the Commonplace* (Cambridge: Harvard University Press, 1981).

20. Danto, *The Transfiguration of the Commonplace*, pp. 1-3.

21. See Carroll, "Art, Practice and Narrative"; Levinson, "Defining Art Historically."

5

Art and Context

In previous chapters we have discussed art in terms of its relation to the audience, the world it represents, and the artist. We have seen that philosophers have thought that art can be defined and interpreted in terms of its relations to these three kinds of things, though they have not agreed on just how to do this nor on which relation is the most significant. We have reviewed disputes about how each relation should be construed and the general consequences for the interpretation of artworks. In this chapter we will consider what might be thought of as the extreme possibilities with respect to the relations of art. The first of these is the view that an artwork should be interpreted without reference to anything else, as an independent object with no relations at all. This view is called formalism. The second, in some ways the antithesis of the first, is the view that an artwork has no independent existence at all but has its status and identity as an artwork only because it has been brought within the ambit of the institutions and conventions of an art world. In this view, anything can be an artwork so long as it is brought within an art world in the right way; and outside an art world nothing is an artwork. This is usually called the institutional theory of art.

Formalism

Formalism first became important in the early part of the twentieth century. It was originally motivated by the desire to focus on the artwork itself and not on aspects of it that were thought aesthetically irrelevant. It was a reaction to the way that critics, affected by both representation and expressionist theories, seemed to subordinate the value of art to the value of other things. These tendencies had reached considerable heights by the end of the nineteenth century. For example, it was common to praise artworks for the sentimental or historical value of what they pictured and also because of the faithful realism with which they did the picturing; these criteria were supported by representational theories. At the same time there was a strong tendency to praise art because it was created by great artists and to romanticize the lives of those artists, telling of their burning ambitions and tragic loves; this tendency was fostered by expressionist theories. The formalist reaction began by wanting to get rid of all such considerations, thinking them irrelevant to what was really important, that is, the work of art itself. It asserted the independence of the artwork from all such relations and sought to focus only on what could be seen in it. The formalists were preoccupied with the quest to clearly identify what is aesthetic in art and in the enjoyment of it and with the insistence that everything else should be disregarded as irrelevant. "Form," in the beginning, was simply their name for what is aesthetically valuable in art.

Their assumption was that there is one feature that all works of art have in common, in virtue of which they are considered works of art and in virtue of which they will be valuable. Many people in addition to the formalists have felt that the question "What is a work of art?" calls for the identification of such a feature. This way of understanding the question is called essentialism. It presupposes the idea that there is an essence of art to be discovered. Clive Bell, an influential early formalist, was quite explicit about this. He said:

> For either all works of visual art have some common quality, or when we speak of "works of art" we jibber. Everyone speaks of "art," making a mental classification by which he distinguishes the class "works of art" from all other classes. What is the justification for this classification? What is the quality common and peculiar to all members of this class? Whatever it be, no doubt it is often found in company with other qualities; but they are adventitious — it is essential. There must be some one quality without which a work of art cannot exist; possessing which, in the least degree, no work is altogether worthless. What is this quality?[1]

For the formalists, the central philosophical problem of art was to define the essence of art ("form") more exactly, and they spent a great deal of effort trying to do so. They began, as we have suggested, by rejecting both representation and expression as irrelevant. Whatever form was, it could not derive from either the subject matter of a work nor the personality of the artist because both of these require reference to things that lie outside the work. What remains after one subtracts these possibilities seems to be mostly the elements of the medium itself and the way they are organized within a particular artwork. In the case of painting, these elements are principally lines, shapes, colors, and textures. When we attend to an artwork but disregard its subject matter and its expressiveness, we approach it as an arrangement of these elements. There are many things we can discover about a work in this way: what the dominant colors are, how those colors relate to each other, how the shapes are arranged on the two-dimensional surface, what forms it contains, the ways in which it suggests a third dimension, what the overall patterning of parts is. The formalists advocate that we attend to such things exclusively.

It might seem obvious that this approach is best suited to abstract works. So, for example, one might well approach a Mondrian painting as a formalist. In that case, one would look at its arrangement of shapes, the patterns of lines, the color relations, and the complex relations among these elements of the painting, how each interacts with the others, balancing, harmonizing, setting up clashes, tensions, and so on. We would be looking at the painting in much the same way we listen to music and in fact many of the formalists held, for this very reason, that music was the highest of all the art forms. They thought that the other arts should strive to emulate the formal, abstract character of music and that the growing modernist tendencies toward abstract, nonrepresentational painting and sculpture actually justified this view. The formalists argue that this is the "purest" way to approach art since it values the artwork alone and doesn't confuse the aesthetic pleasure of art itself with other, nonaesthetic, pleasures.

It is clear, however, that the formalists intend that their view should be applied to all artworks, not only nonrepresentational ones, that we should look at works like the Albright (fig. 1), the Picasso (fig. 2), or the *Madonna of the Meadow* (fig. 11), in just the way that we look at a Mondrian. In fact, it often appears that the most important non-aesthetic consideration that formalists are concerned to guard against is subject matter — our interest in what is represented. Roger Fry, for example, held that a large part of what we normally take to be a delight in art is really just an intrusion of other interests, such as sex, patriotism, or religion.[2] With many paintings, he said, what we are really respond-ing to is the appeal of a beautiful body, the horror or glory of war, or the adoration of a religious icon. He puts the irrelevance of such things in strong terms: "Now I venture to say that no one who has a real understanding of the art of painting attaches any importance to what we call the subject of a picture — what is represented."[3]

Clive Bell is hardly less severe: "The representative element in a work of art may or may not be harmful; always it is irrelevant. For, to appre-ciate a work of art we need bring with us nothing from life, no knowledge of its ideas and affairs, no familiarity with its emotions. Art transports us from the world of man's activity to a world of aesthetic exaltation. For a moment we are shut off from human interests; our anticipations and memories are arrested; we are lifted above the stream of life."[4]

Figure 11. Raphael, *Madonna of the Meadow*, Kunsthistorisches Museum, Vienna. Foto Marburg/Art Resource, New York.

It is clear that the formalists thought of art as being quite uncon-nected with the ordinary world and having little to do with the concerns of ordinary life. Art for them was pure and exclusive of other interests. Aesthetic experience was equally rarified and unconnected with ordinary experience. This view is often thought to have been reflected in the exclusive atmosphere of museums in the first half of this century.

Bell was aware that he was being evaluative and not descriptive here, that is, he was not describing the experience ordinary people have of art but rather giving an account of what he thought that experience should be like. He deplored the fact that in practice many people don't have such experience but are heavily influenced by what is represented. He said:

> I have noticed a consistency in those to whom the most beautiful thing in the world is a beautiful woman, and the next most beautiful thing a picture of one...The art that they call "beautiful" is generally closely related to the women. A beautiful picture is a photograph of a pretty girl; beautiful music, the music that provokes emotions similar to those provoked by young ladies in musical farces; and beautiful poetry, the poetry that recalls the same emotions felt, twenty years earlier, for the rector's daughter.

In short, formalism is a movement bent on reforming rather than describing the way people usually respond to art. Its heart lies in an essentialist conception of the absolute independence of the artwork and its champions commonly deplore the failure of ordinary people to live up to that ideal.

Formalism in the beginning was a response to the new, avant-garde movements in art that swept the European art world in the early years of this century. Roger Fry, for example, was a great champion of the postimpressionists and especially of Cezanne. Formalists have continued to defend and encourage abstract and nonrepresentational painting and sculpture throughout the twentieth century. Clement Greenberg and Michael Fried, two modern American formalists, have had great influence in the United States defending midcentury nonfigurative art. They have provided an influential account of the history of modern art as a progressive evolution away from representation toward abstraction. Their writings have encouraged artists to push this evolution to its completion. To eliminate representation, they argued, it is not enough to reject the portrayal of recognizable objects: one must also eliminate the portrayal of three-dimensional space as well. They were able to show that in fact there has been a gradual flattening of the picture space from the late academic art of the mid-1800s to the abstract art of the 1960s.[6]

At about the same time, artists like Frank Stella and Jasper Johns began to work toward completely nonrepresentational art. They wanted to create works that were things in their own right, not to be interpreted in light of their relations with other things. Previously, art had always been understood to be *about* something, even when it was nonrepresentational, as music might be about a mood or an attitude. It had always had some kind of reference to something else. These artists wanted to create works that did not refer in any way but simply existed, in the way rocks and trees exist, that did not require to be interpreted at all. They were to have "presence" rather than meaning. As Fried put it: "paintings are in no essential respect different from other classes of objects in the world."[7] The minimalist movement adopted the goal of creating works that met this description. In this way, formalism has provided a justification for a particular artistic impulse, in much the same way representation theories defended and encouraged representational painting in the Renaissance and neoclassical periods and expressionist theories defended and encouraged romantic art of the nineteenth century.

Content and Subject Matter

Formalism has been subjected to a number of criticisms. A. C. Bradley, an English scholar and literary critic, articulated a central objection in his discussion of two key concepts: form and subject matter. He argued that we cannot separate the form of the artwork from its subject matter *as it appears in that particular poem or painting*. There are some things that can be distinguished in one's mind but that cannot be separated in fact, like the shape of a cup from the clay of which it is made. You cannot lay side by side on a table some clay which has no shape whatever and next to it a cup shape made out of nothing. In order to have a shape you must have some material that has that shape, and in order to have some material it must have some shape. The form/content distinction in art, Bradley claims, is like the shape/material distinction. You may be able to *think* of the two items separately but you cannot have one without the other. They are mutually dependent. Therefore the debate whether we should consider form alone is misconstrued. Since the form always goes together with the content, there is no point in arguing that we should do without one of them because we cannot.

The reason philosophers have made this mistake, Bradley thinks, is that they have confused the *subject matter* of a work with its *content*. The subject matter is that part of the real world that the work refers to, while the content is the way in which the subject matter appears in that particular work. The subject matter is truly separable from the work, consisting in matters that lie quite outside it. But the content is a part of the work and cannot be separated from it. Content depends on the particular arrangement of colors, lines, shapes and textures that make it up, and these arrangements are exactly what we mean by the form. So, to repeat, the form and content cannot be separated. For this reason, Bradley argued, the formalists are right about the subject matter but not about the content of a work. Perhaps the subject matter should not be considered in an aesthetic response but certainly the content should.

An example of how Bradley would apply this distinction might help. There are many paintings of Mary and Jesus in our art history. Mary and Jesus did exist some two thousand years ago, quite independently of any artwork. As independently existing persons, they are the *subject matter* of many thousands of paintings of the Madonna and Child. But they are presented differently in each of these paintings. In one Jesus is an infant; in another he is a child of five. In one Jesus is playing; in another he is nursing. Sometimes Mary looks fondly at Jesus; sometimes she looks off abstractedly. Sometimes she looks protectively at Jesus as any mother looks at her baby; sometimes she looks with awe at the Savior. In each painting Mary and Jesus appear differently and their particular appearance in a work is the *content* of that piece. In Raphael's *Madonna of the Meadow,* for instance, (fig. 11) Mary is looking at the child with a particular expression; she has a particular gesture; the child has a particular look on his face. In these particularities, they are different from other representations of Mary and Jesus and so, Bradley says, the content is unique although the subject is common. And what matters about this work is the particular content it has, the exact way it portrays Mary and Jesus, and not the fact that it shares a general subject matter with many other works.

Bradley claims that subject matter and content are easily confused because ordinarily we refer to them with the same words. How do we refer to the figure in the lower left-hand corner of the *Madonna of the Meadow?* We say it is John the Baptist. But John the Baptist was not a piece of painted canvas; he was a prophet who lived in Palestine two thousand years ago. We say both that John the Baptist lived in the desert *and,* looking at the painting, that John the Baptist is in the bottom left corner and has had to be repainted several times. No wonder the two are commonly confused. And no wonder — this is Bradley's point — the formalists spoke as if they wanted to exclude the content of artworks from consideration when all they meant to exclude was the subject matter.

The contrast that formalists *mean* to draw, Bradley argues, is not between form and content, which are inseparably linked within the work of art, but between the work of art (which includes form *and* content) and the subject matter, which lies outside of it. The formalist principle, he says, is that we should consider only those aspects of a work that are internal to it and ignore everything that is external to it. In Bradley's view, both form and content are internal to the work, and so they should both be considered. Subject matter is what is external to the work and should not be considered.

What is External and What Internal?

But here the formalists encounter another problem. It is really a version of the same problem we encountered when discussing the relevance of the artist's intentions. The fact is that it is hard to say in general what kinds of things are to be counted as internal and what as external to the artwork. The formalists need to have a usable distinction between what is internal and what is not because they use it to describe what kinds of things are irrelevant to consider when looking at art. Much the same thing is true for those who want to ban consideration of the artist's intentions. But how are we to tell what lies outside a work and what does not? Once again, this turns out to be difficult and is perhaps impossible, especially if we insist on general answers.

Consider again Raphael's *Madonna of the Meadow* (fig. 11). In the previous discussion, aimed at explicating Bradley's distinction, we distinguished between the general story of Mary and Jesus and the particular way Mary and Jesus are presented. Only the latter was, according to Bradley, internal to the work and actually part of it. This accords with what we might ordinarily say on first thought. Neither the story of Mary and Jesus nor the Christian religion as a whole (these two can hardly be separated, one is so much a part of the other) seem to be a part of the painting itself. We would normally say that the religion and the story are a part of the cultural context in which the works were created and are not internal to the work. They were not created by the artist; they are what he took for granted. Nor can they be seen in the work or deduced from it; they have to be known beforehand. Clearly, a formalist would want us to declare them external to the work and to ignore them.

Yet we have to ask, on second thought: can we understand such a painting without knowing something of the Christian religion and the story of Mary and Jesus? And the answer is surely not. Otherwise we will see an ordinary baby in the painting, not one who is also divine; and we will not understand the tension between the human and the divine that the mother feels. This affects directly what we see, the way the work looks to us. For example, we will not see in the painting the particular poignancy of Mary's glance, if we don't know who her baby is. Her facial expression is not just the look of an ordinary mother for her baby. It is a combination of human love and religious awe, embodying an awareness of the simultaneous human frailty and divine strength of her baby. And we can see this combination there in the painting, though it is there in the work to be seen only if we know the religious story. So it is hard to deny that the knowledge of this apparently external material is relevant to the interpretation of the painting.

Consider another example, from another medium. How far could we read poetry if we knew the language but not the cultural information that the language is saturated with? Wordsworth famously compared Lucy with a violet: "A violet by a mossy stone / Half hidden from the eye!"

We could hardly understand these lines if we didn't know what violets are and what their associations are in the English language. The notion that violets are beautiful but shy, virtuous but modest, is a part of our culture and it might seem to be external to the poem. Nevertheless, it is required to understand what is said about Lucy and it changes the way Lucy appears in the poem. Suppose Wordsworth had compared Lucy to a sunflower?

The conclusion seems to be, as it was in the discussion of artists' intentions, that one can't decide what kinds of things are internal or external to artworks *in general*. It seems more to the point to discuss what the viewer needs to bear in mind when looking at particular works. But this would be unacceptable to the formalists. What the viewer needs to consider obviously depends on what the viewer already knows. If the viewer already knows enough about the Christian religion and the story of Mary and Jesus, we could say that the *Madonna of the Meadow* contains within it all that the viewer needs to consider. Similarly, if the reader already knows about violets and their cultural associations, all she needs to consider can be found in the poem. In these cases, the references can be taken for granted and the formalist program might be satisfied. But if the viewers do not know the cultural background, then they must go "outside" the work for the relevant knowledge and bring the two together. Otherwise they cannot interpret the work appropriately. It looks as if formalists expect the viewer already to be knowledgeable about such things, an expectation that in our day appears either elitist or ethnocentric; or, more likely, they simply overlook the need for it.

In any case, it appears that what for some viewers is internal is for others external. Talking about internal and external things presupposes a spatial metaphor that seems to be misleading. An artwork is not like a box, of which we can say that some things are inside it and others are outside. Nor are meanings physical items like marbles or patches of paint. An artwork is more like a symbol than like a box. It is something that has to be interpreted and cannot reasonably be said to have an inside and an outside. To interpret a work, we must have some background knowledge, a "cognitive stock," as philosophers sometimes say, because to interpret a work is precisely to relate it with something we already know. And so the key questions are what it should be related to and what the viewer already knows, rather than what is "internal" to the work.

This problem seems insuperable for the formalists. If art were independent of all contextual relations, then the only meanings it could have would derive from the relations of the parts to each other. This formula may account for a part of the appeal of some works, like those of Mondrian and Stella. But it gives a poor account of most works, which require of the viewer a richer kind of interpretation and a knowledge of context. More generally, the formalist program runs counter to the fact that meaning is inherently a relational affair. Meaning is the significance we grasp in the relation between two things. It follows that deliberately to ignore the relations of an artwork with its context is to rob it of much of its significance. Formalism simply is not an adequate account of our experience of art.

The best way to think of formalism is as a reminder of *one* of the sources of value in art. Artworks are often complex structures and the formal relations of their parts are often an important part of their significance. Formalism reminds us of this basic fact and, consequently, of part of what we should look for in artworks. The reminder is helpful because it is easy not to pay attention to form. It is easy to pay attention only to the representation or the expression of a work and even to be distracted away from the work by the interest of the subject matter or the power of the artist's personality. This is especially true of children. Formalism began as an insistence that we should focus only on what is truly relevant to the work and it may still be valuable in that way. But it loses its value when it passes from a helpful reminder about one important aspect of art to a general doctrine about what is exclusively valuable in art.

Antiessentialism

At this point, it may be useful to ask whether what we have just said of formalism is true of the other theories of art we have discussed.

We said that formalism is useful because it isolates one of several sources of value in art but is misleading when it asserts itself as an exclusive theory of aesthetic value. Could we not say the same thing of the other major historical theories of art, the representational and the expressionist? Each of these theories, as we have seen, has problems defining its key idea, respectively of representation, expression and form, in a sufficiently clear and general way. Each is an essentialist theory in that it holds that the key to understanding art is to be found in its essence, which is understood as, respectively, what the work represents, what it expresses or its form. We have argued that, in the case of formalism, essentialism fails, that is when formalism is understood as an account of the one quality that all artworks must have in common. The thought is inevitable: might not the same thing be said of each of these theories?

In a famous paper published in 1956, Morris Weitz reached just this conclusion. He pointed out that each of these three theories was a response to the art of their time. Representational theories make good (but not exclusive) sense of the realist art that began in classical Greece and in the Renaissance. Expressionist theories make good (but not exclusive) sense of the romantic art of the nineteenth and twentieth centuries. Formalism makes good (but not exclusive) sense of the abstract and minimalist art of the twentieth century. Each has been useful in helping us to see new kinds of value in art movements as they arose and, retrospectively, valuable aspects of all art. But each is essentialist in ambition; each claims to give a complete account of all art. In this respect, each is surely wrong. To suppose that any one of them were right would be to deny that the others had any valuable insight to offer, however partial. Weitz's conclusion was that the theories were valuable but they were all wrong in their essentialism.

Weitz went further than this. He argued that any essentialist attempt to define art was doomed to failure. There is no one quality that all works of art have in common. The assumption that there must be one, he argued, is based on a false view of language, according to which language consists of names for qualities and enables us to identify things by spotting the particular quality that is named. The word "red" names the quality of redness and our perception of redness allows us to use the word correctly. But in the case of ideas more complicated than redness, including the idea of work of art, language may not work this way; it may not be a matter of naming at all. It seems to be impossible to identify any one quality that all artworks possess because someone can always think up or create a counterexample. In fact, this must be so, Weitz argued, because new works are constantly being created so that, even if you found some one quality that all works presently have, another might be created tomorrow that does not have it. In fact artists seem to have been motivated to create such works, transcending boundaries that had previously been accepted, deliberately making art of materials that previously would have been rejected. One could almost write the history of twentieth-century aesthetics as the attempt of philosophers to keep their definitions up to date with the innovations of artists.

Weitz claimed that we should therefore think of art as an "open concept," one whose boundaries could never be finally drawn and whose future could not be predicted. It would not follow that the expression "work of art" has no meaning, only that it has no single and final meaning. We can think of artworks as things that have one or more of a number of qualities, chief among which are those identified by the major historical theories of art we have considered. A work may have some of the qualities identified as important by the representational, expressionist or formalist theories, no one of them being essential, any one of them being sufficient.

This antiessentialist view has been much discussed and has had wide influence in recent aesthetics. It is attractive because it makes sense of the major historical theories of art and of the twentieth-century history of art and aesthetics. The outcome is to suggest that it is a mistake to persist in asking the question "What is art?" The mistake is to suppose that there is an answer that can account for all art in the manner assumed by essentialist theories.

The Institutional Theory

More recently, philosophers have tended to question Weitz's antiessentialism. One reason is that, on further inspection, the argument concerning the open-ended character of art seems lacking. It is true that new works of art are constantly being created and even that new kinds of works of art are being developed. Since the time that Weitz wrote we have had the development of, for example, electronic art, conceptual art, and performance art, all of which in one way or another cross definitional boundaries previously thought essential. But this only shows that previous definitions of art were not satisfactory. It does not follow from this that all definitions must fail. We may discover new varieties of fish without having to change our definition of what fishes are, so long as we have a good definition to begin with. The problem has seemed to many that we have not had the right sort of definition of art, rather than that no definition is possible.

Previous attempts at the definition of art have all assumed that the problem is to identify one quality that all artworks possess, one characteristic that we can see and that also is their source of value. This is what Clive Bell, in the passage cited above, says explicitly, and it is what both representational and expressionist theories also assumed. But those who respond to Weitz say that the defining characteristic of art may be relational rather than simple. That is, it may consist in some relation artworks have to something else rather than in some quality they themselves display. The characteristic we are looking for may not be analogous to redness, which is a simple property. It may be analogous to a relational property like, for example, having the same kind of origin or being the result of similar intentions. Things that have the same origin may not have any other quality in common and yet they are definable as members of the same class. This might be true of decisions of the U.S. Supreme Court, for example. Similarly, things that are the product of certain intentions may have no other necessary features in common: insults, for instance. Relational properties like these are more complex than nonrelational properties like redness because they make reference to the relation between two entities rather than just one. For this reason they are often called two-place, rather than one-place, properties. The institutional theory is probably the best known of the attempts to define art in terms of a relational property rather than a simple one.

Notice that relational definitions are in a sense the direct opposite of the formalist approach. The latter is an attempt to define artworks as independent objects, as having essentially no relations with anything else. A relational approach is one that says that they are *essentially* related to something else, though there may be considerable debate about what that something else is.

The institutional theory, identified originally with the work of George Dickie, holds that artworks are essentially related to the art world.[8] The art world is the combination of institutions and ideas that surround the social practice of art in our culture. A work of art is anything that is considered to be a work of art by the art world, no matter what qualities it has. Let us consider how this comes about.

Suppose we begin with an ordinary plank of wood that is found lying unnoticed on the beach. It is bleached by the sun. Would we normally consider it a work of art? Probably not. Suppose someone stood it on end in the sand and placed stones around it? Most of us would still hesitate to consider it a work of art. What if someone takes the plank home, paints it with red paint, mounts it on a wall and illuminates it with several lights? We are getting to a point where many people are willing to think of it as a work of art. And finally, let us suppose that it is displayed, with a title, on a wall in the Metropolitan Museum of Art. It may not be a favorite but it surely is now a work of art. The point of this series of examples is to show the factors that are influential when we decide to consider the plank as a work of art. According to the institutional theory, the crucial thing is that it is both intended to be and is received by the art world as a work of art – that is, a relational property. When it is hung on the wall at home and illuminated with spotlights, the intention becomes clear. When it is hung in the Metropolitan Museum with a title, its acceptance as a work of art also becomes clear. It has been placed in a social context that is governed by traditions and expectations that pertain to the art world. That makes it an artwork. That is all that is required. And the same thing is true of all works of art.

The point of this theory is that, after all, a work of art is not simply a physical object, like a plank of wood or a colored piece of canvas. It is an object that has a significance of some kind, as a gesture does. It is the expression of some human intention and it is understood to be so by its audience. In the same way, raising one's hand is only a physical action without meaning until it is understood in terms of some system of conventions, such as the semaphore code or a public school classroom. Within those systems of conventions raising one's hand can be a symbolically charged act, being part of a message or a request to ask a question. Similarly, a physical object becomes significant as an artwork only when it is related to the art world.

At this point we might ask what exactly the art world is. Is it clear who or what is a part of the art world and who or what is not? The curators at the Metropolitan Museum of Art may be a clear case, but what about the art gallery that my uncle Sergio opened in a small rented space just off High Street? Do we want to say that any object he hangs in his gallery is an artwork? The answer seems to be that it depends on his success within the art world. Are the kinds of works he shows accepted elsewhere as artworks? Does he show works created by persons who are already considered to be artists? Are they bought by persons who are recognized to be art connoisseurs, reviewed by persons who are accepted as art critics? This may seem to be a circular answer. It says that a person or an institution is part of the art world if it is accepted as such by the art world. For the institutional theorist this circularity is not so much a problem as a necessity required by the facts. Art is a matter of convention and social practice, much as language is. A usage in language remains part of the language only if it continues to be used. If it is not used, then it is not part of the language.

The same sort of thing is true of art. Many things are proposed as artworks. The ones that are accepted are the ones that *are* artworks.

Warhol's *Brillo Boxes* is a well-known example of how this works.[9] The Safeway store displays Brillo boxes and they are ordinary commodities. Andy Warhol displayed them in an art gallery, with the title *Brillo Boxes*, and they were artworks. One of the differences in this case, in addition to the difference between the Safeway store and the Museum, is that Warhol was already known as an artist and the store manager is not. An object is more likely to be counted as art if it is proposed by an artist. We are more likely to take it as meaningful in some way, even if it is not clear exactly what its meaning is. Of course to say that art is what is made by an artist is another case of circular reasoning. It prompts one in turn to ask how we know who is an artist and who is not. The answer is again that this is a matter of historically situated social practice. One gets to be an artist by going through a training that is recognized to be the kind of training that artists go through, and what this kind of training is will vary over time. Art training was once mostly a matter of apprenticing with an accepted artist; then it became a matter of going to art school. Folk artists usually have a different history. And this again, in the same circular way, is a matter of what is accepted at the time by the art world.

The outcome of the institutional theory may be felt to be disappointing. It tells us that we have an institutionalized system that decides what is to count as art, but it says nothing about the criteria that the system uses to make the decision. Why, we might want to ask, does the museum curator choose the plank to hang on the wall? Why this and not something else? The institutional theory tells us nothing about this. Its only reply is that the curator chooses those things that best fit her sense of contemporary art. What her criteria are is not part of the theory. Her criteria are probably quite varied and may change over time, so that there are no necessary and permanent criteria to be identified. There is only the art world and its traditions and the works that it finds meaningful. This answer acknowledges that our idea of art is often disputed and is historically determined, and yet it insists that we can give a stable definition of art.

We may still feel some disappointment with this answer because, although it gives us a definition of art, it tell us little about the value of art or the criteria that artworks should meet. It is important to see that in this case, unlike the case of formalism, whose definition of art was evaluative, the institutional theory is an attempt to be purely descriptive. It purports to describe accurately what we currently mean by the word "art," to reflect our actual practice. The art world in our time has become a matter of conflicting movements and tendencies, characterized by change and pluralism, affected also by contact with commercialism and mass media. The criteria used to decide what is art are not wholly clear and may vary. In such a situation, philosophy can still achieve a definition of art by describing the mechanisms we use for making decisions about what art is, rather than trying to define the criteria used.

Formalism, on the other hand, was not content with providing a descriptive account. It was an attempt to influence our artistic practices by identifying what is important about art. It offered a definition of art that was more evaluative than descriptive; that is, one that focused on the value of art rather than the way we decide what things are artworks. By identifying what it saw as important about art, it wanted to influence the way we decide what things are artworks rather than simply to describe it. In fact it did not clearly distinguish these two options, the descriptive and the evaluative, but seemed to assume that they amounted to the same thing. And, looking back, we can see that the representational and the expressionist theories did the same thing: they also attempted to provide simultaneously a descriptive and an evaluative account of art.

This lack of distinction between the descriptive and evaluative approaches is not surprising because in many cases the same definition achieves the both results. If we were asked to define automobiles, we might very well choose to describe what they are valuable for, their function. In that case, we might say something like this: automobiles are vehicles intended to transport people and small goods safely and efficiently on paved roads. This is both a descriptive and an evaluative definition because it helps us both to identify automobiles and tells us the criteria on which they may be evaluated. Until recently, this is the sort of definition that philosophers assumed they were looking for when trying to answer the question: What is art?

The present situation, however, appears to require us to separate the descriptive and the evaluative questions. It is as if we are unsure what is valuable about automobiles because the way we use them varies — as if, for example, sometimes they are more important to us as fashionable accessories and sometimes as spaces to live in, and especially as if new functions for them are constantly being invented. Then we might try a descriptive definition for automobiles. We might describe where they are made and sold, for example, or the places they are characteristically seen. This might be found disappointing by people who expect the definition to help them understand why we value automobiles so much. The philosopher might well answer that there are

two quite different questions at issue: (1) How do we identify automobiles or artworks? and (2) What is it that makes automobiles or
artworks valuable? They were once treated as if they were one question
but now we need to address them separately. George Dickie has recently
attempted to do just this.[10]

There are other recent accounts of art that attempt to improve on
the institutional theory but adopt the same descriptive logic. For
example, Noel Carroll is unhappy with the idea of the art world, arguing
that it overstates the institutional and formal character of what actually
happens in our society.[11] Art is not as formally controlled as the institutional theory suggests, he argues. Consequently he substitutes the
idea of social practices that are concerned with the making of artworks.
Then, he says, we can identify something as a work of art if it was
produced in accordance with those social practices. What the social
practices actually are varies over time, of course, just as does the nature
of the art world in the institutional theory.

Similarly, Jerry Levinson believes we can identify an artwork in terms
of the kind of intention that the artist had in mind when making it.[12]
We look at artworks in characteristic ways, he argues, though of course
those ways change over time. Artists' intentions are at least partly
related to those characteristic ways we look at artworks: artists intend
their works to be regarded in one of the ways characteristic of their
time. An artwork, he concludes, can be described, roughly, as an object
created with that intention. The purpose of this definition is, once again,
to loosen the rather formal restrictions of the institutional theory and
to insist that an artwork may be produced in relative isolation, without
the apparatus of galleries, museums, and critical reviews. It does, however, use the same basic logic, in that it is a purely descriptive definition
and refers to a relation of the artwork with something else — in this
case with the artist's intentions.

There is a further point one might make about these post-Weitzian
definitions of art. They each acknowledge the way our ideas of art
change over time, the way historical context affects what is considered
art. This also makes them different from the three major traditional
theories we have considered, which seemed to assume that art is essentially the same at all times. The history of twentieth-century art has
made it abundantly clear that what counts as art is partly a matter
of when it was produced. There are so many movements and styles
of art that would have made no sense if they had been produced fifty
years earlier; one cannot imagine minimalism, abstract expressionism
or cubism as nineteenth-century phenomena, for example. The appeal
of the institutional theory to the art world, of Carroll to social practices

and of Levinson to artists' intentions regarding how their works are to be looked at, all take account of the changing historically based idea of art.

The Logic of Interpretation and Evaluation

We have now distinguished descriptive from evaluative readings of the question What is art? and we have described several attempts at supplying a descriptive answer. It seems appropriate therefore to say something here about the evaluative side. The evaluative question in general is: With what criteria should we evaluate artworks? or; How can we argue reasonably about our evaluations of artworks?

One important point to notice at the beginning is that questions of evaluation and of interpretation are often closely related. This is because the reasons we offer for evaluation usually depend on our interpretation and often follow rather obviously from it. Consider again, for example, the photographs of Cindy Sherman (fig. 4). The interpretive question is clearly the most important one here. If we decide that the photographs are simply portraits of Cindy Sherman, they do not constitute a very interesting work. If, however, we decide that they are about some historically based cultural stereotypes of women, according to our previous discussion, then they are a much more complex and interesting work. The phrase "complex and interesting" is an evaluative one and follows almost directly from the interpretation. In this case, we can surely say that the reasons for interpretation are more important than the reasons for the evaluation. We can also say that, as far as teaching goes, we do not need to go beyond interpretation in such a case. If we help our students make good sense of the work, there is no need to pursue explicit evaluation.

However, it is also important to see that this does not relieve us of having to defend our judgments. Interpretation is as much a matter of judgment as is evaluation. We make judgments to decide what a work means as well as to decide how valuable it is. For example, in the Chagall *La Grande Cirque,* there is a figure in the foreground that appears to be juggling its own head. We could interpret this in many ways: that life is like a circus, for example, wherein we constantly juggle our ideas, trying to keep them in balance. Such an interpretation requires a judgment and the judgment ideally should be supported with reasons. Is this is a good judgment? How could we argue for or against it? The point is important because it is often thought that we can avoid sticky questions of judgment if only we avoid evaluation. This is not so. Judgments are involved throughout our response to an artwork.

We could even extend the point to descriptions of artworks: descriptions also require us to make judgments. For example, it requires a judgment to describe the figure in the Chagall as juggling his head, as we did. This appears to be a descriptive statement, but it is possible that his head is just floating away or falling down. To decide which is true requires a judgment, even though it may be an easily defended one. In short, judgments are involved whenever we talk about art.

It is a major philosophical question how we can defend judgments of any kind about artworks, when they are challenged. How objective can these judgments be? There are several parts to this question. First, there is the *formal* sense in which judgments may be objective. Do they have the *form* of an objective judgment? Judgments like "I like chocolate ice cream; I don't like strawberry ice cream" do not; they have the form of a subjective judgment. This is because they do not purport formally to be about the object (the ice cream) but are about how the ice cream strikes the speaker. They are formally judgments about the speaker, saying something like "I am the kind of person who finds chocolate ice cream pleasing and strawberry ice cream displeasing." On the other hand, judgments like "This figure is a juggler" or "This gesture suggests that circuses turn your ideas upside down," or "This work is delightfully ironic," are objective in form since they are about an object rather than the speaker.

The formal distinction is important because when judgments that are formally subjective differ in content, they do not need to be defended. Suppose you like chocolate ice cream and I like strawberry ice cream; there is no contradiction here and no dispute is involved. It is just that you are different from me in this respect, as you are in other ways that need not be resolved. I have brown eyes and you have blue; I am short and you are tall. It is different when judgments that are objective in form have different contents. A contradiction results and there is generally felt a need to resolve it through discussion, to find out which is right and which is wrong. You may say that the juggler figure is juggling his head and also the other thoughts of the circus represented around him, and I may say that it is simply a carelessly done figure in a loosely organized painting. Then we are saying conflicting things about the figure and the organization of the work as a whole. Of course, if we want to avoid an argument, we may retract our claims and say that we were really only talking about how the figure seems to us. This would make the judgments formally subjective and avoid having to give reasons for them. However, so long as our statements are formally about the figure, they are in conflict and call for justification.

Justification of formally objective judgments means the giving of reasons. "*Why* do you think the figure is juggling all these aspects of the circus?" The implication of the question is that if your reasons are good enough I will change my mind, and vice versa. But what would make your reasons good reasons? You might point to the central location of the juggler and the way it forms the point of a major inverted triangle of the elements of the painting. Is this a good reason? What makes it good? Much of the philosophical discussion of judgments in art focuses on the character of reasons that can be offered for them.

The question of what makes a reason a good reason in art is notoriously difficult. This is because reasons in art seem to be different from reasons in other areas in that they do not generalize in the same way. If I say that a cue stick is good because it is straight, I imply that all straight cue sticks are good or at least that straightness is in general a good feature of cue sticks. Reasons in discussions of art do not seem to work like that. They do not generalize with the same ease and often seem to be applicable only to particular works.

Suppose a critic praises a painting because it creates exciting tensions and offers as a reason its "steeply rising and falling curves."[13] Abstractly analyzed, the critic's argument is that the steeply rising and falling curves create exciting tensions in the work, and this idea might seem to imply that all steeply rising and falling curves create exciting tensions in all works that have them. Is this the case? Clearly not. In another work, such curves might be found bombastic and pretentious, as Robert Hughes finds them in the work of Clifford Still.[14] There is no reliable generalization about the effects of steeply rising and falling curves in all artworks. In fact, one might well disagree about their effect even in the same work, one person finding them exciting and the other bombastic.

Disagreement can occur at a number of places in the passage from description through interpretation to assessment. We could disagree, for instance, that the work has steeply rising and falling curves, though we disagree about descriptions less often than about other kinds of statements. More often we might disagree that the curves create exciting tensions. It is also possible to agree that the tensions are there but to disagree that they are a positive feature of the work. They might, for instance, be out of keeping with the harmony and peacefulness of the rest of the work or be merely distressing. In each of these cases, the judgments at issue, though they are judgments about the work and so are formally objective judgments, nevertheless depend on reactions to the work that include feeling and emotion, that are personal and inward and that may not be shared. In this sense they seem to be subjective judgments.

It does not follow that arguments involving such disagreements are hopelessly irrational. The question of objectivity does not depend on whether judgments rest ultimately on personal and intuitive reactions. After all, that is also true of the judgment that something is colored red, a judgment usually thought objective enough. Objectivity of reasons has more to do with whether and to what extent we can ourselves appreciate the force of reasons given by others. Do the reactions that reasons are based on, subjective in the sense that they must be individually appreciated, depend on features of the work that others can see? Are they reactions to the publicly accessible properties of the work, these properties being interpreted in terms of accepted conventions of the relevant genre and in light of reasonable assumptions about life and society in the culture of the work's origin? If so, or if many people have the same response to a work and point to the same features of it as the reason, then it is likely that the response, though in each case subjectively experienced, is objectively based. And if the relevant conventions and assumptions can be articulated, we can probably learn to appreciate the response even though we do not initially understand it. In this sense there is still the possibility of objectivity to reasons for judgments about art.

Another way to say this is that reasoning is objective if it follows recognized procedures that are capable of resolving disagreements. If we have a way of reaching agreement, that may be sufficient rationality for our purposes. Art criticism, it has been argued, is capable of rationality in this sense. Most critics point to particular features of a work when they offer interpretations or evaluations, as Isenberg's critic pointed to the rising and falling curves as a reason for the exciting tensions he saw. Pointing is often sufficient to secure agreement because it gets us to notice the features we may have overlooked.

Sometimes, of course, differences of opinion remain after critics have pointed out all the features of a work that support their different interpretations or evaluations. Do we have a way to resolve these differences? Well, we can ask that each consider the evidence that the other points to. This is a way of saying that they should take account of all of the evidence, should look at the work as a whole, should be reasonably flexible in attitude, and should try to make sense of it in a consistent way. In addition, we can ask that they remain consistent with known contextual features: artistic conventions, historical traditions, the artist's other works, and cultural beliefs and practices of the time. We can also ask that the relevant facts be carefully researched, if they are not known or acknowledged to be unavailable if they are so. Many differences of interpretation will be resolved by these methods.

But, it may be said, there are times when we are left with two inter-pretations that meet these criteria equally well and are still incompatible with each other. Or perhaps there are none that meet the criteria fully and several that meet them partially. What do we have to say then? We have to say, it seems, that though we have proceeded objectively to this point we can do so no further. We can not rationally decide between the alternatives. This situation happens in art, and it is not intellectually such a disgrace as it is in science or morality, where it can also happen. After all, the fundamental purpose of criticism is to help viewers understand the work accurately and to see it more richly. Seeking the best interpretation is usually the best way to this end, but in these rare and difficult cases it may be more rational to accept the two incompatible interpretations. It may be best to look at the work in two incompatible ways because that will enrich our understanding more than continuing the search for the one correct way.

There is another kind of disagreement that occurs especially in connection with judgments of evaluation rather than interpretation. Sometimes critics agree that a work has some particular qualities or meanings but disagree about their relative importance. Then the dif-ference of opinion lies in a difference about which criterion is the more important. The argument is not so much about the particular work as about the appropriate criteria for art in general. The critics are dis-agreeing not so much about the artwork as about what qualities are more important. One gives priority to expressive power, say, the other to compositional unity. They have, in effect, different theories of art. One is an expressionist, the other a formalist. At this point, criticism itself can go no further and the discussion must proceed as a part of the philosophy of art.

Contexts and Relevance

We have seen that artworks are related to a variety of contexts, including the world they represent, the artist who made them, the audience, and the art world and various aspects of the culture in which they were produced. We could order the major philosophies of art according to which of these relations they consider crucial for inter-pretation and which they consider unimportant or irrelevant. In a rough sort of way, this order can be thought of as a set of concentric circles, each containing what the previous one thought relevant and adding something further to it.

In such an ordering, the most extreme case would be formalism, which wants to consider the work by itself as an independent object with no relations to anything else at all. The only relations that a formalist considers relevant are the relations of the parts of the work to each other. These parts notably include lines, shapes, colors, textures; and their relations with each other are what is often meant by "form." As we have seen, there is a strong case for adding to these elements certain aspects of what is represented. These aspects are the particularities of things represented in the work that we can readily recognize without some culturally specific background knowledge. The least controversial example would be three-dimensional space; slightly more controversial would be mothers and children, trees and rivers, if we think these to be universally recognizable. Some formalists are willing, and some are not, to include these sorts of things among the elements whose relations to each other should be considered in an artwork.

The next circle would contain representational theories, which add an artwork's relations with the world it represents to what formalism considers relevant. These representation theories include more than the limited aspects of representation that some formalists accept. They include, for example, not only how this mother and child look in this particular work but also how mothers and children actually look, in particular or general, in the real world. The actual is the criterion for the represented. We judge the mother and child in the artwork in terms of how either a particular mother and child looks or mothers and children typically look in the actual world.

Notice that this criterion does not have to include culturally specific material, though it may. We could perhaps have a general idea of how mothers and children look that is not dependent on culturally specific knowledge, or if this is implausible, then a culturally nonspecific idea of how trees and rivers look. And we could use this culturally nonspecific idea to evaluate artworks. On the other hand, we might want to add to the criterion a knowledge of the particular cultural background in which the work was created. We might expect artworks to represent, say, mothers and children as they are thought of in the Western tradition, rather than mothers and children in general or in some imagined universal state. We might even, as in the example given earlier, expect them to represent Mary and Jesus in terms of the Christian religious tradition. If so, we have added another layer to the circle of relations that have relevance for interpretation. For in this case the artwork is to be considered in relation to the attitudes and beliefs of the culture in which it was created, as well as to the material included in the previous formalist and representational circles. This is still a representational theory, however, because the key criterion is still the way things are thought to look, though this latter is particularized to a particular culture.

The institutional theory adds still more kinds of considerations to the list. It asserts that the artwork should be considered in relation to the art world in which it was created. The art world includes the ideas and conventions that, at the time the artwork was created, governed the particular art genre. For example, there were a host of conventions surrounding the Renaissance tradition of representing three-dimensional space in painting. It was a convention, for example, that smaller in size means further away in space and that the viewer should stand in a particular place with relation to the work. In ancient Egyptian art there were other conventions in force. Difference in size indicated difference in importance and not distance in space, and it did not much matter where the viewer stood. The art world also includes conventions and expectations regarding function and behavior. In the case of the present Western art tradition, the art world includes expectations about the buying and selling of art, about displaying it in homes, museums, galleries, about how we should regard it, as well as about what is to count as art and who is to count as an artist.

The institutional theory regards all of these matters as importantly related to the artwork. The theory is potentially more accommodating of cultural differences than are the formalist or representational views, because it implies, though it is not always made explicit, that we should interpret works according to the criteria of the art world of the culture in which the works were originally produced. It implies, in other words, that we should use Western kinds of criteria in connection with artworks of Western origin, the criteria of the Chinese art world with Chinese works, and so on.

A different kind of contextual relation has to do with the artist. The expressionist theory finds the meaning of an artwork in its relation to the intentions and state of mind of the artist who created it. As we have seen, these intentions may include far more than the conscious thoughts of the artist. They may include emotions and desires not understood by the artist and states of mind that are taken for granted by many of the artist's contemporaries. These states of mind will also be considerably influenced by the culture and artistic conventions of the time. For example, one can have had the desire to express the anxieties of a nuclear age or to explore the artistic possibilities of automatic writing only during the twentieth century. In fact, because the artist's states of mind are in this way so intertwined with the artist's culture, the expressionist theory sometimes comes close to the institutional theory.

Postmodernist theories choose a different set of relations to focus on. For them, the significance of a work is determined by its relation with the viewer and sometimes with the viewer's culture. All the previous theories have, in one way or another, looked for the meaning of a work in some aspect of its origin. Looking at the conditions of its reception can produce very different results. Obviously, it maximizes the possibilities of variation in interpretations of the same artwork, since there may be great variation in the conditions of reception. A work can have only one origin but many receptions. In the case of the social version of postmodernism, the restrictions on what can reasonably be said about the work will derive from the conventions and expectations of the culture of the viewer, including its art world. This, as we have seen, makes least difference if the artist and the viewer are contemporaries from the same culture and if the viewer is assumed to have the appropriate set of attitudes and understandings. In this case, the results may not differ greatly from the results of the institutional theory, since the same conventions and expectations of meaning will apply. It is different with the individual variant of postmodernism, according to which the restrictions on meaning are those of the viewers' actual understanding, whatever the viewers' attitudes and understandings and whatever the viewers know of their own culture and art world. This seems to allow that anything that the viewer reads into the work is legitimately its meaning. If the artist and the viewer come from greatly different cultural backgrounds, then the difference in culture may produce a great difference in meaning.

If we think of the different theories we have looked at this way, we can say that the debate among philosophers is about which of its relations are the most important for interpreting an artwork. There are arguments for and against most of these theories, few of them appearing to be conclusive. A teacher does not have to answer the question decisively: Who is right in this dispute? For educational purposes, it is more important to understand the different reasons and arguments for each position, and the way in which the discussion is conducted, than to attain a final answer.

There is an analogy here with a somewhat different question that teachers are very familiar with: the question of what context to dwell on when teaching about particular artworks and movements. What kind of information and ideas should we give students to help them understand a particular work? This is a characteristic question of teaching. There are many possible contexts in which one can discuss artworks and it is hard to say in general which is better.

Consider a single painting. It exists, we may say, as a particular object, by itself and we can get the students to understand it in terms of what they already can see in it. But we can also teach it as part of the work of the artist; we can teach the work of the artist as part of a historical art movement; we can teach the movement as part of an international art style; and we can teach the art style as part of a social movement related ultimately to the military, economic, political, religious, educational, social history of the human race. The teaching question is: which is the most appropriate level to help these particular students understand this particular painting? The answer obviously depends on the needs of the students and the goals of the teacher. What kind of context to give a topic depends on what the students already know and what the teacher is aiming at in the long run. Teachers understand this intuitively because they are constantly adjusting their material to their students and their overall goals. They also understand that it helps to have as many alternatives available as possible, though they cannot all be used.

Suppose we want to help our high school students appreciate a work of Hans Hoffman. Surely we would want to consider it in the context of other works by Hoffman. And since his work is nonrepresentational, we might think it useful to discuss it as part of American abstract expressionism in the 1940s. But in one way that may seem too broad, and in another way it may seem too narrow. On the one hand, Hoffman's work is not identical with other abstract expressionists; his work is unique and has its own qualities. On the other hand, he might seem eccentric if not placed in the company of similar spirits. We may even feel that it is difficult to explain abstract expressionism without placing that in the context of the older tradition of European abstract art beginning around 1912 or in the context of social discontent in the 1940s and 1950s. What is the appropriate context? If the students are familiar with the older European abstract movement, then we may want to introduce American abstract expressionism as a form of abstract art and Hans Hoffman as one of the abstract expressionists, similar in some ways to other abstract expressionists but different in other ways. If the students are familiar with abstract expressionism but are unfamiliar with Hoffman's work, we may start with Hoffman's work as a whole. Or we may choose just one work on which to focus. And if we have a beginning class, we may feel the need to begin with the historical shift from representational to nonrepresentational painting, going back to the late nineteenth-century impressionists.

We are suggesting that, at least for the purposes of teaching, there is an analogy between this question of the appropriate material to give students and the question of the appropriate theory about the interpretation of artworks. As a teacher, one does not have to make a final and general choice. It is more important to be aware of the range of possible answers than to choose one of them in a final way. One chooses instead to dwell on one of them in light of the particular work at issue and the particular students being taught. Warhol's *Brillo Boxes* might call for an institutional theory, Albright's *Into the World came a Soul Called Ida* might call for an expressionist theory, and so on.

Summary

In this chapter we first discussed formalism as an attempt to focus attention on the artwork as an independent object with no necessary relations with other things. According to this view, the significance of a work derives only from its form, which is understood as the relations of its elements with each other. In the original and most restrictive version of the theory, these elements include only the lines, colors, shapes, and textures of the work. We reviewed a criticism of this that added some aspects of the world represented to the list of elements; that is, the particular way the objects or events represented appear in the particular work. This version of formalism still allows no reference to the world outside the artwork.

We contrasted formalism with the institutional theory, which holds that a work should be interpreted in light of the ideas and conventions of the art world in which it was created. The contrast is that in this view whether something is an artwork at all is a contextual matter, depending wholly on the art world at the time. Anything can be an artwork provided that it meets the current expectations of the art world.

We also found that formalism, the institutional theory and the theories we have previously discussed are all essentialist theories in that they try to identify the property that all artworks must have if they are to be artworks. We reviewed Morris Weitz's argument that no essentialist theory of art could be successful because new kinds of artworks are constantly being produced. The institutional theory and several recent others can be seen as answers to this antiessentialist view. They have the peculiarity that, in order to meet the antiessentialist challenge, they are purely descriptive in their account of art, having given up the attempt common to previous theories to combine a descriptive with an evaluative account. For contemporary theories of art, the question of what is valuable about art is quite separate from the question how we identify something as an artwork. Accordingly, we briefly reviewed some of the logical aspects of interpretive and evaluative judgments.

NOTES

1. Clive Bell, *Art* (1913; reprint, Capricorn Books, 1958), pp. 7–8.

2. Roger Fry, "The Artist and Psychoanalyst," *The Hogarth Essays* (London: The Hogarth Press, 1924).

3. Ibid.

4. Bell, *Art*, p. 25.

5. Ibid., p. 15.

6. Clement Greenberg, *Art and Culture* (Boston: Beacon, 1961); Michael Fried, *Three American Painters* (Cambridge, Mass.: Fogg Art Museum, 1965).

7. Fried, *Three American Painters*, p. 40.

8. George Dickie, *Art and the Aesthetic* (Ithaca, N.Y.: Cornell University Press, 1974); *The Art Circle: A Theory of Art* (New York: Haven, 1984).

9. See Arthur Danto, *The Transfiguration of the Commonplace* (Cambridge: Harvard University Press, 1981).

10. George Dickie, *Evaluating Art* (Philadelphia: Temple University Press, 1988).

11. Noel Carroll, "Art, Practice and Narrative," *Monist*, 71.

12. Jerry Levinson, *Music, Art and Metaphysics* (Ithaca, N.Y.: Cornell University Press, 1990).

13. Arnold Isenberg, "Critical Communication," *The Philosophical Review* 58 (1949).

14. Robert Hughes, *The Shock of the New* (New York: Knopf, 1982), p. 316.

6

Aesthetics in the Classroom

The Purposes of Introducing Aesthetics

Teachers need a reasonable grasp of the subject if they are to incorporate aesthetics into the teaching of art. In this book we have tried to help develop that grasp. It is a book about aesthetics for teachers of art, not about how to teach aesthetics, not even about how to use aesthetics in teaching art. We doubt that at the present time such a book could be written because the attempt to introduce aesthetics into the art classroom is so recent. Nationally, there is little sustained experience with the enterprise, no consensus on the most appropriate curriculum and no significant body of research findings.[1] We hope that, given a basic understanding of aesthetics and some confidence with it, teachers will find ways of using the material in the art class and of adapting a curriculum that is appropriate to their students. There are a few things we can say that may help teachers think through some of the issues involved. That is the purpose of this last chapter.

First, we will briefly restate our underlying beliefs about aesthetics in the art classroom. There are perhaps three of them. The first is that the basic purpose is to help students understand art better, both particular artworks and art in general. It is not, in other words, to teach them aesthetics as a separate school subject. It is not primarily to acquaint students with the history of aesthetics or with what important philosophers have said about art. Nor is the primary purpose to teach students to reason better in general, though this may be a desirable side benefit.

Earlier, we gave reasons why understanding art often requires the sort of thinking represented by aesthetics and why incorporating aesthetics into the art classroom is a reasonable aim. In the first place, art gives rise to various puzzles and controversies because of its powerful and varied nature. This is especially important if we remember that the aim is to help students understand the activities of art in general as well as particular artworks. Secondly, there are reasons to think that the contemporary art scene is conceptually more challenging than it ever has been. We discussed these reasons under the broad titles of the postmodern condition and multiculturalism. Twentieth-century art is more varied in its premises than art used to be, and many people think it has lost its sense of direction. And we are now exposed much more frequently to art from other cultures, which naturally raises questions about interpretation, the relation of art with culture, and the relativity of judgment. For these reasons we think the philosophy of art should be incorporated into the art classroom.

A second basic belief is related to the first. It is that aesthetics should be integrated into what otherwise happens in the art class. It should deal with issues that are already present, if unacknowledged — issues that are encountered in making, looking at and talking about artworks. This includes issues that arise when we teach art history and criticism. It should not deal primarily with unrelated matters imported from articles or books on aesthetics, out of a concern for teaching the discipline or for covering a curriculum. The other side of this belief is that, of course, the issues that do arise in the classroom and are chosen for discussion should be genuinely philosophical. One of the abilities needed by the teacher is to spot the fruitful philosophical topics as they arise and to have a sense of how to discuss them. This requires the teacher to know considerably more of the discipline of aesthetics than she intends to teach to students and it requires her to think about that material in a philosophical way. In short, the ability to relate philosophical topics and arguments to students' concerns is more important, to both teacher and students, than a detailed knowledge of the standard textbook answers. Teaching should be oriented more toward articulating and exploring these concerns than toward settling on the right answers.

Our third basic belief is that aesthetics should be related to students' experience. Discussions of topics should be at the level of students' understanding and should relate to opinions that they really hold or are tempted by. This implies that teachers should understand how their students think about art and should listen carefully to what they say. It is easy to assume that if we teach children a particular vocabulary, we are teaching them ideas. A good teacher will be constantly aware of the difference.

These three principles enable us to discuss several themes having to do with teaching. They include children's abilities, the teaching role, encouraging discussions, asking questions, and modifying the curriculum.

Children's Abilities

We begin with the question of children's abilities. We have already said that to incorporate aesthetics into their teaching a teacher needs to know how her students think about art. They need a sense of what their students think about particular works, what topics are of interest to them and what their abilities are to deal with those topics. A good teacher can acquire this sense in the course of teaching by listening to students carefully and trying to understand what they have in mind. It is one of the joys of teaching art in this way that it enables one to understand how students are thinking better than does almost any other activity.

The best way to develop an understanding of students is to talk with them in a deliberate and preplanned way. This means choosing an important idea or a provocative work, introducing it to students and persistently asking them questions that are designed to clarify their ideas about it. The questions should be about the meanings of what students say and their reasons for believing it. They should be simple questions, such as "What do you mean by that?" "Can you give me an example?" "What's your reason for saying that?" or even "Can you say more about that?" It may help to invent counterexamples and see what students say about them. It is necessary to think ahead of time about the kind of thing students can be expected to say and to devise questions to clarify their expected responses. Afterwards one should try to say accurately to oneself what students meant to say on key points. It may help to make notes on this and about the questions that did not get clarified.

This may sound like part of a prescription for teaching a discussion lesson. We would be pleased to think so. Certainly conversations like this can be had with the whole class and would likely constitute good teaching. If well prepared, they can be illuminating to both students and the teacher, the latter acquiring a sense of how students think, what their philosophical problems are and the range and diversity of their opinions and abilities. Conversations like this can also be conducted with students individually. This takes extra time but it can also give a more detailed grasp of typical thought patterns and problems. It may be possible to choose just one student in a class to "interview" in this way occasionally. This is helpful both in planning lessons and in finding out how well they have been understood. Similarly, reading work written in answer to such questions is a useful way to learn how students are thinking. After a short while, conversations and exercises like these may become a natural part of one's art-teaching activities. They greatly help to focus class discussions and to pitch assignments at a useful level of difficulty.

In addition, there are some general things one can say about children's understandings of art. The arguments of children sometimes seem naive or illogical to an adult. There are several reasons for this. For one thing, children have relatively little experience and information to draw on. As a consequence they may have difficulty, for example, telling the difference between cliché and originality. In fact, they often appreciate works that adults see as trite or cliché-ridden and may even find it difficult to see why clichés are in general undesirable. Similarly, they are unlikely to appreciate the value of simplicity or to understand the sense in which some kinds of simplicity are hard to achieve. An important kind of simplicity that is relevant here is fidelity to the material, the apparent simplicity of work that displays the qualities of the medium rather than tightly controlling them, such as we find in, for example, the work of Paul Klee or Jacob Lawrence. Children are unlikely to appreciate art that conceals its sophistication with apparent naïveté, as the work of these artists does. They are more likely to value the apparently complex, the painstakingly worked, the obvious exercise of skill. Such tendencies may be due simply to the fact that children have had little experience of art or life. It could be argued that there is a necessary sequence in which one has first to learn to appreciate the obvious exercise of skill before understanding its subtler manifestations and before realizing that skill can be overemphasized and complexity too deliberately developed.

In fact, it appears that there are several typical developmental trends in the way children think about art.[2] We have alluded to some of these in earlier chapters. One of the more general trends has to do with the ability to take the point of view of another person and to empathize with their feelings and state of mind. Children sometimes find this hard to do. They have difficulty imagining what things look like from the point of view of another person if that person differs from them significantly. Instead they tend to assume that others feel the same way they do. If it is obvious that others feel differently, they may recognize that as a fact but find it hard to tell what the differences are. For example, children may have difficulty understanding the point of view of an artist who paints in an unfamiliar style or of a critic who interprets a work very differently from themselves. Young children find it hard to read anything of the artist's intentions or feelings in a work and usually pay little attention to them. They tend to be more interested in its subject matter. In so far as they do understand the expressive character of works, it is often through the subject matter or the use of conventional symbols: dancing, fighting, smiles, fists, weather. Children do not easily grasp what artworks tell us about artists and the times they lived in. The extent to which they do is a key question for teachers because it will greatly affect their goals and strategies.

This means that ideas that link the work with the artist are difficult for young children to deal with. Style and expression are two important such ideas. Style is our way of thinking about what a work says about the artist, and expression is our main concept for thinking about a work's emotional impact. There is a fairly clear sequence in which children come to construct the meaning of both of these ideas.

With regard to style, they tend to think of it at first as telling them only about the artist's behavior. For example, June, nine years old, talked about Klee's *Head of a Man* (fig. 5). She could see quite clearly that the style was not meant to be realistic, but she could find no reason why this should be so. She found the style unintelligible except as behavior, seeing nothing in it of the artist except his habits. She said:

> *Why would an artist paint a painting like this?*
> I don't know. I guess that's what he paints. Some artists paint trees, some artists paint lines. Depends on the artist.
>
> *How do they decide what they are going to paint?*
> I guess they just get into it somehow . . .
>
> *Why would he want to paint it like this?*
> It's his style.
>
> *Why choose this style rather than another one?*
> It's what he's used to.
>
> *How did he get used to it?*
> I don't know. I'm not him.

The striking thing about this interchange is that June knows the word "style," recognizes the style of the Klee, but she cannot connect it with the artist's state of mind or its effect in the work. It is for her just a manner of painting that she can see no point to: "They just get into it somehow."

For an older student, perhaps one in junior high school, the same style may suggest something of the artist's thoughts and feelings: that he felt confused, for instance, or that he was in a humorous mood. For still older students, it may reveal characteristics of the artist of which he himself was not conscious: his boldness, perhaps, or his peculiar simplicity. They may also be able to relate the work to other styles, such as cubism, or to techniques, such as the use of the palette knife. The development just described is in the direction of an increasing empathy with the artist. At first, the style reveals only his behaviors, then his conscious thoughts and feelings, and then his character and influences. This is a general pattern for the development of the idea of style.

A similar development occurs with the idea of expression. At first, emotion is found only in what is depicted. If a person is shown playing with a little dog, then the work is happy; if the work depicts fighting, it is bloodthirsty. We quoted Dunstan in chapter 3, who assumed that a painting of a meadow with flowers would be happy and one of a dragon would be angry. In his way of thinking, the meaning of the work lies in the subject matter; it lies on the surface, we might say, as something not to be interpreted but to be seen. Older students have more empathy with figures represented in the work and more ability to sense the emotions involved; a good example would be the contrast between Debbie and Eric in chapter 3, who found Ida in Albright's painting (fig. 1) repulsive and Betty in chapter 4, who found her compellingly pathetic. Older students are also more aware that the artist has particular intentions and feelings that she is trying to get over. They are likely to think, for example, that if the artist were feeling sad even a field of flowers could express the sadness and to understand that, in general, the artist may have feelings that are not identical with those of the figures depicted.

Preadolescence, in general, brings a greater ability to understand the point of view of others and a greater interest in their emotions. This means, among other things, greater interest in the expressiveness of artworks and in what artists may be trying to say. An understanding that an artist may be trying to express an idea or a feeling in her art is an important milestone in the development of aesthetic understanding. The same pattern of development occurs as with the understanding of style. At first expression is understood only in terms of what is pictured, then in terms of what the artist is consciously trying to say; then in terms of attitudes and feelings that the artist may not have been conscious of and perhaps did not understand herself.

There is a similar developmental history to ideas like creativity, originality, inspiration, all of which have a reference to the character and inwardness of the artist. Originality, for example, at first has reference only to things depicted. It means to many elementary school children that the objects or events depicted aren't real or didn't happen. For example, twelve-year-old Dexter said that the painting by George Bellows, *Dempsey and Firpo*, is original because it shows an event that didn't happen (in the painting Dempsey knocks Firpo clear out of the boxing ring). He said:

Would you say this is an original painting?
Yes. Because, well, I could paint some person in a boxing match, but I
   don't think I would ever paint someone falling into someone else's lap.

*What if that really happened in the fight? What if he really hit him out
of the ring, and the artist is painting a picture of it?*
Yeah, that would not be so original. It would just be painting the picture
as you remembered it.

Would it be original if he just painted it out of his head?
To be original, you have to make something up.

At a somewhat older age, the meaning of originality usually has
a more inward reference, meaning roughly, having deep, genuine
feelings or thoughts about something. Whether, in order to be original,
the feelings need to be new as well as deeply felt is often a question
that students are interested in discussing. Even traditional feelings and
thoughts can be new to the person having them and it is not clear how
a person decides when a feeling that is deeply felt is a new one anyway.
Sometimes students find it hard to see how any criteria, including
relevance, legitimately apply to feelings, so long as they are deeply
felt. Later, originality may come to be thought of in a more public
way, as, for example, extending a tradition, making variations on
previous achievements, having new insights that can be publicly understood and evaluated or having to do with the novel use of a style or
medium.

It may also be worth asking students why, at any point in this
sequence of understanding, originality should be considered a good
thing in an artwork. Why is it a good thing to show things that didn't
happen, to think new thoughts or feel deep feelings, or to extend
traditions? Why shouldn't we be content to have the same experiences
as our ancestors? This topic can lead to the heart of contemporary
discussions of the values of modernity, the idea of progress and our
culture's constant desire for the novel.

Another developmental matter has to do with self-awareness. Self-
awareness is the ability to reflect on one's own actions, to describe one's
state of mind for others, or to take the perspective of others on what one
is doing or feeling. It is the opposite of taking one's actions and feelings
for granted, of supposing that their motivation and character is obvious
to everyone. Self-awareness in this sense comes gradually as students
grow up and it can greatly affect aesthetic understanding. For example,
children of elementary school-age are usually not aware that they are
interpreting artworks and do not appreciate the extent to which they
themselves contribute to their interpretations. They tend to think that
they *see* works and don't *interpret* them, that whatever they see is
obvious and undisputable. Similarly, they usually think of their own
studio works as representations rather than as interpretations of a

subject. To them, their works tell the viewer about their subject matter, not about their creator.

This is true even where the students' values are clearly involved. For example, if a work is thought ugly, it is reported as fact rather than judgment. "No one wants to see stupid things like that in paintings" said one little boy of the Albright (fig. 1), as if its ugliness was an objective fact rather than in part a product of his own values. When there are differences of opinion about the same work, the avoidance of reflection is harder to sustain. The differences in opinion might seem to call for an account of the different interpretations that lie behind them and perhaps even raise the question as to what are the influences on people that explain why they have different interpretations. This is the epitome of self-awareness, to reflect on one's own interpretations, on the assumptions that shape them, and on what has influenced one's assumptions. It is also ideally a part of doing aesthetics. But a teacher of young children must learn to be patient, even while trying to foster such abilities. Young children may well explain differences of opinion about an artwork simply by appealing to the well-known fact that people like different things, an explanation that is basically a repetition of what is to be explained. Dennis, eleven years old, was asked why there are differences of interpretation and said, with an air of announcing the obvious: "A painting is just a thing. People have to decide for themselves if they like it or they don't like it. It is just a thing that you have."

In the same way, presumably, he thinks of a response to the painting as just a thing that you have, a learned habit or in-born predisposition, rather than as a meaning you construct.

Preadolescence tends to be the time when the role of interpretation becomes more apparent. Students become aware that different judgments reflect different interpretations and that interpretations are influenced by individual character and personal background. Then interpretation is a more inward affair, something meaningful in the mind either of the artist or of the viewer. This idea can often be seen behind what older students say. For example, Craig, who was seventeen, was a little unclear about the meaning of a Chagall painting. He was asked whether he thought it should be hung in a museum, and why, and he said:

> Well, I guess, like, I don't know, a museum isn't really important. I think the main thing that is important is if the artist is satisfied with what he has done, and if he can look at this painting and, like, he sees clearly what he has tried to say. And so I imagine he would like people to look at it and try to get what he is trying to say. I guess that's what museums

are for. But then it would be hard to say, like, if this picture made it, or what.

Craig is here clearly aware of the need for interpretation and that the meaning of the work is more than what can simply be seen. He thinks interpretation must occur inwardly and invisibly, in someone's head, and therefore that it would be hard to know exactly what the artist intended. And since Craig assumes that authority belongs with the artist's intention, interpretation is "hard to say."

A similar set of assumptions lies behind the following remark by Carie, talking about the same work. Carie disagreed with Craig about the importance of the artist's opinion but had the same awareness of interpretations, their inwardness, and individual differences. Carie said this about the same Chagall painting:

> You know, I think it's all in the person who's looking at it, and their interpretation of it. The artist might even paint something and say: "Oh! This is a bad painting! I didn't put a lot of work into it." And someone else might see it and say: "Oh! That's a great painting! I love the way you put those colors." So I think it would be hard to judge. But I like this painting. It makes you think about things. You could look in every corner, there is so much activity going on; you can interpret different things out of everything you see there.

There are many ideas in these two short extracts that a teacher could fasten on for educational purposes. Which to choose depends in part on where the teacher thinks Craig and Carie are in their development. They both take for granted, for example, that the artist was trying to say something, that the viewer might not interpret it correctly and that different viewers might have different interpretations. If they were at a slightly earlier stage, where these ideas were not so obvious to them, one could have students contrast these ideas with Dennis' view, previously quoted, that everyone sees the same thing ("a painting is just a thing"). This would make the act of interpretation more visible and raise questions about the role of the viewer. With Craig and Carie, on the other hand, for whom these appear no longer to be issues, more appropriate questions might be about how interpretation works, that is, how artists convey meanings through their works or why viewers' interpretations vary with their background. One good approach is to get students to speculate on the factors that have influenced a particular interpretation of their own. If the students are still further along the general path of development, one might raise questions designed to get at the difference of opinion between Craig and Carie; that is, whether the artist's or the viewer's interpretation is the more important.

Is meaning really all "in the person who's looking at it"? Is there some way in which the artist or the work itself limits the meanings that can be found in it? Can some of the thoughts and feelings of the viewer be more relevant than others? These questions, of course, circle around the issue of the "intentional fallacy," which Craig assumes and Carie, equally without argument, denies.

The general point here is that students develop their understanding of fundamental ideas like interpretation in typical patterns and the curriculum should respond to their particular level of development. This means that teachers need to be in touch with their students' developing understandings of some basic ideas, to know which they take for granted and which they have not yet grasped. The best choice for class discussions are ideas that students have become aware of but have not yet thought through. It is a good strategy to pick a few key ideas, such as expression, beauty, and style, and a few typical students and to focus on how those students understand those ideas. This gives one a reasonable marker on how most of the class are likely to be thinking.

Sometimes it helps to make a tape recording of what is said during class discussions and to bring back key passages to class. Much can be learned by both students and teacher by examining an extract from a discussion that was not clear but was on an important topic. Some of the passages quoted in this book would serve the purpose well, especially if they had originated in the class. One can also learn much about how students are thinking by reading what they write, if one structures the writing task carefully. It is important to break the question into small parts and to ask for both particular examples and general statements and to give good feedback by passing out interesting answers for everyone to see.

One of the things that students can learn from the discussion of extracts from their own conversation or writing is how much difference it can make exactly how a point is phrased. Philosophy requires that one take care with words, and important differences often lie behind *exactly* how one says something: whether to say, for example, that a work portrays or conveys an emotion, whether the work expresses outrage or it makes one feel outraged. Such differences of phrasing can be crucial, and students can be brought to see that. It is a valuable learning in itself. On the other hand, such differences are crucial only when the students understand them. It does not help if the teacher insists on the importance of clear phrasing if the students do not grasp the issue. When this happens, students will learn only that philosophy is a matter of "merely verbal distinctions." All distinctions may be verbal but *merely* verbal ones are those that do not mark a difference of meaning.

We will briefly turn to a somewhat different question about children's abilities. It is sometimes questioned whether children can do philosophy in a meaningful way. Isn't philosophy too abstract for children? Some people think that young children cannot think abstractly and therefore that they cannot do philosophy. In their view, young children reason best when they reason concretely and teachers should avoid discussing ideas with them and get them to deal with concrete things as much as possible. Some people even think that developmental psychology has demonstrated the value of this advice. The name of Piaget is often raised in these discussions, since he is probably the most famous of developmental psychologists.

Are children unable to do philosophy? Have developmental psychologists proved this? The answers to both questions is no. With respect to the first, there is plenty of evidence that children can do philosophy. If one stops to talk with young children, or listens to them closely, one finds them talking freely about questions such as whether it is right to be cruel to animals, whether it is reasonable to believe in witches and whether frogs look beautiful to other frogs. These are philosophical questions regarding, respectively, ethics, science, and aesthetics. Children talk about such questions from an early age; they raise them spontaneously and discuss them with spirit. Moreover, they speculate abstractly about such questions and can give reasons for their beliefs. We have quoted enough examples of children talking abstractly about art in this book to demonstrate that this is true and we do not believe that more formal evidence is required. Of course, children do philosophy in their own way. Their ideas are often different from those of adults and are often more limited. But this is true in any subject and is not particular to philosophy.

In fact there has been an active movement to teach children philosophy in schools for more than a decade,[3] and there are several books reporting the philosophical talk of children.[4] This movement has gradually grown in influence. We see it as only tangentially related to our interest in this book because it has a rather different purpose. Our aim is to help children understand art better; the aim of the children's philosophy movement is to help them do philosophy — to reason more carefully and scrupulously in a general way. This is a worthwhile goal but a different one. Nevertheless, the existence of the movement shows that children have the abilities required to do philosophy. And some of the materials developed by the movement may well be useful for teaching aesthetics. Unfortunately, the movement has, on the whole, been more interested in teaching children ethics and epistemology than aesthetics, but a teacher may find it interesting to consult some of the literature.[5]

The second question was whether Piaget and his followers deny that children can do philosophy. Many people — including many teachers — think that they do. Even major figures associated with the philosophy for children movement believe this.[6] But it is a misinterpretation of the main thrust of Piagetian thought. Piaget was a pioneer in the study of children's ideas. He and his followers were the first to show in detail that children understand things differently from adults. But they also extensively explored children's abilities to deal with ideas and to think abstractly. For instance, Piaget wrote a book on children's abstract reasoning about moral problems, a book that is still worth reading.[7] Because of work spawned in part by this book, there has been great progress in understanding just how children think about abstract moral ideas like justice, punishment, conscience, and responsibility.[8] Other developmentalists have looked at how children think about abstract ideas like God,[9] or the self.[10] The conclusion of all this work is the same: children think about the major topics of philosophy, their ideas are often different from those of adults, their interest is genuine, and their ability to think philosophically is not in doubt.

We have already spoken of our view that the basic motivation for doing philosophy arises with the puzzling situations we meet in real life. This view is consistent with the conclusions just reviewed. When we encounter facts that do not fit our ideas, we are prompted to raise questions either about the facts or about our ideas. These latter kinds of questions are basically philosophical in character. Children as much as adults puzzle about facts that don't fit their conceptions of reality. In fact, children may do this more than adults, since their ideas are based on a more limited range of experience and so they more often fail to fit the facts. Children and philosophy are not strangers.

The Teaching Role

The role of the teacher in aesthetics is not that of an authority who can provide students with answers to philosophical questions. It is more a provocative and facilitative role whose function is to help students identify and discuss philosophical issues related to the artworks they encounter. The attitude required is antidogmatic, for dogmatism is the enemy of philosophy. Philosophy has always required a speculative and open-minded attitude, in which the interest is as much in getting the question clear as in securing answers. It requires an interest in playing with alternative ideas and in considering counterfactual situations, even when the eventual answer seems obvious. Philosophers value clarity of thought for its own sake and are usually willing to follow a line of argument just to see where it leads. Equally, they do not much respect unexamined convictions and dogmatic assertions, even where these convictions and assertions seem be true. A good teacher will try to model this attitude, which we could call deliberate open-mindedness.

There is some tension in such an attitude. We all have opinions about things that matter to us. We think that our opinions are true and feel that others should agree with us. We may feel a kind of discomfort when people question what we take for granted. In this sense everyone has a desire to reach answers and a tendency toward dogmatism. And certainly philosophers *aim* to find answers. They want to find the truth. Much philosophy is written to establish particular theories or in defense of particular views. But the interest is always also in the quality of the arguments, the clarity of ideas and the consistency of positions, as well as in the content of the conclusions. Philosophy is good only when conducted in the spirit of deliberate open-mindedness.

This spirit may require a change in the teacher's and the students' roles. The traditional role of the teacher is that of an authority figure who knows what the right answers are. Students are the learners and are to pick up their cues from the teacher. But one cannot teach philosophy that way. Teachers must avoid imposing their solutions on students and be content to leave them at times with unresolved problems. Students must be willing to assert their own doubts and understandings and often be content with incomplete answers.

Such a role may not be difficult for art teachers because the tradition of teaching art has been less authoritarian than in other subject matter areas. Most art teachers already value independent thought more than conformity to authority: the spirit of art and of philosophy are in many ways similar. But putting the value into practice is not a simple matter. Many teachers intend to encourage their students to think independently but nevertheless, in a variety of subtle ways, they make it clear which ideas they think are sensible and which are not. It is easy to convey the feeling that an idea is silly by a style of questioning, a tone of voice or a quick gesture. Worse, it is easy to suggest, without intending to, that a question is inappropriate or an attitude unwelcome. Teachers and students both are used to the notion that the teacher knows best and it is not always easy to defeat this assumption in practice.

One thing that deliberate open-mindedness requires of teachers is awareness of their own assumptions. Sometimes our students are more aware of our beliefs than we are. This happens when we believe in something deeply and have come to think that it is obvious: for example, that Johns is a great painter; that women artists are as good as men; that Marxist criticism adds nothing to our understanding; or that art should be expressive. In cases like this, we may not recognize that our mind is actually closed to further discussion. Our students will pick this up, even though we *say* that we want them to think through all opinions for themselves.

This is especially true with beliefs that we have acquired more by socialization than by conscious argument because for us they have the character of assumptions. Assumptions are the truths we find most obvious and think least about. They support our behaviors and patterns of life and that may make us unwilling to clarify them or to take questions about them seriously. Uncertainty about such basic things can provoke anxiety. When the truths we live by are challenged we may feel threatened, the threat being that the world in which we live will change. As John Dewey used to say, all thinking involves risk and any thought followed through may put the whole world at risk. For this reason it helps teachers to be aware of their own assumptions and to be prepared to discuss them in a spirit of open-mindedness.

One common case of the failure of open-mindedness may seem paradoxical. It occurs where a teacher is committed to a view that itself seems open-minded but the commitment of the teacher is not. For example, many teachers hold a relativist view of interpretation that says something like this: any interpretation of a work is valid so long as it is honestly held because it is the result of the experience of the viewer and is therefore justified for that viewer. This idea seems open-minded, since it appears to let everyone say what they like and it avoids disagreeing with them. It might even seem to be a paradigm case of open-mindedness. But it is not so. Open-mindedness is a property of persons, not of views. Relativism can be as much a dogma as any other view, depending on the attitude of the person holding it. It is a standard topic in aesthetics and there are as many good arguments against it as for it. As we have seen, the discussion usually centers on the question what should count as a good reason for an interpretation or a judgment and there is no clear consensus about this. So it would be dogmatic to pass relativism on to students without debate. The better thing to do is to help them examine the arguments for and against it and to decide for themselves.

To become aware that one has assumptions of this sort is hard enough. To prevent their affecting students is still harder. It helps to examine one's own behavior to see what subtle messages it gives. One interesting way to do this is to ask students to write an account of what they think the teacher's views are on a topic that has been discussed. This may reveal whether they have been able to pick up hidden prejudices and how open-minded one is managing to be. Sometimes it is sufficient just to let students know what one's prejudices are and to make it clear that it is OK to disagree with teacher. Sometimes it helps to play devil's advocate and to argue the opposite of what one believes. In any case, teachers should learn to resist the anxiety of leaving students with a belief that teachers feel is a poor one. It is better to return to the subject later than to become dogmatic.

The other side of this endeavor is getting students to abandon *their* authoritarian habits and assumptions. It is often harder for them to change roles than for the teacher, and there is no quick formula for success. Students have to learn the attitudes and skills both of discussion in general and of philosophy in particular. The attitudes are a matter of trust and expectation, the skills of particular abilities and habits. It is helpful to think of this learning as a matter not of individual change for either the teacher or the students but as group learning, of the class changing as a whole, the students and teacher together learning to have fruitful discussions. And like most worthwhile learning it will happen a little at a time.

Good discussion requires a supportive classroom atmosphere, one of positive regard between students. Creating such an atmosphere is part of good teaching in general but philosophical discussion especially requires tolerance and emotional support. Without encouragement, students may not be willing to be open about their feelings on topics that are important to them or to say when they don't understand. They may be embarrassed to admit being confused about matters that they think are obvious to others. They make be anxious about what is acceptable to say. They may voice opinions mostly to impress others. Adolescents are particularly likely to feel embarrassed by the apparent naïveté of philosophical questions. They should be helped to feel safe asking all kinds of questions and to see that it takes insight to ask questions about what others take for granted. Feeling confused may be a sign of having penetrated beneath the surface. Sometimes those who do not understand are actually more perceptive than those who think they do. Socrates famously said that his chief distinction lay in knowing that he did not know, whereas others mistakenly thought they did. The figure of Socrates can be attractive to adolescents and the story of his trial can help to get this point across.[11] In any case, it is important that students learn to be tolerant of each other and not to feel defensive speaking in front of their peers.

This learning can begin with the teacher modeling acceptance of students' opinions. The message a teacher wants to give, both verbally and nonverbally, is that she is both interested in and nonjudgmental about students' thoughts and feelings. One good tactic is to restate feelings when a student talks about them, before asking a question about them. "You are saying that you feel annoyed by this artwork? Can you say more about that?" Rephrasing feelings in this way can help students understand what they are saying and reassure them that their feelings are acceptable. Another tactic is to ask others to compare their feelings: "Crystal, do you feel the same way?" This engenders a sense of being understood by one's peers. It is also helpful to distinguish between feelings that are responsive to an artwork and other kinds of feelings. "Is there something about the work that makes you feel that way? Can you tell what it is? Or is that just the way you are feeling this afternoon?" Reflecting on what influences one's thoughts and feelings is an important habit in both art and philosophy.

Another part of creating a supportive classroom atmosphere is teaching communication skills. These include listening and questioning skills. Students should be encouraged to listen carefully to what others say and to think about their own comprehension of what has been said before they respond with another opinion. One can model this by rephrasing what a student has just said in a slightly different way. One can also ask a student to do it: "Derek, can you tell us what Anita just said? What was her most important point?" In extreme cases, one can institute a temporary rule that before students make any further contribution to a discussion, they must restate what the person who has just spoken has said. This makes the importance of listening well obvious to everyone.

Students should also be encouraged to ask clarifying questions of each other as an active part of listening: "I don't know what you mean by violent. Where is the violent part?" "I lost you when you talked about form. Can you say it again?" An important point about these questions is that they begin with a statement about one's understanding and not with a judgment about what the other said. Compare the rather negative tone of the alternative form: "You were unclear about violence. Where is the violent part?" "Your talk about form was confusing. Can you say it again?" Learning to ask facilitative questions takes a while and may need to be taught as a skill in itself.

Another clarifying move is to ask for an example. This is often useful in philosophy. Or one can describe a case and ask if it *is* an example of what is meant. One can try to find a counter-example, a case that clarifies by *not* being an instance of what is being talked about. One can also ask for connections: "How are the two things you've talked about connected with each other?" "Is that different from what Vesta just said?" "How does that apply to the painting we were looking at yesterday?" It helps to get students to distinguish between kinds of questions: between, for example, clarifying questions, aimed at getting

a better understanding; substantive questions, aimed at more information; and argumentative questions, which are really ways of
challenging a point. One useful tactic is to ask students to state what
kind of question they are about to ask before they ask it.

Asking Good Questions

We have already started talking about asking questions and the
tactics of discussion. A discussion should begin by identifying the issue
to be discussed. It is worth spending time getting the issue stated
explicitly and understood clearly. It may be worthwhile having students
formulate their conceptions of the issues and writing some of these
on the board. Then one can ask questions about these formulations:
"Is there more than one issue on the board? Are there several versions
of one issue? How do the versions differ? How do they relate to the
artwork we began with? And which version shall we focus on today?"
It would be a mistake to think that clarifying the issue in this way is
just preparation for doing philosophy; it is an important part of it.
Furthermore, it can help to keep the discussion on track if one leaves
the different versions on the board where everyone participating in
the discussion can make reference to them.

Once the discussion has started, it is important to keep the focus
on reasons for opinions. We all find it easier to give opinions than
to give reasons for them, yet it is the reasons that are the more important. Posing this question sometimes takes persistence because it asks
students to look beneath the surface of their opinions to their more
general assumptions. A skeleton of a question and answer sequence
might go as follows: A student praises a work and the teacher asks
why the work is good. The student says it is because of the detail and
the teacher asks why so much detail is a good thing. The student says
it shows the artist's skill and the teacher asks why skill is the important
thing. This sequence in practice may take a while to get through but
it is only at this point that the student is likely to have reached an
assumption she has not thought much about.

Many children, whose own art making is often dominated by an
awareness of their lack of skill, take it for granted that skill is a primary
virtue in art and that the more skillful the artist the better the work.
In response one might decide to thematize the idea of skill, asking for
examples (compare talking, making paper airplanes that fly, cooking
with recipes, winning a lottery: which of these require skill?) and asking
what skill really is (is skill dexterity of hand, the application of knowledge, patience, a perfectionist control of the medium?) One might return

from time to time to such a topic over the course of a whole year, collecting examples and counter-examples and trying different formulations.

It is worth remembering that often we have several reasons for an opinion and we don't always know which reason is the most important. It is important for students to realize that several reasons may be relevant to one issue and that the problem is often not finding a reason but weighing which of several is the most important. A good group discussion exercise is to collect several reasons for an opinion and list them; then to ask students which are the more important. It can be a group exercise to come to agree on a rank ordering of reasons. This has the advantage that it focuses students on the reasons rather than simply on the opinion. It may reveal, too, that students who agree in their conclusion nevertheless disagree about the reason for it. Sometimes the way in which reasons are stated becomes crucial. In one instance some sixth-graders agreed on a position about the relativity of judgments written by a small group of students. It read: "What is good in art depends on what people like. If you like something, that means it's good for you. If someone else doesn't like it, that means it's not good for him." The sixth-graders agreed with this statement but gave two rather different reasons for it (but some thought they were just two versions of the same reason). One version had to do with taste: that people like different things and this is a simple fact about them, rather like the color of their hair. The other version had to do with interpretation: people understand things differently and this is because of their different background and experience. Recognizing that there is a real difference between the two versions proved to be hard work for some of the students and the issue kept recurring over the course of a quarter.

Often a group of students will volunteer reasons both for and against some particular view. In such a case one can write the reasons out in two columns, the pro and the con. This helps students to see that the issue is not so much whether they have a reason for their view as which reason is the more weighty. The discussion can proceed by discussing each reason one by one, assessing both its relevance to the issue and its importance. This itself may become a matter of disagreement and therefore of the attempt to produce arguments for the importance of a particular reason. It is likely that some reasons will drop out of the list, some will be qualified or changed, and others will rise in significance as the discussion proceeds. One may wind up with only one good reason left but it is equally possible that there will be still some reasons in the pro column and some in the con column. It is good for students to appreciate the complexity of this situation and not to

Aesthetics and Education

assume that finding one good reason, pro or con, settles the matter. It is not always easy to accept that there are several arguments that are relevant to an important issue and that they do not all point in the same direction. Understanding such situations requires that one make one's judgments in a more tentative manner and consider the arguments on both sides.

Encouraging Discussion

There are many kinds of discussions in class. Two main kinds are student-to-teacher and student-to-student. Both are useful. A good way to stimulate the latter is to structure small group discussions. Talking in small groups (of somewhere between four and seven) gives more students a chance to talk than does a full class discussion, it encourages them to listen to each other carefully and it allows for the expression of more points of view. In addition, it provides opportunities for collaborative learning and the practice of democratic skills: taking turns, asking questions, giving reasons for one's point of view. Also, for many older students, talking in small groups is not as threatening as talking in large groups. Small group discussions are, therefore, an important device.

Success with small group discussions, though, requires careful structuring until the students are used to it. One kind of structure is a clear set of directions about what to do. At the beginning it is not enough simply to ask students to discuss a topic. It is necessary to create an exercise that has specific tasks to it. For example, one can ask students to create a list of reasons for and against some particular view that is already written down for them or to think of all the similarities and differences between two ideas. Other tasks might be to agree as a group on prioritizing a preestablished list of examples of an idea, or of reasons for a conclusion, or to decide as a group which is the best and the worst argument from a written list. They can be asked to paraphrase faithfully a written extract from a class discussion or a book, or to identify and categorize the various claims in it, using some simple category system, for example, philosophical/factual, general/particular, value-laden/neutral. It is better at first to write out a short set of clear and specific instructions for such tasks than to give them orally.

Good discussion questions have two somewhat contrary characteristics. They focus on ideas rather than on things and they are couched as specifically as possible. So they ask, for example: "What is a caricature?" rather than: "Describe the characteristics of these three caricatures." This helps students keep the focus of discussion on the idea rather than on the examples, something that becomes important when there is disagreement about details regarding the examples. At the same time, it is well to add: "Give examples of the characteristics you mention from these three caricatures." It is also better to contrast two ideas than to ask about one; better to ask "What are the differences between a caricature and a photograph?" than: "What is a caricature?" and even better to ask: "What are three important differences between caricatures and photographs? Give examples of your points from these caricatures and photographs." Sometimes the small group discussion is better if students are asked first to sit for a few moments to think about the question and to write down some initial answers. They then each have something to say when they go to the small group and can begin by reading what they wrote.

Another kind of structure for small groups is to assign some roles. One is the role of discussion leader, whose job is to facilitate discussion. We have already spoken of the desirability of teaching the skills required by this role: the skills of listening carefully, of being able to repeat what was just said, of asking clarifying questions. These can be taught by rotating the role of small group discussion leader and, of course, discussing with the class what that role is. Another role is group secretary, who makes notes on the important things that are said and reports them later to the teacher or the class. A part of this job is to keep the group focused by asking how various points relate to the issue at hand; making a summary of a discussion requires keeping it clear what the issue is. Such roles can rotate among students from day to day. It is also helpful sometimes to ask students to think or write about how they performed in a discussion. Did they talk a lot, listen well, ask questions, tell anecdotes, withdraw? Did they focus on the issue, get side-tracked, become emotional, act as if bored? One can list these functions or these modes of performing on the board and ask students afterwards to decide which they most did themselves. They can also be asked to think about the group process as a whole: Did the group stay on the topic? Were there awkward silences? Did one person dominate the discussion? Did people listen to each other? What role did each person play? This stimulates an awareness of group process, which is worthwhile in itself and is also related to awareness of the kinds of substantive reasoning going on in the group.

A different kind of structure has to do with time. Small groups should know how long they have to complete the tasks asked of them and what will follow. At the beginning, a simple task and a few minutes in small groups is probably enough. It is better to have students wanting more time than for them to have more than they can handle well. After a while, as they learn appropriate behaviors, they can deal with larger tasks and take more time. A typical class structure is to spend some minutes identifying the question for discussion, whether it has been written out in advance or the class is to identify it. Then the small groups meet for discussion, at the beginning for perhaps ten to fifteen minutes only. Then it is good practice for the whole class to reassemble for debriefing. A traditional method is to have each group secretary report briefly on what was said or decided in the group. It is often helpful to focus these reports on some particular topic, such as what was agreed to be the best reason or the top priority and why. Reports can also focus on some aspect of group process. It helps to write these summaries on the board as the secretaries report. This gives the class a better sense of perspective on the topic and of closure to the process, without bringing closure to the substantive discussion. In fact, this reporting often opens up the issues again, as students see that the small groups disagree with each other and that leads naturally to a further discussion.

At this point, or in a later lesson, the teacher might choose to continue the discussion with the whole class. She can restate in her own words what she thinks the students are saying. This gives them perspective on their own thoughts and it is a check on whether the teacher has interpreted them correctly. She can also try to make connections clearer by asking further questions. For example, one can categorize arguments in different ways or compare two different arguments and ask whether they are alternative versions of the same argument. One can add considerations that the students have not thought of—new examples, new arguments, connections they have overlooked. And frequently there is a need to focus the discussion, to keep asking what the issue actually is.

One purpose the teacher sometimes has at this point is to prevent premature closure, if she feels that the students can make further progress with the issue at hand. It does not help if they leave the class with the feeling that they have reached the truth if it is clear that they have ignored some accessible considerations. Better yet, the teacher should keep them thinking between classes. On the other hand, how much to do of this is a matter of judgment because too much could make students insecure or frustrated. But it is appropriate for them to understand that some philosophical problems require a long and persistent effort to reach a reasonable conclusion.

After a good discussion, one can ask students to write out some of their conclusions, either as answers to questions or as further questions they would like to discuss. This is especially useful if the discussion has been lively because the writing requires each student to think through for herself what she has heard. And, of course, what is written can then become the substance of further exercises another day.

The Curriculum

We have said several times that the philosophical questions discussed in class should be related to two kinds of variables: the artworks made and studied in the classroom and the students' concerns and abilities. This means that teachers will have to adapt and devise a curriculum from whatever resources they can. No textbook can be expected to do what is required. Fortunately, there are many ways of raising philosophical questions in the course of making or discussing particular works or art in general. In addition, discussion can easily be structured around what the students themselves have said or written previously. This latter source may be the best of all. This does not mean that one cannot use books or other outside sources such as newspapers and art journals.[12] The more sources consulted the better, provided that the resulting materials are relevant to the students and are genuinely philosophical in their bearing. It does mean, however, that the teacher must expect to keep adapting and experimenting with different topics, materials, and exercises.

This requires more of the teacher than a more textbook-dependent approach would require, but it is also more rewarding. It requires some awareness of the students' levels of understanding and interests and a reasonable anticipation of how they are likely to respond to artworks and topics. It also requires a sense of the important issues in philosophy and of where they surface in the classroom. Curriculum development lies exactly in bringing these two sorts of things together. This book has tried to help especially with the latter but there is no substitute for experience and reflection. Incorporating aesthetics into the art class this way is possible because one can learn as one teaches. This can be very rewarding. Not only do the students have more meaningful learning but so does the teacher: learning about the interests and understandings of the students and how they relate to the important issues in aesthetics.

With practice, one can develop the ability to spot the fruitful philosophical questions that permeate everyday classroom situations. They lie behind many ordinary encounters with artworks. But they do not lie on the surface and they are not apparent to most people because philosophy is about what we usually take for granted. So we need to look at the interactions that already occur in our classroom rather deliberately to find the philosophical issues that lie behind them. For example, when two children disagree about an interpretation, the simplest thing is to treat their disagreement as being about the specific work. That is the way they will understand it. In that case one might do art criticism with them and discuss the work in greater depth. But one might see that the disagreement rests on a difference in assumptions, and in that case it might lead to a philosophical discussion. Perhaps the students have different assumptions about whether the artist's intention should be taken into account. Perhaps they disagree about whether their personal circumstances should influence the meaning of the work. One might think it is important to know when the work was made and the other not. Such differences in assumptions may not even be noticed in the discussion unless the teacher deliberately focuses attention on them. This means, of course, that the teacher needs to be alert for such situations and to be ready to unpack them.

After practicing a while, one begins to see philosophical themes everywhere, behind every interpretive statement and critical judgment. And then the difficulty becomes not how to spot the themes but how to decide which are most worth discussing with students. There is not much time in class and not all topics are equally worthwhile. To be worthwhile, a topic should be both important in aesthetics and also at the right level of difficulty and interest for students. The question whether this is a good topic for now, how much to do with it, when to move on to some other activity, is not always easy to answer. It depends on the context. It is a matter of judgment and not of rule, the sort of question that makes teaching such a demanding but interesting occupation.

Even so, there are some tips deriving from the experience of others. One needs to adopt an experimental attitude and not to mind too much if the students do not respond with interest every time. The point of experimenting is to learn something. After an unsuccessful episode, one can ask: Why did they not respond well? Was it the difficulty of the topic? The developmental level of the students? The lack of good examples? One way to answer these questions is to choose one student and interview her: to ask what she thinks about the topic, what she did with the instructions, how she would change the example. This is a chance to check one's intuitions about interest and difficulty level and to get a better sense of how students understand an issue. One can think of a lesson as a test of the interest of the topic or the clarity of instructions, and use it as an opportunity to learn. There is little doubt that teaching aesthetics at the beginning requires some experimenting and willingness to accept disappointments.

It also helps to create a group memory. The simplest form of this is a running list of the questions that have been discussed with interest in class. This list can be kept on the board or elsewhere for public view or students can keep their own versions in notebooks. One can also keep a list of the arguments that have been discussed pertaining to one issue. Such lists serve a number of purposes, one of which is to keep the issues and arguments in students' minds and to stimulate their further thinking. It also gives a sense of structure and progress to topics and in effect defines the curriculum.

One such list of questions, kept in a fifth grade class by a teacher we know, was titled "Philosophical Questions." At the end of the first quarter it read as follows:

— How can you tell scribbles from abstract works? What is a scribble, exactly?
— Does it matter how much time a work took to make?
— Does the artist need to have skill? What is skill? Is it using tools well or is it thinking out things to do?
— Does it matter if an artist makes a mistake? How can mistakes sometimes be good?
— Can earthworks be artworks? Can you walk in or on artworks?
— Why do different people like different things?

On another part of the wall, the teacher had a different list of questions that had also arisen in class. She called this list "Other Questions." It read:

— Did Picasso ever make mistakes? Did he use an eraser or paint over things?
— How long did Picasso take to paint a painting?
— Who decides which works go in museums?
— Why are earthworks sometimes out in the desert where you can't easily see them?
— Do people in every country make drawings?
— Who invented painting?
— Why are some paintings worth a lot of money?
— Who has the most paintings in the world?

Making these two lists was the teacher's way of reminding students that there are different kinds of questions. She told the class that the first set were philosophical because they called for a discussion of ideas and the second set was not because they could be answered by finding out some facts. Using this distinction, the class at times debated which list a question belonged to. All of the questions had been rewritten by the class several times and some had been moved from one list to the other in the course of the quarter. For example the questions: Who decides which works go in museums? had been moved from the first to the second list by class vote following a discussion. This discussion itself, of course, was philosophical in character.

Another function of a memory device like a list is to help students make connections. Important issues are connected with each other in complex ways and discussions are usually about one issue at a time, often a rather specific one. Keeping a list in front of students may provoke them to make connections in their mind. It allows the teacher to ask students, when they ask a question, whether the question is related to one that is already on the list or whether it is a completely new one. It also allows the teacher to refer to the list during discussions, asking whether there is anything relevant already there. Students can be encouraged to think of other examples of topics on the list or of similar questions that have occurred to them since the discussion. In these ways, a list can be a source of continuity, generalization, and further provocation.

Another kind of memory device is to ask students to keep a list of the conclusions they have reached about art and the reasons for them. This can be done after class discussions, making a quick record of their conclusions, their puzzles, and their reasoning. It can also be done, at greater leisure and in a more careful way, in a philosophical diary. Keeping a philosophical (or a more generally artistic) diary through the year helps students to see where they have changed their minds and where their opinions conflict or generalize. To realize that they have answered a question in contrary ways can provoke further thought; to see that they have had some progressive insights over time can lend a sense of power.

The teacher can also help students to make connections by reminding them of their previous arguments ("Malcolm, isn't that the same argument you made last week about the earthworks?" or "Isn't that the same sort of question that bothered you when we made prints? Is this case like the prints?"). This kind of connecting helps students generalize their own beliefs. It is a variant of the tactic we mentioned earlier of restating students' arguments so that they can see them in a slightly different perspective. The same result can be fostered by having students read another student's philosophy diary and restate its main issues, conclusions, and reasons. The aim is to put these into one's own words but to be as faithful as possible to the original meaning.

Summary

We have argued that the main challenge of incorporating aesthetics into the classroom lies in relating genuinely philosophical issues to students' levels of understanding and interest. This requires of the teacher a grasp of the important philosophical issues and a sense of where they might arise in the art classroom. It also requires an awareness of the way students think about art and of their interests. We gave a brief account of some typical developmental patterns of thought and urged that there are various ways for a teacher to learn about students, including during the course of teaching itself. Learning how students think is a part of the pleasure of engaging them philosophically.

We also argued that the teacher's role is an antidogmatic one, oriented toward provoking questions and clarifying ideas. This role requires self-awareness of teachers if they are to avoid defensiveness or the subtle indoctrination of favorite views. Several ways of achieving this were suggested. It is also important to help students change their expectations about learning and to adopt habits and attitudes supportive of good discussion. Methods of doing this were discussed.

The kinds of questions to ask focus on ideas and reasons. Students should learn that reasons for opinions are often more significant than the opinions themselves. At the same time, good questions are usually relatively specific. Several examples were discussed. Methods of organizing small group discussions were also discussed.

The teaching of aesthetics in schools is a relatively new enterprise and there is little established curriculum material available. In any case, we argued that teachers will always have to adapt material to their students' needs and to the students' overall sense of the art curriculum. This requires experiment and reflection. Teaching aesthetics is a demanding task, but it is also a rewarding one, one through which teachers may come to understand more about their students and about art itself.

NOTES

1. But there are a few resources that teachers may find helpful. Two are particularly notable: Louis Lankford's *Aesthetics: Issues and Inquiry* (Reston, Va.: National Art Educators Association, 1992), which particularly addresses how to bring aesthetics into the classroom; and Mary Erickson, Eldon Katter, and Marilyn Stewart, *A Basic Curriculum for Art*, (Kutztown, Pa.: Art Education Dept., Kutztown State University, n.d.), which includes a general curriculum outline.

Other articles that may be useful include: Mary Erickson, "Teaching Aesthetics K-12," in *Pennsylvania's Symposium on Art Education, Aesthetics and Art Criticism*, ed. Evan Kern (Harrisburg, Pa.: State Department of Education, 1986); Carmen Armstrong, *Aesthetics Resource: An aid for Integrating Aesthetics into Art Curricula and Instruction*, School of Art, Northern Illinois University, 1990; Louis Lankford, "Preparation and Risk in Teaching

Aesthetics," *Art Education* 43:5 (Sept. 1990); and Robert Russell, "Children's Philosophical Inquiry into Defining Art," *Studies in Art Education* 29: 3 (1988).

2. An extended discussion of the development of children's ways of thinking about art is to be found in Michael Parsons, *How We Understand Art: A Cognitive Developmental Account of Aesthetic Experience* (Cambridge: Cambridge University Press, 1987). See also H. Gardner, E. Winner, and M. Kirchner, "Children's Conceptions of the Arts," *Journal of Aesthetic Education* 9:3, 60-77; Abigail Housen, "Levels of Aesthetic Development: A Study of Museum Visitors" (Unpublished manuscript, Harvard Graduate School of Education, 1977).

3. See, for example, Matthew Lipman, *Philosophy Goes to School* (Philadelphia: Temple University Press, 1988); Matthew Lipman and Ann Sharp, eds., *Growing Up with Philosophy* (Philadelphia: Temple University Press, 1978).

4. See especially Gareth Matthews, *Philosophy and the Young Child* (Cambridge, Mass.: Harvard University Press, 1980); Matthews, *Dialogues with Children* (Cambridge, Mass.: Harvard University Press, 1984); Michael S. Pritchard, *Philosophical Adventures with Children* (Lanham, Md.: University Press of America, 1985).

5. For a useful discussion and adaptation of the Philosophy for Children approach, see especially Sally Hagaman, "Philosophical Aesthetics in Art Education: A Further Look toward Implementation," *Art Education* 43:4 (July 1990).

6. One of the main problems with the books by Gareth Matthews, which are otherwise quite charming, is that he believes that Piaget denies that children can do philosophy, and he spends a large part of both books complaining about how foolish this is. This material seems to be unhelpful and is based on a misunderstanding of Piaget.

7. Jean Piaget, *The Moral Judgment of the Child*, trans. Marjorie Gabain (Free Press, 1965).

8. See especially Lawrence Kohlberg, *Essays on Moral Development*, vols. 1 and 2 (San Francisco: Harper and Row, 1991).

9. See James Fowler, *Stages of Faith* (San Franscisco: Harper and Row, 1981).

10. See John Broughton, "The Development of Conceptions of Subject and Object in Adolescence and Young Adulthood" (Ph.D. diss., Harvard University, 1974).

11. A good place to find the story is in Plato, *The Apology, from The Trial and Death of Socrates*, trans. G. M. Grube (Indianapolis: Hackett, 1954).

12. A useful source of problems for discussion is Margaret Battin, John Fisher, Ronald Moore, and Anita Silvers, *Puzzles about Art: An Aesthetics Casebook* (New York: St. Martin's Press, 1989).

Suggested Further Reading in Aesthetics

Anthologies

Two leading anthogies of contemporary writings are Joseph Margolis, ed., *Philosophy Looks at the Arts* (Philadelphia: Temple University, 1987); and George Dickie, Richard Sclafani, and Robin Roblin, eds., *Aesthetics: A Critical Anthology* 2d ed. (New York: St. Martin's Press, 1989). Both of these books represent the contemporary analytic tradition. Both emphasize the problem of the definability of art, the possibility of establishing "essentialist" theories of art, and the emergence of the "institutionalist" theory of art. Margolis's anthology was first issued in 1960 and has gone through many editions since then, which together represent a minihistory of the analytic movement in aesthetics. Margolis has recently become one of the few prominent analytic philosophers of art attempting to respond to the challenge of postmodernism, and this attempt appears in the latest edition (1987). Margolis's book is entirely contemporary, containing nothing before 1950, whereas Dickie et al. balances the contemporary emphasis with selections from the historical classics.

The most recent contemporary anthology in aesthetics is Gene Blocker and John Bender, *Contemporary Philosophy of Art* (Englewood Cliffs, N.J.: Prentice-Hall, 1993). This includes recent articles from both the analytic tradition and postmodernism.

History of Aesthetics

Three useful histories of aesthetics are Katherine Gilbert and Helmut Kuhn, *A History of Esthetics* (New York: Dover Publications, 1972); Harold Osborne, *Aesthetics and Art Theory: An Historical Introduction* (New York: Dutton, 1970); and Monroe Beardsley, *Aesthetics from Classical Greece to the Present: A Short History* (1966; reprint, Birmingham: University of Alabama, 1975). Any of these histories, in conjunction with an anthology such as that of Dickie, et al., is a good place to begin a study of the classics such as Plato, Aristotle, Hume, Kant, Hegel, and Schopenhauer.

Modern Classics

There are a number of important twentieth-century classics in aesthetics that are still well worth reading. These include John Dewey, *Art as Experience* (New York: Putnam, 1958); R. G. Collingwood, *The Principles of Art* (Oxford: Clarendon Press, 1938); Leo Tolstoy: *What is Art*, trans. Aylmer Maude (Indianapolis: Hackett, 1960); Nelson Goodman, *The Languages of Art* (Indianapolis: Bobbs-Merrill, 1968); Susanne Langer, *Feeling and Form* (New York: Scribner, 1953). Each of these modern classics has the traditional essentialist ambition of constructing a grand theory of art in general and in that way is basically preanalytic.

Recent Classics

Important recent works include George Dickie: *Art and the Aesthetic* (Ithaca, N.Y.: Cornell University Press, 1974), which rejects the traditional notion of the aesthetic; George Dickie, *The Art Circle: A Theory of Art* (New York: Haven, 1984), which gives an account of the institutional theory of art; Arthur Danto, *The Transfiguration of the Commonplace* (Cambridge: Harvard University Press, 1981), which analyzes conceptual art and the artworld; and Arthur Danto, *The Philosophical Disenfranchisement of Art* (New York: Columbia University Press, 1986), which discusses the "end of art" and its dependence on history.

Three important works in the earlier continental tradition include Mikel Dufrenne, *The Phenomenology of Aesthetic Experience*, trans. Edward Casey et al. (Evanston, Ill.: Northwestern University Press, 1973); Martin Heidegger, *Poetry, Language, Thought*, trans. Albert Hofstadter (New York: Harper and Row, 1971); Henri Arvon, *Marxist Esthetics*, trans. Helen Lane (Ithaca, N.Y.: Cornell University Press, 1973).

Postmodernism

The best approach to postmodernism is probably by way of a good general introduction. The best of these are Vincent Leitch, *Deconstructive Criticism: An Advanced Introduction* (New York: Columbia University Press, 1983); Mark Poster, *Critical Theory and Poststructuralism: In Search of a Context* (Ithaca, N.Y.: Cornell University Press, 1989); and Hugh Silverman, ed., *Postmodernism: Philosophy and the Arts* (New York: Routledge, 1990).

For a more detailed look at the sources of postmodernism, the following are recommended for the serious student: Umberto Eco, *A Theory* of Semiotics (Bloomington: University of Indiana Press, 1976); Hans-Georg Gadamer, *Philosophical Hermeneutics,* trans. David Linge (Berkeley: University of California Press, 1976); Jurgen Habermas, *Knowledge and Human Interests,* trans. Jeremy Shapiro (Boston: Beacon Press, 1971); Victor Burgin, *The End of Art Theory: Criticism and Postmodernity* (Atlantic Heights, N.J.: Humanities Press, 1986); Hal Foster, ed., *The Anti-Aesthetic: Essays on Postmodern Culture* (Port Townsend, West Australia: Bay Press, 1983); Agnes Heller. ed., *Deconstructing Aesthetics* (Oxford: Blackwell, 1986); Jacques Derrida, *Speech and Phenomena,* trans. David Allison (Evanston, Ill.: Northwestern University Press, 1973); Peggy Brand and Carolyn Korsmeyer, eds., *Feminism and Traditional Aesthetics* (special issue of *The Journal of Aesthetics and Art Criticism,* [Fall 1990]); Gisela Ecker, ed., *Feminist Aesthetics,* trans. Harriet Anderson (Boston: Beacon Press, 1989); Claire Duchen, *Feminism in France: From May '68 to Mitterand* (London: Routledge and Kegan Paul, 1986).

Journals

Most work in aesthetics is written as short pieces for scholarly journals and is later anthologized or incorporated into books. The best way to keep abreast of new developments is to consult three main journals: *The British Journal of Aesthetics, The Journal of Aesthetics and Art Criticism,* and *The Journal of Aesthetic Education.*

Index